The AS/400 & IBM i Pocket Developers' Guide

QuikCourses: Architecture, AD Setup, CL, PDM, SEU, DFU, Work Management, SDA, Subfiles, etc.

A Comprehensive Book of QuikCourses for the new and experienced AS/400 and IBM i Application Developer.

This book is based on WebSphere Development Studio for IBM I and the Kelly Consulting QuikCourse™ AS/400 classroom education modules.

Brian W. Kelly

Contains significant reference material, how-to's, and insightful tutorials.

IBM i Pocket Developers' Guide   Author Brian W. Kelly
All you need to know learn about how to build applications with AS/400 & IBMi
                                                  Editor Brian P. Kelly

Referenced Material: *Standard Disclaimer:* The information in this book has been obtained through personal and third party observations, interviews, and copious research. Where unique information has been provided or extracted from other sources, those sources are acknowledged within the text of the book itself or at the end of the chapter in the Sources Section. Thus, there are no formal footnotes nor is there a bibliography section. Any picture that does not have a source was taken from various sites on the Internet with no credit attached. If resource owners would like credit in the next printing, please email publisher.

Published by: LETS GO PUBLISH!
Editor in Chief: Brian P. Kelly
Email: info@letsgopublish.com
Web site: www.letsgopublish.com
Address: PO Box 621 Wilkes-Barre PA 18703

Library of Congress Copyright Information Pending
Book Cover Design by Michele Thomas,
Editor—Brian P. Kelly

ISBN Information: The International Standard Book Number (ISBN) is a unique machine-readable identification number, which marks any book unmistakably. The ISBN is the clear standard in the book industry. 159 countries and territories are officially ISBN members. The Official ISBN For this book is

978-0-9980848-7-9

The price for this work is   **$ 19.99 USD**

10   9   8   7   6   5   4   3   2

Release Date: November 2002,   October 2016

Dedication

To my great friend and a recent addition to God's Corps of Angels, a good and wonderful man, a committed and giving father, a dedicated husband, a loving son, a cherished brother, an honorable family man, a lover of COMMON, and one of the first eternal members of the Legion of AS/400 Rightful Bigots.

Al Komorek

Acknowledgments

I would like to thank many people for helping me bring this work to fruition.

I would first like to thank my family, starting with my lovely and wonderful wife Patricia whom I love dearly. She always helps me in more ways than can be mentioned in a simple acknowledgment. During the writing of this book, Pat contracted Mononucleosis, which she dealt with as the strong and wonderful person she always is. She always encourages me to do my best, even when she does not see the benefit. Thanks Pat.

I would also like to thank my eighteen-year-old daughter Katie, my twenty-year-old son Michael, and my twenty-two-year-old son Brian who, with enough prodding will always come through. I am proud of them all.

Boy, have I got friends! And, they are all willing to help. The long list includes Dennis Grimes, his daughter "Wizzler," Barbara Grimes, and Viola Grimes. More than worth a mention is Joe and Peg McDonald. Without them, there would be no acknowledgments.

Of course, the long list includes Jeanne and Joe Elinsky, John and Carol Anstett (Carol is also known as "et ux."), Carolyn and Joe Langan, Connie and Jerry Rodski,.Karen Komorek, Bonnie and George Mohanco, Josh Mohanco, young Dame Kiev- Lililya, Bob Lussi, Patricia Singer, and of course, Frannie and Mike Kurilla. And, don't let me forget Pierre Le Kep, Nancy and Jim Flannery, Mary and Bill Daniels, Dianne and Joe Kelly, Ed and Eudart Kelly, Bill Rolland, Bill Kustas and Shelly Bartolomei.

Special acknowledgments to Steven Dressler and Howard Klein, the Top Management team at Klein Wholesale Distributors in Wilkes-Barre, PA. Their vision, foresight, and execution have brought Klein to the enviable position of being the fifth largest candy and tobacco wholesaler in the U.S.A.
The Klein IT Staff has used this book in various training sequences. In alphabetical order, by first name, these fine folks are as follows:

Adrian Koehler, Amy Latona, Barb Chaderton,
Bill 'Curly' Kepics, Bob Plonski,
Brian Kelly, Cindy Dorzinsky, Cindy 'Yours Truly' Goodwin,
David Dakin, Dennis Grimes, Eric Priest,
Gay Maron, Jeff Massaker, Jennifer Jones, Jerry Cybulski
Jerry Reisch, Jessica Webb, John Robbins, Joe Byorick,
Joe Rydzewski, Joe Wilk, Paula Terpak, Ray Giovagnoli,
Rod Smith, Rosalind Robertson, Steve Bartolomei, and Steve Safka.

Special thanks to Nancy Lavan, and Michele Thomas from Offset
Paperback, our printing company, who assured that this project
would be successful.

I would like to sum up my acknowledgments, as I have in every book
that I have written. I am compelled to offer that I am truly convinced
that "the only thing you can do alone in life is fail." Thanks to my
family, good friends, and a helping team, I was not alone.

The most current acknowledgments which include Wiley
Ky Eyeley are found at www.letsgopublish.com

Table of Contents

Preface:

This pocket guide introduces the traditional notion of the WebSphere Development Studio for IBM i to the AS/400 RPG400/COBOL programmer, and perhaps more importantly, to the prospective programmer. Yes, a non-AS/400 programmer can also use this book to gain a tremendous amount of insight into (1) the way application development (AD) is typically performed with an AS/400, and (2) the sheer beauty of the traditional tools in the WebSphere Development Suite. This book is clearly designed from an AS/400 programmer's application development (AD) perspective.

This book is for both entry level and existing programmers. A general notion of how computers work is certainly helpful. However, if you are new to AS/400 and IBM i, and want to be a programmer, you can be typing in source programs within 24 hours. You can gain the right idea of how source programs are stored and how objects are created. In fact, if you are uncomfortable with the term "object," you may even learn just what an object actually is and what it is not. Along the way to becoming a developer or becoming a better developer, you'll also learn how the AS/400 gets its work done. This systems administration secret is one that many programmers never get to learn.

This book is a series of independent, quick, yet reasonably comprehensive courses, sequenced in the order in which you should take them. These QuikCourses are designed to make it easy for you to learn AS/400 application development tools and techniques. They were originally designed as slides and notes for stand-up education modules. This book is the result of their conversion to a stand-alone tutorial / reference format with plenty of action and plenty of examples.

You can learn from just reading this book. But, if you can convince your systems administrator to give you some real authority, you can type in and execute the same commands and see the results as shown in this book. There is no CD, since we start you with tools in which you need entry practice. There's not a lot of it, but there's enough to make you wish there was a little less. Once you hit that point, of course, you have achieved the objective. Go ahead and leaf through the book now. You'll see it is chocked with examples and many screen shots are taken in tutorial sequence so you can play along with your server.

Before we ask the manager readers to consider a "new" "old" way of creating new programmers using this book as an aid, the next section of this preface takes a look at each of the QuikCourse modules which make up this book. The purpose for the courses and each course's content are explained in two introductory chapters.

We wish you well in your endeavors, and we hope to see you again reading our next two books in this series: the Database Pocket Developer's Guide and the Query/400 Pocket User's Guide.

Brian W. Kelly
Wilkes-Barre, Pennsylvania

Chapter 1   Create Your Own Business Programmers From Your Smartest People.

Who should read this book?

New programmers, existing programmers, supervisors, and advanced end-users should all read the courses in this book — or a selection of Lets Go Publish and Kelly Consulting Quik courses made by IT management. In fact, IT management should consider reading or browsing this whole book to better understand how they can match personnel with the areas of study included in these QuikCourses.

IT managers need to consider creating programmers. With all of the smart, yet sometimes clueless PC technicians running around every business and institution, there are many who would appreciate the opportunity and who would do well if redeployed.

This book can help. If you've always wanted to be able to tell your team what you know about application development on the AS/400 and now IBM i, but you did not have the time, as your author, I have done this job for you. I've said what you would have said if you had the time to say it. Moreover, you'll like what you would have said.

Consider creating a home-made programmer. It may be a good deal for you and for your company.

Home-Made Programmers?

If you need one, make one! That's what Jay Leno used to say about the corn chips. "We'll make more!" It's time to make some more programmers. Have you ever thought of making one of your own employees a programmer? Years ago, it was done all of the time. Nowadays, there is a perception that you must hire a "professional" if programming is the requirement.

Not true! It may take time. But at least it's an investment. Other than the completed project, what does your firm gain when it contracts with an outside programmer? Make your own programmer and you build an asset for the organization. A programmer trained in-house does not need to be a full-time programmer... at least initially.

☺ TIP General Benefits of making a programmer:

1. Employees, trained in-house do not need to be full-time programmers
2. Great employees become great programmers
3. Hard working employees become hard working programmers
4. Choose from Technicians, System Operators, IS Supervisors, Web Builders, Former dot gone types, others
5. Home-made programmers are loyal to the firm
6. Home-made programmers do not command exorbitant salaries
7. **Home-made programmers know your business better**

Home made programmers are a great deal for the company!

- ✓ What's the risk?   – Little
- ✓ What is the opportunity?   – Big
- ✓ Who are your candidates?   – Bright Users etc.

The fact is programmers are tough to find, and it's getting tougher. AS/400 programmers are the toughest to find though the system is the best for a business to us.

The technology boom is on us again. Moreover, it is not expected to let up for at least ten years. Industry estimates of one year ago show a 1.3 million Information Technology person shortage. The "dot coms" may be "dot gone," but IBM i talent is not easy to find. Businesses are asking help from government, academic institutions, and trade schools to bring more technicians on board. Unfortunately, not much help is in sight. See how long want-ads for AS/400 programmers remain being advertised!

The solution is not necessarily to offer all programmers $100,000 and up, per year. If farmers stopped growing food, we'd grow our own. If the bakers stopped baking bread, we'd bake our own. If our favorite restaurant stopped preparing food, we'd prepare our own. We'd figure a way. Likewise, since the schools do not produce many IBM i programmers, why should we not produce our own.

With demand for even more IT skills to help solve today's eBusiness problems, clever consultants are suggesting that businesses consider training in-house personnel for technical positions. Over all, it may be the most economical choice. Investing in staff typically pays off in increased loyalty and greater output. Moreover, the cost of the training plus the cost of a hand-picked, newly trained, IS technician, from your existing staff, is substantially less than hiring a professional programmer when such skills are still in such high demand.

So, how do you go about getting this training? You know the answer. This is the book. Without leaving the shop, with The IBM i Pocket Developers' Guide, you can teach yourself and your AS/400 and IBM i job candidates about how to develop applications using the system. Like the spaghetti ad said: It's in there! It is designed to take a bright candidate from little knowledge, or knowledge of other systems, and give the candidate the skills to use the traditional set of the WebSphere AD Studio tools quite effectively. This is certainly the right starting point.

Moreover, you and your charges gain through success. Your hand-picked in-house professionals will begin to contribute more and more to the success of the organization, without you being chained to the want ads, hoping someone will call. This is the same educational material which has been used for ten years in a proven training regimen. The Kelly Consulting team have used this material successfully in many businesses and institutions in the form of on-site stand-up QuikCourse offerings. Now, the same starter set for this successful formula is available in this book.

One of our major objectives from the outset was to present the program development tasks clearly so the student would not get bogged down in things that are nonessential to the program development mission.

AS/400 programmers typically learn what the IBM IBM i ADTS tool set (now called the WebSphere Development Studio for IBM i) is all about either by performing these tasks on their own machines or by following somebody's ad hoc directions in a semi-tutorial fashion.

The problem is that somebody on your staff has to create those ad hoc semi-tutorial exercises — if the new players even get to have a few dry runs before you cut them loose. Otherwise, your existing programmers do one-on-one education with the new folks. Mentoring is tough enough on your staff, but the three tasks of creating material, then monitoring, and then mentoring, hit development teams where it hurts - in productivity.

You could take very expensive formal "away game" courses or you could buy the expensive tutorials which are out there. (Your mentors also have to install and learn these first.) For shops with tight budgets, as is the case in most organizations, it is tough to convince anybody to spend a few thousand dollars for formal material. Moreover, IBM formal, stand-up education, though highly worthwhile, is very difficult to justify to management.

It would be nice if the Colleges offered AS/400 and IBM i courses. Most do not. They continue to be hung up on Windows and Unix. Where there are Colleges, such as Luzerne County Community College and Marywood University that offer quality AS/400 education, this book is the perfect adjunct to the learning process.

So, how do you educate new people or help give your existing team more knowledge. If you've got colleges close by with AS/400 curricula, take advantage of them. You could also go to COMMON, which is always a good option. However, this education is fairly specific and highly topically oriented. It is also not free. You could theoretically cheap-out and send your new folks to the IBM Web documentation sites. There is certainly enough material out there to learn something. But what?

In less than 400 pages, this book touches on each of the areas necessary to learn or sharpen your AS/400 Application Development (AD) skills — one QuikCourse at a time. You and your team can gain an appreciation of how to work with simple applications using traditional AS/400 and IBM i development tools. Then after the basics are covered, you will be in a position to create a successful development team better than ever before.

The Step Often Forgotten

It helps to remember that before anybody can work on their first program at your shop, they have to understand the AD environment and the tools that are in the shop's development kit. By supplying sample databases and sample programs in the nine separate QuikCourses within this book, we prepare your team to use the IBM i development tools.

When your prospective programmer takes all nine of these QuikCourses, he or she can then move on to learn a programming language such as RPG/400 or ILE RPG (RPGIV) or even COBOL. The fact is most shops do it the other way around. They send a student to programming school or put him on a   real project before he has yet to learn the IBM i system or the system's essential AD tools.

If your objective is to teach a programming language, consider that a programming language such as RPG equates to just one learning objective. There are nine QuikCourses about different development topics in this book. Therefore, you might well conclude that a good percentage of your training (9 out of ten areas) has already been covered when your prospective programmer successfully walks out of this book, a graduate of <u>The IBM i Pocket Developers' Guide</u>. The point is that there is lots more to know than just a programming language. This book helps you get to the point where learning the language is the next right thing to do. Just a thought!

Chapter 2   Detailed Abstracts of Eleven QuikCourses for the AS/400 & IBM i.

What is a QuikCourse

QuikCourses were originally developed by your author Brian Kelly in the early 1990's when Brian W. Kelly created the Kelly Consulting Corporation. Kelly is well known for having written over thrity technical books beginning with the goundbreaking The AS/400, The Internet, & Email for Midrange Computing in 1996.

Over the years, after his long career with IBM as a Senior Systems Engineer, Brian Kelly has written books for the complete application development process including pure development, query, data communications, database, SQL, PHP, Joomla, and programming languages. Most of his books came after Brian had built seminars for the topical area in question.

He has presented his QuikCourses at companies all across the United States. Brian was a featured speaker at Midrange Computing Seminars, COMMON, and IBM Technical Seminars. He was a Certified IBM Instructor for years. This book is a reflection of a three-day course (QuikCourse) that Brian built in the 1990's and improved over time. Here are the courses that are presented in this book in a very logical and understandable way. You will be amazed at what you can learn Quikly!

QuikCourse A.   AS/400 and IBM i Architecture

Many developers have never been introduced to the sheer beauty and elegance of the AS/400 under the covers. When you've got the basic tenets of what an AS/400 is all about, well ingrained in your mind, the Intel guy out there looking to make your machine appear to look grey and haggard, better watch his Windows.

In this QuikCourse, you will learn what makes the AS/400 so special. The secrets of the four big AS/400 technology innovations are revealed and you will never again wonder why nobody else has this technology:

- ✓ A high-level machine interface
- ✓ Single level storage
- ✓ An object-based architecture
- ✓ An integrated relational data base
- ✓ Integrated Application Development Toolset

It took IBM over twenty years to build it all. That's one of the reasons why it is so special.

QuikCourse B. AS/400 Work Management

The idea of how an AS/400 gets its work done is cleverly referred to as work management. To navigate around an AS/400, it helps to have a basic idea of work management. In this QuikCourse, you should be smart enough, if you are not already, to be one lesson away from being dangerous.

You will learn the work management rules on AS/400 and the changes you can make which determine what work runs where. You will also learn the notion of competing work as you balance one job against all other work on the system. To learn work management, you will be introduced to a number of object types which you do not need very much for application development but which, if understood, would make you a better developer.

You will taste and feel what only system programmers are permitted to touch and feel. You will create subsystems, user profiles, job queues, output queues, classes, and job descriptions. You'll even learn about routing data, how to use it, and why it is good. By the time you finish this QuikCourse, you will be introduced to all of the work management objects you will need for almost a lifetime. In fact, some may even become your friends.

☺ Note: When you look through the Table of Contents, you won't find this QuikCourse in the # 2 slot. In the technical review of the book, we were asked to componentize this QuikCourse and position it later in the sequence. It is still QuikCourse B. It just happens to follow QuikCourse S, in the book.

QuikCourse C.   Creating an AS/400 Source Development Environment

Unfortunately, this course is missing in most other education paths. Here you learn about libraries and files, and things that go into libraries. You also learn about source files and members and how source files are both the same and different from database files. Along the way you will be exposed to all the ingredients you need to create for yourself, a workable production and development environment. Of course, that's necessary in order to develop. You'll also see the library effect when a source is compiled into an object.

QuikCourse D.   AS/400 Control Language (CL)

In this course you will learn about the power of Control Language, which many in the AS/400 refer to as Command Language or just CL. You'll see how it is used for programming, operations, and systems management. You'll see that it requires no installation or generation and all functions are available at installation time. But, you'll also learn that many implementers change the default values so that they can change the characteristics of the system on the fly.

Since CL is a natural part of the Operating System/400 (OS/400), a developer's guide would be incomplete without helping you understand the constructs and the meaning of the CL language. You'll learn that CL is intuitive, and by the end of the course, you may be able to tell IBM the command for any new function the company chooses to introduce in the future.

You'll learn many of the nuances of this very crisp, concise and *HARD TO FORGET* Control Language (CL). You'll also learn the table driven nature of the AS/400 and how system values contribute to the operating flexibility of the machine. By the end of the course, you will have worked with many commands and you will have built yourself a display file and a CL program with which to drive it.

To top off your experience with CL, we borrowed a CL program from IBM, which we dissect at the end of this QuikCourse. It is the system startup program. Knowledge of this program should come in handy in other areas of your work. Additionally, we use a 50 statement (with comments) home-made CL program as an example of code which would be more typical of that you will write in your shop.

Again, we use the term *dissect,* since we cut this program into little pieces. In it, we introduce a number of helpful CL batch commands. By the end of the full dissection, you will have played the role of one of the "doctors" in a semi real CL operation. This experience should add significantly to your knowledge and your perspective of CL as a programming language.

You can then begin your own CL adventures which may or may not top our fifty liner.

QuikCourse E.   PDM: Program Development Manager

Right from the Work with libraries, objects, and members main menu of PDM, you will learn how this tool enhances a developer's productivity in much the same way as a mouse helps a Windows aficionado. PDM is your mouse on the AS/400. With it, you get to use a bunch of other utilities that you don't have to care much about, since PDM does much of the caring and some of the hard work for you.

You'll find that PDM uses its "type" attribute to decide which other ADTS tool to call in much the same way as your Windows PC uses the file suffix. Based on the suffix or "type" a particular program gets called to operate on the selected file or object. This PDM notion works with all of the other tools in the AS/400 and IBM i AD tool set including the following:

1. Source Entry Utility (SEU)
2. Screen Design Aid (SDA)
3. Data File Utility (DFU)
4. Advanced Printer Function (APF)
5. Report Layout Utility (RLU)

You'll learn how to use the Program Development Manager, as the consummate AS/400 development tool, while it enables you to create, test and maintain an array of AS/400 objects from programs to screens to reports to data files.

QuikCourse F.   SEU– AS/400 and IBM i Source Entry Utility

In this QuikCourse, you get to study and learn about SEU. Along the way, you are introduced lightly to the underlying AS/400 and AS/400 database technology, including physical and logical files– since the examples for SEU are all database examples. At the end of this QuikCourse, you also get a quick look at DFU as seen through option 18 of PDM to prove that the file you create in the SEU exercises can actually hold data.

The format of the course will be to present the facts about SEU first in lecture format, followed by a tutorial type machine exercise segment in which databases are created with SEU and data is entered with DFU. This hands-on approach can be effective whether you are following along step-by-step at the office with your AS/400 (or IBM i) or just reading the material for self edification.

QuikCourses G, & H continue the SEU lessons

QuikCourse I.   SDA–AS/400 and IBM i Screen Design Aid

SDA is a great terminal-oriented screen painter. Having worked with GUI designers, I still find it easier to create a green screen design, first with SDA, than to use the GUI tool first. For me, it is easier to create it or convert it for GUI purposes after SDA has helped me build a prototype. In this course, you will learn how to build non CL-driven menu objects with SDA. You will learn how to build screen panels from scratch and then manipulate your screen objects using the SDA design facilities. You will also interactively design and create, and understand how to maintain display files.

After we build the panel using SDA tools in a tutorial, you will learn how to use the SDA testing facilities to get a look at the screen prototype even before it is used in a program. And, though this is not a programming course per se, as the course capstone, you will learn how to merge your display panel into an RPG program and execute it.

QuikCourse J.   DFU– AS/400 and IBM i Data File Utility

In this QuikCourse, you will use the DFU utility for defining, creating, and maintaining simple data base applications. You will note the facilities in DFU for data entry, inquiry and file maintenance, all without creating a source program.

You will see how DFU is fully aware that the AS/400 is an integrated database machine, and how this helps you be more effective in its use. You will learn how to invoke DFU, and make it a tool for you as a programmer, while understanding its intrinsic value to the user community.

You will discover why the utility is very convenient for developers and more technically oriented end-users who want to quickly develop data entry, inquiry or file maintenance functions within applications – or outside applications. You will see that the utility is a good fit for general entry and update of data and for those times when 'fixing' data requires only simple maintenance.

QuikCourse S.   Subfiles– Creating and Using Subfiles in Programs

This QuikCourse, in many ways, is a continuation of SDA QuikCourse H, into a more powerful area - subfiles. Some may argue that subfiles are an advanced topic and should not be in The IBM i Pocket Developer's Guide. Subfiles are certainly an advanced topic. There is no denying that. However, there is little need for concern in this QuikCourse. Our approach is not threatening. This course is not overwhelming. There is more good news. It is also not underwhelming. We think it is just right.

You will learn how to build an inquiry subfile using SDA and you will then merge the subfile into an RPG program and observe its execution characteristics. You will also be exposed to how to drive database update operations from subfiles. The treatment of the topic in this QuikCourse is a combination of a succinct and pithy lecture with a presentation style which is mostly tutorial in nature. We hope you enjoy this brief Case Study and that you emerge with some good tools to help you become a master of subfiles.

Appendix: How to Find an AS/400 or IBM i AD Manual

This appendix is designed to help you locate the AS/400 and IBM i manuals which may be of assistance in your development life. All of IBM's books are on the Web, free for the taking. This appendix helps you find those hidden treasures and is worth the read to avoid the frustration of believing the manuals are actually hidden.

QuikCourse A   AS/400 and IBM i Architecture

Course Topics

QuikCourse A addresses the following topics:

A.   AS/400 Machine Characteristics
B.   Software Architecture

From 1978, with the introduction of the System/38, the AS/400 and now the IBM i achieved its *advanced systems architecture* while never abandoning the notion of small system ease-of-use. The objective has always been to allow applications to be built today that will last long into the future.

At the core of the AS/400's machine and software architecture are four advanced principles:

1. High-level machine
2. Single level storage
3. Object-oriented architecture
4. Integrated relational data base
5. Integrated Application Development Tool Set

These features provide a platform for flexibility, ease-of-use, and non-disruptive growth. Let's examine each of these in detail.

High Level Machine

Quite simply, a high-level machine implementation works in favor of the user, rather than the computer designer. To get a picture of this, let's look at Figure A-1. This gives a side-by-side comparison of traditional architecture and the AS/400 advanced architecture.

Now that you have seen a picture, let's try less than a thousand words. Just what is the High Level Interface anyway? It is another way of saying that user functions are built into the machine. The traditional approach is to use add-on software. If you need a database – buy one! If you need a transaction processor – buy one! If you need compilers – buy them! A traditional approach is an ala carte approach. You never get a full dinner. Most vendors, including IBM with its other system models found it easier over the years to just add function patches with some new software, rather than start over and design the system the right way.

Future System

That changed in the late 1970's with the System/38. IBM had studied the best possible architecture and ingredients for a new system replacement for its mainframe processor line. However, the Future System project was too advanced for mainframe customers and IBM dropped support of the project.

The IBM Rochester team picked up the remnants of the project and designed the System/38 as a small system embodiment of all these future system ideas. The System/38, the predecessor to the AS/400 and the IBM i is the only system originated from scratch since the 1970's. Since it was an effort from scratch, IBM could approach the task in a way it should be done instead of how things had been done.

Their efforts were quite fruitful. There still is no machine built today, other than a System/38 descendent, such as the AS/400 and IBM i, which has the elegant architecture that is designed into this machine. So, for starters, a high level machine is one which provides integrated function, which looks like it is meant to operate together, as opposed to a patchwork quilt of convenient add-ons.

Figure A-1 Traditional Machine Compared to the AS/400

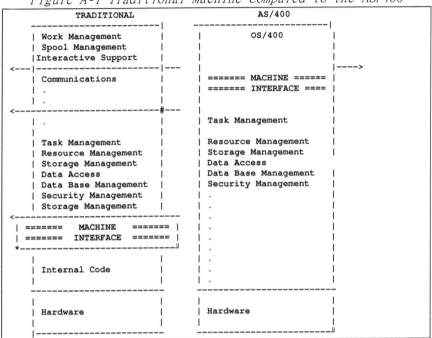

Access to the powerful system function is provided by a powerful, consistent interface a.k.a. *the high-level machine interface.* Programmers love it and don't want to give it up because they don't have to learn cryptic machine code and silly names for normal functions. Even the machine instructions are more Englishlike. As explained by IBM, the interface is at such a high level on the AS/400 that machine instructions, not add-on programs, are used to get data base records, perform multiprogramming, handle storage management, query a data base file, or create an index over a DB file.

If you know it is needed in the design phase, you can build it into the machine. When you do,   it runs much better rather than when you simply add function by adding software packages. The AS/400 system is "smarter," It can be told to query a data base with just one machine instruction.

Some other facilities handled by high-level machine instructions are as follows:

- ✓ Supervisor and control
- ✓ Language functions
- ✓ Symbolic interactive debug
- ✓ Data base management
- ✓ Communications

———

Advantages of High Level Interface

By building your interfaces at the top rather than the bottom, another advantage is that new technology does not affect existing application programs. Who cares what is in the pit when your interface is on the platform?

The advantages are many:

1. Fewer programming interfaces are required.
2. There is greater potential for non-disruptive growth.
3. Underlying hardware technology is not important.
4. You and your programs can move easily into the future.
5. You can take advantage of both new hardware technology and new software – without worrying about changing your programs.

Building A High Level Interface Is Not Easy

If it is easy to achieve, then why did WordPerfect have to rewrite its package to go from DOS to Windows, and again to go from Windows to Windows 95. If they could have made the transition without rewriting, they surely would have. Windows does not have a high-level interface. More than likely, in order to take advantage of 64-bit Intel technology and the 64-bit Windows when it finally arrives cleanly, WordPerfect, will again have to rewrite its software. It isn't easy.

In 1995, IBM changed the AS/400 from CISC processors to RISC processors. It changed from 32-bit processors to 64-bit processors. Programs written in 1978 for System/38 were already RISC ready and 64-bit enabled without any rewriting. That is a high-level interface, and it means investment protection. Code does not need to be rewritten for system changes.

Single Level Storage

Most of us understand the notion of virtual storage. It has been used in computer systems since the very early 1970's. Virtual storage permits computers to run programs that are bigger than the memory of the machine itself. It also permits memory to be over-committed, running many different programs. This has many advantages including never being shut down for inadequate real resources. Single Level Storage takes this one step further.   It takes virtual storage an evolutionary step beyond traditional architectures.

The capabilities of AS/400 and IBM i have extended the notion and the usability of the single level storage notion even further than IBM even thought it could go. For our purposes here, we discuss this concept in terms of the System/38, which was the most limited of the three advanced architecture machines since it depended on the most simplistic and the weakest hardware.

Big Time Addressability

The System/38 with single level storage believed that all of its objects existed in a 281 trillion-byte memory continuum. That's pretty big. In 1979, I recall my first presentation about the System/38 as an SE with IBM. The presentation guide suggested that the 281 trillion bytes represented the sum total of all of the disk drives that had ever been sold. I was impressed for sure. It took mainframes twenty more years to reach this level of addressability.

The notion of single level storage was originally conceived at a time when bubble memory appeared to be the storage of the future. If this were the case, there would be no spinning disk drives with cylinders, tracks or sectors. There would be just one huge blob of memory.

And, that is exactly how single level storage is implemented. At the high level interface, the system is unaware that it has disk drives. It does not care. It accesses all objects by their single level storage address and then huge system vector tables resolve the memory addresses to either real memory or disk cylinders, tracks, and sectors.

When an object is created, it is given an address across this continuum, and that object has that one address as long as it exists. Way back with the System/38, the addressability was theoretically set at a 48-bit level to match the 48-bit System/38 hardware. It was expensive to build processors with high addressability. The official word at that time was that the 48-bit hardware had been augmented with 64-bit software addressing, but it was not all being used.

Lots of Bits

Today the hardware is 64-bit, but the software still accesses the machine at a higher level. Just recently IBM began to openly confess that the software was not built at a 64-bit level. Actually, IBM had achieved 128 bit software addressability way back in the 1970's with the high level interface of the System/38. With real memory being so scarce when the System/38 made its debut, I can appreciate why the company chose to wait so long to become so frank about how it used up so much memory back then – carrying around big addresses in each instruction.

What Good Is Single Level Storage?

One of the first things you see when you use the system is that it frees you as a programmer or a user from managing disk storage. The system manages the disk storage all by itself. Since real disk storage is treated as a   large main storage area, the system doesn't even know that disk storage is attached. Moreover, since there is just one storage blob, regardless of how many disk drives are on the system, you don't have to worry about "C" drives or "E" drives or "F" drives. If you get a new disk drive, the system begins to use it. You don't specifically have to put anything there. Thus, you can take advantage of new technology faster. You can put in a new fast disk drive without moving your data to it. The system will automatically use it. None of your programs or procedures are affected when you add or change disk because it all looks like one space both before and after the change. All objects are shared in single level storage.

More than one user shares the same program code in storage. The system, not the user or programmer makes the most effective use of main storage. It avoids having to manage multiple copies of the same program. Data is also shared in virtual storage, not just programs. The end result is improved system performance and a much easier way to manage the application development environment.

I have a copy of IBM's old System/38 chart for single level storage. As you can see in Figure A-2, all of the objects are in an address continuum and are fetched into main memory as needed. The user does not know or care to know where they actually are located in storage. Thus, the system is substantially easier to manage.

Advantages of Single Level Storage

There are even more advantages to single level storage than you could imagine. Keeping in mind that the storage vectors do not care where they locate an object, if the object is found in main memory, for example, that is where the object is used. Thus, main storage serves as a direct access buffer (cache) for the most frequently used objects. Programs, data and other objects are effectively cached in main memory.

When you add main storage or disk storage, the system automatically uses it to further improve system performance. There is no requirement to partition or create regions in the virtual system because of the very large set of storage addresses. All objects can be shared among all users on the system. Thus, there is no need to make multiple copies of programs or data.

On top of all this, the system uses object-based security so that access to objects is not limited by system restrictions. It is   controlled by system security. Single level storage makes everyone's job easier than a traditional approach, whether you are a programmer, an operator, or a user.

Figure A-2 Single-Level Storage

```
                       VIRTUAL ADDRESS SPACE
@------------------------------------------------------------$
|  /----\                                                     |
|  |====|                              -------|               |
|  |====|                              |      |               |
|  |====| DB FILE                      | PGM1 |               |
|  |====|                              |      |               |
|  |====|                              *------JJ              |
|  *----JJ                                                    |
|                                                             |
|      ---------|                                             |
|      |        |                      /----\                 |
|      | MENU   |              DB FILE  |====|                |
|      |        |                       |====|                |
|      *--------JJ                      |====|                |
|                                       |====|                |
|        -------|                       |====|                |
|        |      |                       *----JJ               |
|        | PGM2 |                                             |
|        *------JJ                                          . |
|  .                                                       .  |
|   .                                                     .   |
|    .                                                   .    |
|     .                                                 .     |
|      .                                               .      |
|       .                                             .       |
|      @-------------------$         _____        .         |
|      |                   |        /       \ .               |
|      |                   |       |_____/|               |
|  *---|    MAIN           |-------| AUX STORE |-----JJ        |
|      |  STORAGE          |       |           |               |
|      |                   |       |           |               |
|      |                   |        _____/                 |
|      *-------------------JJ                                  |
```

Systems expertise is not required for disk or memory management. This is most often required on other machines. Windows has caught up a little, but not completely. You may recall the DOS days when PC Memory Management was a full day, difficult course.

The "Car" Analogy

To help us take a look at the "hugeness" of single level storage in a proper perspective, let's use an analogy about a car.

If a car could go one inch per address, then a car with a 24 bit address space would go 264 miles. Let's say we double the size of the address width to 48 bits. A car with a 48 bit address space could go 4.5 billion miles. In other words, the car could go to the Sun and back about 24 times. Can you imagine where a RISC System with its 64-bit address would take us?

Object-Based Architecture

In 1978, IBM Systems Engineers spoke of the AS/400 as having an object-oriented architecture. Since that time, as we all have learned more about the notion of objects, the System/38, AS/400 and IBM i have been recast more correctly as object-based systems.

What Is An Object?

So, just what is an object anyway, and why is it good? An Object is a package containing structured data, a set of instructions, and rules for that data. A simple view of an object is shown in Figure A-3.

Object-oriented and object based computing are all about objects. The best way of looking at an object, from my days of teaching comparative programming languages, is to think of an object as a "black box." Oh! It is not a solid black box. It has an opening for input messages, and it has an opening for messages, which it must send out. Thus, it can be thought of as a "black box," which receives and sends messages.

Many computer science classes are taught about the idea of hiding implementation details from the user of a computer subroutine. For example, just like a hardware instruction, the user should not be concerned how the instruction does the *ADD*. Additionally, the user should not be concerned about modifying the *ADD* instruction to do special things that the designer of the *ADD* never intended to be done. There may be lots more to an *ADD* than just addition. On the other hand, there may not be anything more. The point is that it does not matter. An *ADD* is an *ADD* and that is all it is. The same applies to the black box notion of all other objects. They are built to be used, not to be toyed with.

Figure A-3 Object Package

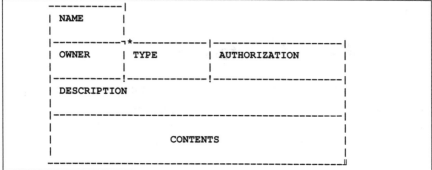

Internal O-O Communication

A black box (object) actually contains code (sequences of computer instructions) and data (information upon which the instructions operate). But, unless you developed the object, you don't get to see any of that. Traditionally, code and data have been kept apart. For example, in many programming languages, units of code are called functions, or subroutines, while units of data are called structures. Functions and structures are not formally connected outside of their use together in a program. A function can operate on more than one type of structure, and more than one function can operate on the same structure. Thus, the link is not permanent between the program function and the data structure.

Not so for object-oriented software! In o-o (object-oriented) programming, code and data are merged into a single indivisible thing – an object. So how does the code know what to do? That's one of the secrets of o-o. All communication to and from an object is done through messages. The object receives a message which instructs it to do something. In a sense, messages define the interface to the object. Everything an object can do is represented by the messages it can receive. Therefore, you don't typically have to know anything about what is in the black box in order to use it. You tell the black box what to do via a message, and it does it. Then, it gives you information back via a message.

By not looking inside the black box, you are not tempted to change what is inside. Let's say you looked inside and found a better way to perform the task of the object, and you changed its implementation details. Then later on the original programmer decided to make the object even more capable while preserving the original message interface. Your software would no longer work correctly! You would be in trouble.

The same goes for packages of all kinds. If you stay away from the implementation details and you use an object only through its interfaces, then that object can be enhanced over and over and your interfaces will continue to work, thereby preserving your code investment.

Experience has taught us the popular adage that "software is not written, it is rewritten." Many of the costliest mistakes in computer history have come from software that breaks when someone tries to change it. If you can let it be, and work with the building blocks of objects, then your investment in software is better preserved.

IBM Rewrites Object Oriented Microcode

In 1995, IBM introduced RISC-BASED AS/400 machines which were highly o-o oriented, and in order to do so, the company had to change the implementation details of many low level objects. The System/38 and CISC-based systems were not truly object oriented though they used real objects. They were called object-based.

Because the system already was object-based and high-level when IBM converted the low-level OS to object-oriented, Despite this major change in hardware architecture, the company did not have to rewrite OS/400 to achieve its goal. Because the operating systems were already based on high level objects, only the low-level primitives (IBM estimated about 5% of the code) had to be rewritten in o-o. IBM began to call this *licensed internal code* rather than *microcode* during this time period.

If IBM had not developed its AS/400 and System/38 machines with an object basis, the transition to RISC would have been as difficult for IBM as it seems to have been for Intel. Seven years after IBM put RISC AS/400s into production, Intel still does not have their game perfected

Object Type Examples

To say the least, IBM, with the AS/400 and the IBM i have perfected the object game. Examples of familiar object types in this architecture include:

1. User profile
2. Subsystem description
3. Job description
4. Queue (message, output, job)
5. Program
6. Library
7. File
etc.

There are more than 200 different object types on the AS/400 and IBM i. Among other facilities, the object orientation of the AS/400 makes the box a very special machine compared to the machines many small businesses choose to use - PCs. Since most of us have a good feel for the power and limitations of PCs, let's compare the object-based AS/400 with the file-based PC machines.

Objects vs. PC File Orientation

All computer systems, including PCs, have different types of data structures:

1. Programs
2. Queues
3. Data files.

However, on most systems the type of object is not specifically identified as to whether it is a program, a file or a queue. Instead, the determination of what type of object is stored on a PC, as an example, comes from how it is used at any given time. Since the data and the methods of processing that data are separate, there is no control in the item itself (program or file) to prevent you or the PC system itself from making mistakes.

For example, a PC system permits programs to be processed as if they were data and vice versa. This can lead to serious program and data integrity problems. The reality is that there is only one object type on a PC - the file. PCs support all objects as long as they are files! Thus it is easy to ship a virus around in a PC because it can be masked as something which it is not. This is much more difficult to do with object-based technology.

Within object-based technology systems, the AS/400 object orientation is unique. In fact, object integrity is not known to be an issue on the AS/400 and IBM i. On a PC, as we have noted, a program is a file and a file is a file. On an OS/400 object-based system, a program is not a file. It is a program. When a program object receives a message to send a record to a requesting object, the program object checks its valid methods, and it says: "no can do! Sorry!" The program itself knows that it is not a data file and it does not let itself get treated as a data file. So also, a file is a file. Therefore, when it gets asked to execute itself, it knows that the request is not one of its valid methods and it respectfully declines. Not so with PC systems whose identities change as quickly as the three character suffixes of the file name changes.

With AS/400, objects combine the data and the valid methods of using that data into one entity. Therefore, only valid methods of using that data are allowed. By doing so, the system protects itself from attempts to use a data structure incorrectly. This improves the overall integrity of the system and its data.

Capability-Based Addressing

There is at least one more thing worth discussing regarding objects - their security addressability. The AS/400 uses a computer science facility called capability-based addressing as its object level security implementation. AS/400 object addresses are really not known above the machine interface and thus even security is enforced below the machine interface

The AS/400 handles all security by object. Everything on the system is an object. Everything can be secured very easily at this base level. As noted above, the security mechanism is called capability-based addressing. Capability (authority) must be established to use an object (user profile / object description.) Security checking takes place at the time you attempt to reference the object. If you are authorized, you get it. If not, you are excluded. It's built into the machine itself.

Let's try a little more technical explanation. The actual authority check takes place below the machine interface by the system. First the system locates the object by name, then checks the object. Are you the owner? If not, the system checks your user profile to see if, as a non-owner, you have authority to the object. If so, a capability pointer is passed up allowing you to use the object. If not, use is denied by the system.

This procedure is performed each time a user attempts to touch any system object for the first time in a process. With capability-based addressing, security checking is enforced by the machine and is performed all the time on every object in the system. Unless there is a problem, you never know!

Integrated Data Base

The System/38, in 1978 was the first computer ever built with a relational database integrated within the hardware and the framework of the system. The integrated relational database was and continues to be a hallmark of the AS/400 and the IBM i. There is no other machine in existence, even today, which comes with a built-in database. Can you imagine how far ahead of the competition the System/38 was in 1978 when DB2, IBM's mainframe relational database product had yet to be announced? And with a System/38, it was just there!

Relational databases by definition are flexible, natural, and simple to use. Yet there is a high level of sophistication in the capabilities and the low level implementation. Consider that one of the most frequently used operations in a relational database is index creation. The AS/400 has implemented this function as a hardware instruction. There is no argument that the AS/400 is a database machine since its inherent capabilities come from implementations that are not part of add-on products but, in fact are built into the hardware and the internal code of the system.

AS/400 and IBM i Break DB Rules

Most relational databases use set theory and set oriented operations. Simple features such as the ability to link a compiler read and write operation to the database are not part of the deal. In fact, "compiler reads and writes to a database" are anathemas to the spirit of a relational database. Not only does it read and write naturally to the database, the compilers were written knowing the integrated database would be there.

The AS/400 breaks this big DB rule that data must be processed in a set. Not only does the AS/400 provide high-level SQL facilities and set operations with the data manipulation language, as you would expect any database to deliver, it also provides and in fact optimizes "natural read, write and update record-at-a-time oriented operations" to the database. You do not have to use SQL if you want to use an HLL compiler such as RPG or COBOL with your database. You don't have to define input and output for your RPG and COBOL programs because the compilers know about the database and copy the definitions in from the database at compiling time in much the same fashion as copy books.

Database is a Given

In fact, the compiler writers, knowing that the very fabric of the AS/400 was its integrated database, used the natural APIs in the database, so that normal HLL   reads, writes, and updates to the database occur in the same way that other compilers access flat file systems. In other words, you get the power of the integrated database in program development built-in at the compiler level without having the pay the development burden of an add-on, unnatural facility that the compiler knows nothing about.

Moreover, the operating system provides major database recovery facilities that are just as built-in as the database. High performance journaling, and commitment control are built-ins, not afterthoughts, for advanced recovery scenarios. Many companies have used this support to deploy cross system journaling in which all of the updates on a given computer are mirrored via journaling on a computer in the next room or in the next city.

No Name Database

In the early 1990's IBM did a survey of its AS/400 customers. It is a fact that many AS/400 customers have no or little professional staff keeping their systems running. The company asked AS/400 customers if the AS/400 had a database. Reportedly half of the AS/400 users did not know their machine had an integrated database. That's when IBM decided to use the IBM relational DB brand DB2 for the AS/400. IBM speakers often joked about this fact at conferences, believing that their audiences would see the slam more as a put-down to the unaware AS/400 community, rather than as intended for the enlightened students in the room! After all, they were not at the conference.

If It Has a Name, It Can't Be Integrated?

Of course that ruined one of my favorite pitch lines that I always felt put the AS/400 DB in perspective. Once I was able to say: "If it has a name, the machine knows nothing about it . . .   If it has a name, it is not built-in, it is an add-on." Consider the plethora of databases which fit this mold: DB2 for all other platforms, Sybase, Informix, Oracle, etc. No compilers are aware of any of the hooks in these named databases. IBM wanted to make sure its customers knew that the company supplied a free database and a no-name version was not cutting it. Now, the AS/400 database has a name and it has the power of the best that IBM knows about a database. Corporate IBM's Santa Theresa Labs, where the relational database was invented, are now a big part of this new database for the future. And, it is still integrated with the machine.

Integrated Application Development Tools

When you build a new system from scratch, you don't have to worry about preserving anything from an old architecture. IBM was fortunate and so are today's AS/400 and IBM i users because of this. Knowing that there is a database within every System/38, AS/400, and IBM i permitted the builders of the application tools to use such built-in function within the new tools. For example, the program editors are aware that there is a database and so instead of a cryptic "call interface" to the database, there is a natural device used depending on the language –RPG, COBOL, etc. The same for the display panels. On other systems programs such as CICS and/or Tuxedo are needed to access terminals for transaction processing. With AS/400 and IBM I, the compiler has a natural device interface and no strange coding is required.

Summary and Conclusions

Though this is a very short sample of the innate capabilities of the AS/400, and it is a snapshot taken at a high altitude, hopefully, you now have a better appreciation for what the "Future System Today" has looked like since it was first built in 1978. An honest appraisal by the Windows-loving trade press of the underpinnings of the AS/400, which in conception is still System/38 technology, would render a far more complimentary identifier than the label, "legacy."

AS/400 architecture represents everything IBM knows about computers and wishes it could have rammed into mainframes over the years. It is the most technologically elegant machine within IBM, and in the entire computer marketplace. It is certainly not well understood, and is not marketed by IBM in a way which comes close to the distance separating this system from all others.

Maybe IBM will get it right one day. But, I don't think so! Unfortunately, even IBM does not seem to believe that it is politically correct to actually suggest that its technology is superior to all others. If you'd like to check on that, ask yourself if you have ever heard IBM say one more positive thing in public about the AS/400 or IBM i, than any other IBM product. Many AS/400 aficionados continue to believe that there remain some souls in other divisions of IBM, who would be happy if the AS/400 and its advanced architecture would just go away.

QuikCourse B Information

When I conducted AS/400 training classes at various companies across the US, One of the parts to the training was work management. By having conducted these courses using this material as well as aids such as PowerPoints and transparencies, I was able to learn that AS/400 managers do not always want their programmers and sometimes operators to understand all ther is to know about IBM i Work Management.

Work Management is about how IBM gets things done on the system using operating system commands and objects such as subsystems, queues, job descriptions etc. Since there are an equal number of my accounts that want Work Management training, what we have done is taken QuikCourse B and moved it to the end of the book. SO, the next QuikCourse chapter we will cover is QuikCourse C. It is coming right up.

QuikCourse C: Creating a Source Development Environment for AS/400 and IBM i

File Systems

Before IBM invented the integrated file system (IFS) about eight years ago, everything that I am about to say was absolutely true. Now, in order for it all to be true, you must take it in the context of the native file system on the AS/400, which is also known as the *library file system*. If you are an IFS buff, you may know it as the *QSYS.LIB* file system.

How would you know what file system your AS/400 operates within? It is certainly easy to find out. If you turn your AS/400 on and it seems to work, then you can bet your pay that your machine is operating in native mode, going through its paces in the traditional library/file system. You actually have to do a few special things in order to not use the traditional methods. So, for now, let's pretend that the library file system is all that there is.

The Genesis:

Everything starts someplace. The AS/400 system library name is QSYS. Besides containing the bulk of the operating system code, every other library on the system resides in QSYS. There are no sub-libraries per se, so that you cannot have a library within a library.

Libraries are objects. They provide the same facilities as directories which point to the objects in the library system. There are many different object types on the system such as:

Object type name	System abbreviation
Programs	*PGM
Files	*File
Output Queues	*Outq
Data Comm lines	*LIND
Data Areas	*DTAARA

Again, all objects are located by library, much like the directories on PCs and Unix systems. No useable object in the library file system exists on the AS/400 that is not "contained in a library"

Since it all starts from the QSYS Library, or the system library, you can say that QSYS is the genesis of the library file system. It is the source from which all else spans. Though it is not the root directory, it is the root of the library file system. As we noted above, QSYS is also the only library on the system which can contain objects of the type *LIB.

Let's Create a Library

How do you create a library?   For the first command in this section, in Figure C-1, we show a picture of the AS/400 command line from within the AS/400's main menu, and the command to create a library called PAYROLL. When we suggest typing other commands as this QuikCourse progresses, consider that these commands will be typed from a terminal or PC whose display panel looks like that in Figure C-1.

After you type *"crtlib payroll"* on the AS/400 command line, and you press the ENTER key, the message *Library PAYROLL created* appears right where the IBM copyright is in Figure C-1. A library object named *PAYROLL* now exists in the QSYS library. By the way, AS/400 and IBM i commands can be upper or lowercase. The system does not care.

Figure C-1, Create Payroll Library

```
MAIN                          OS/400 Main Menu
                                                    System:   HELLO
Select one of the following:

     1. User tasks                          .
     2. Office tasks
     3. General system tasks
     4. Files, libraries, and folders
     5. Programming
     6. Communications
     7. Define or change the system
     8. Problem handling
     9. Display a menu
    10. Information Assistant options
    11. Client Access/400 tasks

    90. Sign off

Selection or command
===> crtlib payroll text('This is the payroll library')

F3=Exit    F4=Prompt   F9=Retrieve   F12=Cancel   F13=Information Assistant
F23=Set initial menu
©) COPYRIGHT IBM CORP. 1980, 2000.
```

Though we say that an object is *contained in* a library. This is just a
figure of speech. In reality, just as DOS directories on PCs, libraries
point to locations in which objects are stored. Of course, with a PC
the only object type is a file, so the directory entries all point to files.

For an AS/400 example, since we created it, it is safe to assume that
there is a directory entry in QSYS right now which contains the name
PAYROLL and that it points to a location in single level storage in
which the PAYROLL library object actually resides.

When objects are created *in* the PAYROLL library, for each object, a
directory entry will be created in the PAYROLL library object. The
entry will contain the name, object type, and the location in single
level storage in which the object can be located by the system.

Thus objects "placed" in this library are merely located (pointed to)
via the library entries. They can physically be located anywhere on
any of the AS/400 disks

Since it is just a form of a directory, the amount of space, which a
library occupies is minimal. Each referenced object within a library
consists of not much more than a name and a pointer. It is analogous
to the index at the back of a book

If Everything Is in Directories, Where Is the Data?

We might ask at this point: *Where has all the data gone?*
Unfortunately, Peter, Paul, and Mary are not going to give us the
answer. Since we ask, however, we will also answer. Data is stored in
Physical Files which are stored in libraries. How do we create one of
these files?

Let's Create a Database

The Command *"CRTPF PAYROLL/MASTER"* will create a
physical file called *MASTER* in a library called *PAYROLL*. MASTER
is given a single level storage address, and then it is placed on any
disk on the system. In fact, parts of *MASTER* may be on different
disks. The system keeps track of it all.

MASTER is pointed to (located) by an entry in the *PAYROLL* Library
(directory). Of course having *MASTER* in the library does not really
give us a database. For *MASTER* to be a database file containing the
structure of its data as well as its data, the structure must be
referenced on the *CRTPF* command (create physical file).

The system cannot guess what fields should be in the *MASTER* file so
the programmer enters the field names and attributes into a source
file. The programmer then submits the source for compilation. The
database compiler reads the source file as input and creates the
database physical file as its output.

Database Structures

I like to call physical database file descriptions "structures," since that
is how they have been referred to in PC land since the days of Ashton
Tate's dBase. Database structures, as they are called in dBase, are
part of physical files on the AS/400. A physical file on the AS/400
contains both the structure of the data, and the data itself.

However, unlike dBase, the AS/400 structure can lie about the real
shape of the data. If, for example a database is created properly with
a source definition, the structure, more than likely, will match the

actual shape of the data. This is demonstrated below. However, without a source description to show the specific fields in the database, the physical file would believe that it has just one big field in the file which happens to have a size equal to the record length.

DB With No Structure

There has actually been a lot said in the preceding paragraph. First of all, real native AS/400 databases, with fields known to the system, are created when the CRTPF command is given a source definition from which it can build the actual DB field descriptions within the database file object. However, a database file can be created without source definitions. In this case, the file looks a lot like the flat files you would find on other record oriented systems such as mainframes, and System/36s. For example, a file can be created with a length of 200 characters with the following command:

$$\text{CRTPF FILE}\left(\text{PAYROLL/MASTER}\right) \text{ RCDLEN}\left(200\right)$$

This command creates a database file for sure, since there is no file on the AS/400 that is not a database file. However, there are no field definitions provided to the database compiler. After this command, if you wanted to get a list of the field names in the file, you could use the *display file field description* command or *DSPFFD*. This command would show you that there was, in fact, one field defined for this file. Its name would be *MASTER*, and the field would be 200 bytes long.

High Level Language (HLL) programs are not forced to use the power of the database on the AS/400. Therefore they can describe the record layout (Input in RPG and Data Division in COBOL) of a file within the program itself, just as with a non-database machine. As long as the total size of the internally described data fields did not exceed 200, and the spots carved out in the record for numeric data actually were used for numeric data, using this method is OK on an AS/400. Of course, it does not help when you want to run the Data File Utility or Query against the file, since the file projects that it has just one field.

The ability of an AS/400 database file to be "internally described" within a program has some advantages. For example, this capability can come in especially handily, when you are importing data from other systems. It can also come in handy when you are running programs from another system, which does not have a database, such as an IBM System/36.

Creating and Using Source DB Files & Members

Because it gets a little hairy trying to explain that a source file which describes a database file is actually a database file itself, I will try to do this using a Q&A technique. Hopefully, these are the questions you would ask.

Q & A   - Data Description Specifications

Q1. How is a data description, or structure, made known to the AS/400 system?

A1. DDS - Data Description Specifications

Q2. Where does DDS go?

A2. In almost all cases, DDS goes into a pre created special source file, called QDDSSRC in one of the system's libraries. IBM supplies a default file called QDDSSRC in the QGPL library, when an AS/400 is shipped from the plant. Most AS/400 shops continue to use this name for the source file which contains DDS specifications.

Q3. Can this QDDSSRC file, which holds the DDS, be in any library?

A3. Yes. QDDSSRC can be in any library, and many libraries. The libraries in which the file exists are those specified at the time the create command is entered into the system. The command is

CRTSRCPF. (Create Source Physical File). You can also use the CRTPF command but there is more work to do in order to make the file a source file if you choose this route. The recommendation is to use CRTSRCPF. With the CRTPF command, you would actually have to create DDS in order to build the source file with its record length of 92. The layout of a standard DDS type source file would be as follows:

Length	Description
6	Sequence number
6	Date
80	DDS statement

Since the CRTSRCPF builds the same three-field source file, without you having to define any DDS, it does not make sense to use the CRTPF to achieve the same result since it is more work, and there is more potential for error. So, don't do the unnecessary work. Just type a command such as the following: (AS/400 typically does not care about case)

crtsrcpf payroll/qddssrc
text('Payroll File Source Descriptions')

Q4. How do these DDS statements get into the file, called QDDSSRC?

A4. By Using the Source Entry Utility (SEU)

Q5. What kinda stuff do I need to specify in DDS?

A5. You need to name the file, the   record formats, and the fields. Additionally, you must size the fields and   describe their *attributes* (numeric, alphabetic etc.). There is a set format for the specifications.

Q6. After I get the structure for my file, say MASTER, into the source file QDDSSRC, can I then put data into the File?

A6. No! After using SEU to type the DDS into the QDDSSRC source file, there is one more step required. You must take the description of the file (structure definition in source), which you typed into QDDSSRC, and make an object from it. The file object must be created with the CRTPF command, referencing the name of the DDS member containing the source description, and specifying the name which you want to give to your file object. The CRTPF command would look as follows:

CRTPF FILE(HELLO/MASTER) SRCFILE(HELLO/QDDSSRC) SRCMBR(MASTER)

If the source member were not specified, the system would default to the name of the field to be created which, in this case, is also the name of the source member.

Q7. You mentioned the word "Member." What do you mean by a member, and do I need a QDDSSRC file to contain the DDS for every different file I wish to create?

A7. These questions are related. Just as a library is a directory to system objects on the AS/400, a file is a directory to different sets of data which are all shaped exactly the same. The file determines the shape of the data but not the contents. In fact, files do not contain data at all. Files "contain" members. Members "contain" data.

So, in the file QDDSSRC, there can be many different database definitions, each with its own name, and each contained in a separately named member.

For the MASTER file, for example, more than likely you would name its defining structure member in the QDDSSRC file the same as that of the file object to be created. In other words, because you want to create a database file named MASTER in HELLO, you type up your DDS specifications and store those in a member named MASTER in the source file QDDSSRC.

Sometimes a picture is worth a thousand words. Starting from QSYS, the genesis of the object MASTER, before it is created would look like Figure C2. The genesis of MASTER, after it is created, is shown in Figure C3.

Figure C-2 QSYS Before Creating MASTER

System Library Name	User Library Names	Object Names	Object Types	Members (If file)
QSYS	Payroll	Qddssrc	*File	File1
File2				
Master				
Menu		*Pgm		
Prt01		*Outq		
File1		*File	File1	
Mystuf	QRPGSRC	*File	RPG01	
RPG02				
RPG01		*Pgm		

Figure C-2 shows that *QDDSSRC* is in the PAYROLL library. It is a *file object type. Within *QDDSSRC* are several members, *File1*, *File2*, and *Master*. These are the DDS statements for the three files respectively. Notice that *File2* and *Master* are not yet created as objects in the *PAYROLL* library as shown in Figure C-2. Notice also that there is another library listed called *Mystuf*. This has a source file called *QRPGSRC* with two members, *RPG01*, and *RPG02*. These are source programs. Notice also that *RPG01* has been compiled and it exists as an object in the Mystuf library. Though the source for *RPG02* exists, the figure C-2 shows that it has not been compiled successfully into an object at this time.

Figure C-3 QSYS Genesis After CRTPF PAYROLL/MASTER

System Library Name	User Library Names	Object Names	Object Types	Members (If file)
QSYS	Payroll	Qddssrc	*File	File1
File2				
Master				
Menu		*Pgm		
Prt01		*Outq		
File1		*File	File1	
>>>>	Master		*File	
Mystuf	QRPGSRC		*File	RPG01
RPG02				
RPG01		*Pgm		

After we compile *Master*, notice that in Figure C-3, it exists as an object in the *PAYROLL* library. At this point, *File 2* and *RPG02* have yet to be created, though their source has been typed.

Q8. If we compile source program RPG02 into the Mystuf library, will this chart (Figure C3) change?

A8. Yes, of course, an entry would exist in Figure C-3 immediately after the last line RPG01 *Pgm, for RPG02 *Pgm, showing that it was compiled and has become an object in the Mystuf library.

File / Member Commands

The following is a list of commands and descriptions which are used to create and delete database files and members:

CRTPF	Create Physical File
CRTLF	Create Logical File (an index plus more)
CRTSRCPF	Create Source Physical File
ADDPFM	Add Physical File Member (to a physical file)
RMVM	Remove Member from any type of file
DSPLIB	Display Library
DSPFD	Display File Description (File attributes)
DSPFFD	Display File Field Description - the database field definitions within the file itself
DSPPFM	Display Physical File Member - displays raw data in physical files.

Development Environment

When an AS/400 is to be used for application development, an implementer typically sets up a source library for the developers to use. In addition to the source library, the implementer would also create a library in which the programs and other objects reside. A third library would be created for the data. This is not a rule, but it is a convention that I have seen in many shops.

If, for example an Accounts Payable system is being developed from scratch, the letters *AP* may be used as the defining part of the library names. Three libraries would be created as follows:

CRTLIB APSRC TEXT('Library for AP Source')
CRTLIB APOBJ TEXT('Library for AP Objects')
CRTLIB APDTA TEXT('Library for AP Data')

Within the *APSRC* library, for an RPG and COBOL shop, you would want to create the following source files:

CRTSRCPF FILE(APSRC/QDDSSRC)
TEXT('Source File for DDS')

CRTSRCPF FILE(APSRC/QCLSRC)
TEXT('Source File for CL Pgms')

CRTSRCPF FILE(APSRC/QRPGSRC)
TEXT('Source File for RPG/400')

CRTSRCPF FILE(APSRC/QCBLSRC)
TEXT('Source File for CBL/400')

CRTSRCPF FILE(APSRC/QRPGLESRC)
RCDLEN(112) TEXT('Source File for ILE RPG
Source')

The Procedure

The development routine for creating new modules, whether COBOL, RPG, or DDS, would be as follows:

1. Start the Program Development Manager
2. Select Work With members (option 3)
3. Specify the file (QDDSSRC) and the library (HELLO) to work with.
4. Press F6 to create a new source member

5. Type in the new source member's name (Master, etc.)
6. SEU panel opens up. Enter source statements
7. Press F3 to end SEU, and fill the new member with source statements
8. Create the object. From PDM Work With Members list, type a 14 next to the source member to use as the source for the object to be created.
9. The compiler will create the object, or give you an error message
10. If error, type WRKOUTQ on command line to find printout queue.
11. Type option 5 to view the output queue.
12. Type option 5 next to your printout and 4 next to those you want deleted.
13. Look through the listing to find errors
14. Select Option 3 from STRPDM panel to work with members
15. Pick your source file and library
16. Place a 2 for edit next to the member you wish to change.
17. Change statements as appropriate.
18. Work through steps 7 through 17 until the member compiles error free.

Summary and Conclusions

In this QuikCourse, we outlined the considerations and the steps necessary to create an application development environment on your AS/400. Once you create your environment, you can use the tools in the Application Development Tool set as well as other tools in the WebSphere Development Studio for IBM i to build the source and objects necessary for your applications.

QuikCourse D.   Introduction to AS/400 and IBM i Control Language

What is CL?

Control Language, which many in the AS/400 refer to as Command Language, or just CL, is a very powerful programming, operations, and systems management language and tool. It requires no installation or generation, and all functions are available at installation time. Many implementers change the default values and are pleased to find that the configuration changes are effective immediately.

CL is a natural part of the Operating System/400 (OS/400). Of course OS/400 itself is very efficient and requires no special generation or installation steps, as are required on many environments such as Linux and mainframe systems. In most cases, OS/400 is pre-loaded at the plant and requires no tape or CD or DVD installation time at all.

All functions of the operating system are available at installation time through a very crisp, concise and *HARD TO FORGET* Control Language (CL).

System Values

One of the unique attributes of an AS/400 is that it is *table-driven*. In other words, functions are enabled, disabled, or selected at the system level through a series of options known as system values.

On many other "large" or mid-sized, especially IBM systems, you go through a system generation process when you install an operating system in order to tune it for your needs. In this process, different modules are copied in and, different modules are excluded so that the resulting operating system in one shop is, by definition, different from that in the next shop–with the same operating system.

On the AS/400 and IBM i this is not the case. These values can be changed at any time through natural system interfaces (WRKSYSVAL command). The impact on the system is either immediate, or the change takes effect after one IPL and/or power down/power up sequence.

A sample list of AS/400 and IBM i system values is given below:

System Value	Shipped	Description
QABNORMSW	0	Previous end of system indication
QACGLVL	*NONE	Accounting level
QACTJOB	20	Initial # of active jobs
QADLACTJ	10	Additional # active jobs
QADLSPLA	2048	Spooling block addl stg
QADLTOTJ	10	Additional # total jobs
QALWUSRDMN	*ALL	Allow user domain objects in lib
QASTLVL	*BASIC	User assistance level
QATNPGM	*ASSIST	Attention program
QAUDCTL	*NONE	Auditing control
QAUDENDACN	*NOTIFY	Auditing end action
QAUDFRCLVL	*SYS	Force auditing data
QAUDLVL	*NONE	Security auditing level
QAUTOCFG	1	Autoconfigure devices
QAUTOVRT	0	Autoconfig virt devices
QBASACTLVL	6	Base storage pool activity lvl.

As you can see in the above list, there are quite a few system values. It took 15 values to get through the A's. When you have a chance, get an AS/400 or IBM i command line, and type the WRKSYSVAL command. If you have time read the HELP text about all of these system values and the role that they play, you will be amazed at how much you will learn about your system.

Control functions

CL provides traditional command functions plus more. For example it is the interface for the following important system facilities:

1.   Librarian functions
2.   Utility Programs - COPY, etc.
3.   Procedures
4.   Operator Commands
5.   File and disk space management

On other systems, to perform all of the functions that the one CL interface provides, you may need several different languages. Even IBM's beloved System/36 has OCC (operator control commands) and OCL (operation control language). On some systems, spooling requires another language for its management and control. CL, by contrast, is a single interface to all AS/400 functions. AS/400 CL is made up of many commands that replace the functions of traditional commands. There is only one control language on AS/400 for all functions, and that alone gives it a big plus, over all other control languages, on all other systems

CL Capabilities

Control Language is a single consistent interface to all system functions. It is used in interactive or batch mode. In interactive mode, it provides prompts and command grouping menus to help you find the command you need for a given function.

CL can also be compiled into programs. This is unique to AS/400. All other systems use interpretive forms of control language which means the system must translate the source on the fly to figure out the user request, and then it must execute the request. It is designed for controlling application flow. CL is fast, with powerful logic and data manipulation facilities. CL can also have a built-in direct workstation interface so that CL programs can use the same type of display file as other high level languages (HLL) on the system.

A significant feature is the ability, in interactive mode, for a CL user to be prompted during the formation of a command. Simply by pressing the F4 Command Key, the user is prompted for all command parameters. Along with the AS/400 and IBM i menus and extensive help options, the command prompter makes it almost impossible to forget how to get something done. You can't forget since the system has all of this stuff in CL to remind you how to accomplish tasks that you may only occasionally use. Moreover, this feature helps you avoid many look-ups and searches into the many system reference manuals.

What Makes a CL Command?

There are three basic components of a CL command:

1. Command Name
2. Command Parameters (0 - 50)
3. Blank Separators

How are CL commands structured?

CL commands are designed as mini-abbreviated English sentences. Each CL command has at least two Englishlike, abbreviated components: (1) a verb, and (2) a noun, and sometimes an adjective or two. The noun often represents an object type on the system which the verb is operating upon. For example the command to display a program is DSPPGM Whenever you want to use a verb in a command to display anything, you can count on the three characters, *DSP* beginning the command you choose to use.

Other popular command verbs are as follows:

CRT   Create
WRK   Work with
DLT   Delete
STR   Start
CHG   Change
RMV   Remove

Besides PGM, for program, there are also a number of nouns or objects, which you will find in many CL commands. You will find the nouns to be a little more cryptic than self-explanatory. However, once you know the abbreviations for the verbs and the nouns, you can almost form any command yourself. A sample set of abbreviations for these is as follows:

D	Description
E	Entry
F	File
LIB	Library
ARA	Area
Q	Queue

Verbs, Adjectives, Nouns

You are not done yet. Here's why! Let's say you take the verb DSP and the noun Q. The command would be DSPQ. If you try this on the system, it will fail? Why? The answer is in another question: What type of Q? However if you know that you want to look at an output queue versus a job queue, you can use an adjective in front of Q, such as "OUT" Q (OUTQ),   to hone-in to the specific object that you want to reference. Thus there are adjectives, sometimes several adjectives which are necessary in the formation of a command. Moreover, sometimes an abbreviation for a CL noun is actually used as an adjective. An example of this is file description or "FD."

The adjectives can be 1, 2, or even 3 characters long, depending on the choice of the AS/400 command structure designer in IBM's Rochester Minnesota lab. Let's take a look at a group of common adjective modifiers which are often found in CL commands:

P	Physical
DSP	Display as in display file (also a verb)
MSG	Message (also a noun)
DTA	Data (also a noun)
BCK	Backup
OBJ	Object (also a noun)
F	File (also a noun - meaning in context)
F	Field (also a noun - meaning in context)
JOB	Job (also a noun)

Looking at this again, we have the AS/400 Command Structure made up of a 3-character verb, which denotes the action to be taken, an adjective or two, and a noun. For example, for the verb *create*, use CRT whether you are creating a physical file, a program, or an output queue.

The adjective modifier in the command can be 1 to 3 characters. This distinguishes the type of action to be taken, although sometimes the modifier has to do with the actual type of object to be worked upon, and / or created.

For example, when creating a program or file object, the modifier determines whether the created object is a physical file (CRTPF) vs. a Logical File (CRTLF) . . . or perhaps a COBOL program (CRTCBLPGM) vs. an RPG program (CRTRPGPGM).

The third part of a command is the noun, which often serves as the object of the verb, which causes action to be taken against it. This noun delineates that action is taken on a file, library, description, or other object type.   The noun (object of the verb) can be 1 to 3 characters. Often the noun (object) gets its full object type by combining with the adjective / modifier, as in the case of PF, LF, DSPF. CBLPGM, CLPGM, RPGPGM.

In summary, CL command names are comprised of 1 verb,   0-2 adjectives or modifiers, and 1 object or noun.

Let's play a little game. Cover up the answers below the questions. You fill in the blanks:

	VERB	MODIFIER	OBJECT
Create RPG Program	CRT	RPG	PGM
Create Physical File	___	___	___
Display Library	___	___	___
Start Print Writer	___	___	___

The answers are as follows:

```
Create Physical File  - CRT   P    F     CRTPF

Display Library   -       DSP        LIB   DSPLIB

Start Print Writer -     STR   PRT  WTR   STRPRTWTR
```

Command Parameters

Commands need parameters to actually get work done. For example a CREATE command needs a name for the object to be created. Another advantage of CL is that its parameters can be keyword, positional, or MIXED

Let's take the command *"create library"* as an example:

CRTLIB LIB(liba) TYPE(*prod) AUT(*none) TEXT(*blank)

There are four keywords used in the above example.

Default Parameters, Positional Parameters, Keywords

Now, let's take another example with a mix of keywords and positional parameters:

CRTLIB liba AUT(*none)

In this example, *liba* is positional and AUT(*none) is keyword oriented. A rule is that you can use positional parameters on any command until you use your first keyword. From then on, all prompts must be keyword-oriented. If you want to use positional parameters, the first ones are the easiest to use, since you are just a few commands away from the start. If, however, you wanted to merely change the text of an object, a mythical command might have to be specified with lots of commas, such as:

MYTCMD MYTHOBJ,,,,,,,,,,,'city life'

Programmers are also welcome to create your own commands, such as MYTHCMD above. These commands typically look as nice as those created by IBM but they use your programs to perform their work. Almost all IBM commands have defaults. User commands also have defaults. That is why in the above example, you did not have to fill in between the commas. The default parameter values were used.

An example of an incorrect command is as follows:

CRTLIB AUT(*NONE) liba

The problem is that positional parameters such as *liba* must precede keyword parameters. This one is correct:

CRTLIB liba AUT(*NONE)

Interactive Prompting

Commands can also be prompted interactively by typing the command and then pressing F4. They can also be prompted and completed in an SEU session. They can also be prompted at execution time by placing a "?" in front of a compiled command when typing in the source. Additionally, selected command parameters (parts of commands) can be prompted individually by placing "?" in front of the keywords when typing in the CL with SEU.

Command Alternatives from the Past

To help us gain an appreciation for how nice AS/400 commands are, let's take a look at some System/36 OCL below:

```
// LOAD PGM1
// FILE NAME-APLVND1
// FILE -------------------
// FILE ------------------
// RUN
```

There are five statements for this simple program call with just three files. If there were ten files, there would be twelve statements in the command to run an S/36 program. With AS/400, it is reduced to one statement as follows:

CALL PGM1

OCL vs. CL

When using S/36 OCL you have to include statements, which load the program, define the files to be used, then run or execute the program. Syntax checking occurs each time you execute any set of OCL. On the AS/400 you simply call the program to execute it.   No file statements are required. The virtual addressing scheme used for programs is also used for files.

Let's copy a file using a method from another time era. First, we show the System/3– the first IBM Rochester small system. Then, we contrast it by showing how much less work is needed on the AS/400 and IBM i.

SYSTEM/3 OCL

```
// LOAD $COPY,F1
// FILE NAME-COPYIN,LABEL-APPVEND,
     UNIT-D1,PACK-ABCDEF
// FILE NAME-COPYO,LABEL-APPVEND1,
     UNIT-D2,PACK-GHIJKL,RECORDS-500
// RUN
// COPYFILE OUTPUT-DISK
// END
```

AS/400 CL

CPYF APPVEND APPVEND1 MBROPT(*ADD)

On other traditional systems such as the System/3, and mainframes, if you wanted to copy a file, you would have to specify the pack, unit, and file name. With AS/400 and IBM i, you need specify only the "from and to" files in addition to an indicator as to whether you are adding or replacing records. AS/400 CL is much easier and simpler to use than any other control language.

Sample AS/400 CL Commands

CRTLIB MYLIB
CHGLIB MYLIB TEXT('MYLIB TEXT')
DLTLIB LIB(MYLIB)
?CRTLIB
WRKSYSSTS
WRKACTJOB
CRTDUPOBJ
RNMOBJ
GRTOBJAUT
WRKSYSVAL

The commands above are translated below for your edification:

CRTLIB	creates a library.
CHGLIB	changes object information about the library.
DLTLIB	deletes a library.
?CRTLIB	keyed interactively or inside a program. The "?" Invokes the system command prompter. In fact, a question mark before any command invokes the command prompter.
WRK	is a prefix (verb), which provides a vehicle for working with an object (display, change, delete, etc.)
WRKSYSSTS	displays the status of the system, and provides for changes to be made.
WRKACTJOB	displays the status of all active jobs in the system and allows them to be changes.
CRTDUPOBJ	creates duplicate objects.
RNMOBJ	renames objects.
GRTOBJAUT	grants a user authority to an object.
WRKSYSVAL	displays a list of the system values and allows the user to select a value for display or change purposes.

CL Program Command Statements

Cl can also be also used in programs. CL Programs provide additional commands, which only make sense in a programming environment. They cannot be used interactively. In fact many have suggested that CL looks a lot like the PL/1 programming language, but it does not have the full facility of the super PL/1 language. Since CL is a programming language, you find operations such as the following in its basic makeup:

DO
DATA
IF
GOTO
etc.

What is a CL Program?

CL programs are compiled. This is the first control language to which I was introduced, which operated in compiled form. Rather than interpret CL into machine language at execution time, as most other command processors would do, IBM chose to make CL invocation substantially faster, and for this purpose, built the CL compiler. Arithmetic and data manipulation operations were also made part of the language so that CL stands today as the super model for Control Languages on all systems.

There are a number of commands on the AS/400 such as STRDBRDR (Start Database Reader) and SBMDBJOB (Submit Database Job which can interpret CL that is stored in a source file. However, most AS/400 and IBM i aficionados will go through their whole careers without finding a need for these commands.

Simple CL Program

To give an appreciation for what a CL program may look like, let's examine a simple menu program. For this example, assume that you have already created the display file. If you want to examine the display file first, you can go to the mini lab in Figure D-5. The program is as follows:

```
PGM
DCLF            FILE(VENDSELECT)
START:          SNDRCVF RCDFMT(VENDREC)
IF              COND(&IN99) THEN(GOTO END)
                IF    COND(&OPTION = '1') THEN(DSPMSG)
                IF    COND(&OPTION = '2') THEN(DSPLIBL)
                IF    COND(&OPTION = '3') HEN(WRKOUTQ)
                IF    COND(&OPTION = '4') THEN(CALL DINQ)
                IF    COND(&OPTION = '5') THEN(SIGNOFF)
                GOTO  START
END:            ENDPGM
```

This is an example of a CL program that would be used for a menu application. The CL program writes a display screen, using the send and then receive format - SNDRCVF command, and gives the user five options to take from the menu. At any time, the user can press F3 which turns on indicator 99 in the display file (Figure D-5). Indicator 99 causes a branch to the END: label and the ENDPGM program is executed causing the program to end.

If F3 is not pressed, when the user types in an option and hits ENTER, the program tests the option field (&OPTION) as entered. If the user types in a value of 1 to 5, one of the IF statement commands is satisfied, and the appropriate program is executed. Following execution, the program falls to the bottom, loops, and then sends and receives another menu option. The game continues until the user hits F3.

In this simplified program, there is no test for an invalid option, so if something other than 1 to 5 is entered, the program falls through to the "GOTO." It loops and the user is prompted again to enter another option - with no indication that something was wrong.

Declare File

If you are wondering where the variables (shown beginning with an "&" in CL programs) are defined, look at the DCLF (declare file) statement. This is the Declare File statement. It is the link between the display file (Figure D-5) and the CL program. This command brings in the display file object which defines all of the fields in the Display File named *VENDSELECT* to the CL program.

What about Other Variables?

&OPTION and &IN99 (indicator) are the only two variables in the display file. They are intrinsically defined by the DCLF display file reference. If you wanted to define a variable independent of a display file, you can use the declare operation (DCL). Sample declarations are included below:

```
DCL   VAR(&COUNT)     TYPE(*DEC)    LEN(5 0)
DCL   VAR(&USER)      TYPE(*CHAR)   LEN(10)
DCL   VAR(&JOBNO)     TYPE(*CHAR)   LEN(6)
```

The first field declared is a variable COUNT which is decimal, 5 positions long, with no decimal positions. The next is a variable USER which is character with a length of 10. The next is a field called JOBNO which is defined as character with a length of 6.

Command Prompting and Assistance

Prompting and assistance is available on the AS/400 in a number of ways. First of all, there is a facility which is available at the touch of the attention key called *Operational Assistant*. This is invisible unless you ask it for help.

There is also system assisted command entry via:

1.   Menu Displays
2.   Prompt Displays
3.   Interactive Syntax Checking
4.   Extensive HELP / On-line Documentation

These assistants are available when using:

1.   Command entry display
2.   Programmer / Operator/ Main Menus via the command line
3.   Source Entry Utility(SEU)
4.   Program Development Manager (PDM)

A Look at the Command Prompter

As I suggested above, my favorite CL component is the command prompter, because it makes it impossible to forget about a command. Let's say you are at a display station and you know that you want to create something, for example. All you have to do is hit F4. Don't type anything, just press F4. The system responds with the command grouping menu in Figure D-1

Figure D-1 Command Grouping Menu

```
MAJOR                          Major Command Groups

                                               System:  HELLO
Select one of the following:
      1. Select Command by Name                       SLTCMD
      2. Verb Commands                                VERB
      3. Subject Commands                             SUBJECT
      4. Object Management Commands                   CMDOBJMGT
      5. File Commands                                CMDFILE
      6. Save and Restore Commands                    CMDSAVRST
      7. Work Management Commands                      CMDWRKMGT
      8. Data Management Commands                      CMDDTAMGT
      9. Security Commands                            CMDSEC
     10. Print Commands                               CMDPRT
     11. Spooling Commands                            CMDSPL
     12. System Control Commands                      CMDSYSCTL
     13. Program Commands                             CMDPGM

More...
Selection or command
===>
F3=Exit    F4=Prompt    F9=Retrieve    F12=Cancel    F13=Information Assistant
F16=AS/400 Main menu
(C) COPYRIGHT IBM CORP. 1980, 2000.
```

Command Grouping Menus

Take a look at Figure D-1. This is a programmer's dream. All of the commands and substantial help text are just a finger's touch away. In the example that you are pursuing, you want to create something. To get some help on all of the create commands, you can do a few different things.

1. You can GO CMDCRT. This is a quick means of using command HELP navigation. Use GO as the menu command, CMD as the command menu prefix, and CRT, DLT, etc as the subject you are looking for. In this instance, you are taken to the create menu.

2. You can type 2 in the command grouping menu in Figure D-4, and press ENTER. The next panel is similar to that shown in Figure D-2.

To get to the panel in Figure D-2, just press the ROLL Down or Page Down key on your keyboard.

Figure D-2. Second Page of Verb Command Groups

```
 VERB                            Verb Commands

  Select one of the following:

        15. Cancel Commands                               CMDCNL
        16. Container Commands                            CMDCNR

        18. Copy Commands                                 CMDCPY
        19. Create Commands                               CMDCRT
        20. Create File Commands                          CMDCRTF
        21. Create Program Commands                       CMDCRTPGM
        22. Convert Commands                              CMDCVT
        23. Declare Commands                              CMDDCL
        24. Deallocate Commands                           CMDDLC
        25. Delete Commands                               CMDDLT
        26. Delay Commands                                CMDDLY
        27. Dump Commands                                 CMDDMP
        28. Do Commands                                   CMDDO

  More...
   Selection or command
   ===>
  F3=Exit    F4=Prompt    F9=Retrieve    F12=Cancel    F16=Major menu
```

To get to the *CREATE* menu, select option 19 and press ENTER. You will then be taken to the first CREATE menu as shown in Figure D-3.

When you get to the panel in Figure D-3, you are at the first panel of 13 panels of commands for which you can be prompted. More than likely, you would read these commands and roll from panel to panel looking for the object type you want to create and then you would pick the command by number and be prompted. Let's say you wanted to create a bound C program for example. You would select option 5 on this menu and you would be taken to a panel such as Figure D-4 in which you would be prompted to enter the appropriate parameters for the command. Tell me why you need a book! Tell me why GUI is so good!

Figure D-3 Create Commands Menu

```
CMDCRT                        Create Commands

Select one of the following:

  Commands
     1. Create Alert Table                              CRTALRTBL
     2. Create Authority Holder                         CRTAUTHLR
     3. Create Authorization List                       CRTAUTL

     5. Create Bound C Program                          CRTBNDC
     6. Create Bound COBOL Program                      CRTBNDCBL
     7. Create Bound CL Program                         CRTBNDCL
     8. Create Bound C++ Program                        CRTBNDCPP
     9. Create Binding Directory                        CRTBNDDIR
    10. Create Bound RPG Program                        CRTBNDRPG
    11. Create COBOL Module                             CRTCBLMOD
    12. Create COBOL Program                            CRTCBLPGM
    13. Create Configuration List                       CRTCFGL

More...
Selection or command
===> 5
_____

F3=Exit    F4=Prompt    F9=Retrieve    F12=Cancel    F16=Major menu
©) COPYRIGHT IBM CORP. 1980, 2000.
```

Figure D-4, CREATE C program Prompt

```
                    Create Bound C Program (CRTBNDC)

Type choices, press Enter.

Program  . . . . . . . . . . . .   CPROGRAM      Name
  Library  . . . . . . . . . . .     *CURLIB     Name, *CURLIB
Source file  . . . . . . . . . .   QCSRC         Name
  Library  . . . . . . . . . . .     *LIBL       Name, *LIBL, *CURLIB
Source member  . . . . . . . . .   *PGM          Name, *PGM
Source stream file . . . . . . .   _____


Text 'description'  . . . . . . .   *SRCMBRTXT


Bottom
F3=Exit    F4=Prompt    F5=Refresh    F10=Additional parameters    F12=Cancel
F13=How to use this display          F24=More keys
```

Control Language Mini Lab

To strengthen your knowledge of CL and get some structured machine time, we have built a simple, yet complete CL Lab for you to exercise. We urge you to take this Lab. If things get boring to you, either you started knowledgeably, or you have already "gotten" the material! We introduce some notions in this lab which have not yet been taught. Don't worry about it. You will be able to accomplish these exercises, and you will know CL and how it fits in even that much better. If there's something you don't understand, move through the lab anyway. More than likely, we'll be getting to it soon.

Mini Lab Objectives

The objectives of this little lab are to get you familiar with how to function in an AS/400 and IBM i application development environment while creating a small CL program. In the lab, you will create a CL program to:

1. Display messages
2. Display a library list
3. Work with all output queues on the system
4. Call a mythical RPG III Vendor Inquiry program. Note: We have not created this program yet. In your lab, feel free to substitute another program from your shop.
5. Sign off the system

The source for RPG programs and files should naturally be created as part of previous QuikCourses. However, when appropriate in the Mini Lab, we show how to create necessary objects which may not have been previously created.

☺ Note: Though this is a CL program creation lab. The source for the display file, and the steps to create the display file are shown in this lab for Completeness.

The Lab Steps:

Though this example lab is very simple, it shows the power of CL programming as used in an interactive environment. The same program which we built above is used in this lab. This time, however, you will perform all of the steps necessary to create the CL program as an object on your system.

The steps you will follow are:

1. Signon to the system and start the Program Development Manager (PDM) by typing *STRPDM*. PDM is covered in QuikCourse E in this book.
2. Take option 3 from PDM   (Work with members).
3. Enter file - QDDSSRC, library - HELLO, press ENTER. If HELLO is not built, then you can create it by typing CRTLIB SAMPLE on a command line and pressing ENTER. If QDDSSRC is not in HELLO, you can create it with: CRTSRCPF HELLO/QDDSSRC
4. Press F6 for the SEU ADD member function to add VENDSELECT to the Source File. Then type in your DDS (covered in QuikCourse F).
5. When you have keyed the VENDSELECT Display File DDS, take F3 to end the job and save your work. You will return to PDM member selection menu.
6. Place a 14 next to   VENDSELECT to create the display file for the CL program. Press F4 to assure yourself that this will compile to the HELLO library. If it is not set to do this, change it to HELLO and press ENTER. This will compile the display file named VENDSELECT and place the display file object in the HELLO library.
7. From the PDM Work With Members panel, change the source file name on the top left to QCLSRC and assure the library name continues to be HELLO. Then press ENTER. This should place PDM into the QCLSRC file in the HELLO library. If QCLSRC (the source file for CL) does not exist, then create it with the following command: CRTSRCPF HELLO/QDDSSRC. After typing this, press ENTER to create the source file. When the file is created, change the top of the PDM screen to get into the QCLSRC file as described above.
8. Press F6 for the SEU ADD member function to add the CL program named   VENDSELECT to the QCLSRC source File.
9. Then type in your CL program. When you have keyed the VENDSELECT CL program, take F3 to end the job and save your work. You will return to PDM member selection menu.
10. Place a 14 next to VENDSELECT in QCLSRC to create the CL Program. Press F4 to assure yourself that this will compile to the HELLO library. If it is not set to do this, change it to HELLO

and press ENTER. This will compile the CL Program named VENDSELECT and place the CL program object in the HELLO library.

11. Call VENDSELECT to execute by typing CALL VENDSELECT on your command line and pressing ENTER.

* If there are problems compiling or executing in which a *"file not found"* message is displayed, your library list needs to be changed. If you submit to batch, you can add the library to the list you use in your job description. If you compile interactively, execute this command before selecting PDM option 14 again: ADDLIBLE HELLO.

The display file to be keyed in step 3 is shown in Figure D-5. The program to be keyed in step 8 is shown in Figure D-6, and the display panel for the CL program, when executing, is shown in Figure D-7.

Figure D-5 VENDSELECT Display File DDS

```
Columns   . .:    1   71              Edit                    HELLO/QDDSSRC
 SEU==>.                                                      VENDSELECT
 FMT A*  ..A*. 1 ...+... 2 ...+... 3 ..4 ...+... 5 ...+... 6 ...+... 7.......
         ***************** Beginning of data********************************
0003.00  A                           PRINT CF03(99)
0004.00  A            R VENDREC       BLINK OVERLAY
0005.00  A                        6 34'VENDOR SELECTION'
0006.00  A                        7  2'Select one of the following:
0007.00  A                        9  4'1.  ' DSPATR(HI)
0008.00  A                        9  9'DISPLAY MESSAGES'
0009.00  A                       10  4'2.  ' DSPATR(HI)
0010.00  A                       10  9'DISPLAY LIBRARY LIST'
0011.00  A                       11  4'3.  ' DSPATR(HI)
0012.00  A                       11  9'WORK WITH ALL OUTPUT QUEUES'
0013.00  A                       12  4'4.  ' DSPATR(HI)
0014.00  A                       12  9'CALL RPG/400 VENDOR INQUIRY PROGR+
0015.00                             AM'
0016.00  A                       13  4'5.  ' DSPATR(HI)
0017.00  A                       13  9'SIGNOFF'
0018.00  A                       23  2'Option:  '
0019.00  A            OPTION   3  I 23 12DSPATR(PC)
0020.00  A                       24 22'F3  END OF JOB'
         ***************** End of data********************************
 F3=Exit  F5 Refresh  F9=Retrieve  F10=Cursor   F12=Cancel
 F16=Repeat find      F24=More keys
```

Figure D-6 Program to Display Menu & Accept Options

```
Columns . . . .:   1  71              Edit                HELLO/QCLSRC
SEU==>. . .                                                VENDSELECT
FMT **   ...+... 1 ...+... 2 ...+... 3 ...+... 4 ...+... 5 ...+... 6 ...+... 7
         *************** Beginning of data ********************************
0001.00
0002.00            PGM
0003.00            DCLF        FILE(VENDSELECT)
0004.00  START:    SNDRCVF     RCDFMT(VENDREC)
0005.00            IF          COND(&IN99) THEN(GOTO CMDLBL(END))
0006.00            IF          COND(&OPTION = '1') THEN(DSPMSG)
0007.00            IF          COND(&OPTION = '2') THEN(DSPLIBL)
0008.00            IF          COND(&OPTION = '3') THEN(WRKOUTQ)
0009.00            IF          COND(&OPTION = '4') THEN(CALL VENDINQ)
0010.00            IF          COND(&OPTION = '5') THEN(SIGNOFF)
0011.00            GOTO        START
0012.00  END:      ENDPGM
         ****************** End of data ****************************************
 F3=Exit   F5=Refresh   F9=Retrieve  F10=Cursor   F13=Cancel
 F16=Repeat find        F24=More keys
                                        ©) COPYRIGHT IBM CORP. 1981, 1990.
```

Figure D-7 CL in Action

```
                              VENDOR SELECTION
    Select one of the following:

       1.    DISPLAY MESSAGES
       2.    DISPLAY LIBRARY LIST
       3.    WORK WITH ALL OUTPUT QUEUES
       4.    CALL RPG/400 VENDOR INQUIRY PROGRAM
       5.    SIGN OFF



    Option:    ___
                   F3    END OF JOB
```

Since you will not have created the RPG program (menu option 4) in Figure D-7, prior to executing this CL menu program, selecting option 4 from the menu will cause an OS/400 Function Check. That's OK. When you get the function check, you will know that the menu option in the CL program performed as designed.

Now, perform the steps from step zero until you have completed this mini lab.

Start PDM

0. Signon to the system and start the Program Development Manager. Key the following and press ENTER.

STRPDM

You will see a panel similar to that in Figure D-8

Figure D-8 PDM Main Menu

```
                        AS/400 Programming Development Manager (PDM)

  Select one of the following:

        1. Work with libraries
        2. Work with objects
        3. Work with members

        9. Work with user-defined options


  Selection or command
  ===> 3
  _____

  F3=Exit          F4=Prompt        F9=Retrieve       F10=Command entry
  F12=Cancel        F18=Change defaults
```

Work With Members

1. Take option 3 from PDM as shown on Figure D-8. You will see a panel similar to that in Figure D-9.

2. In the panel shown in Figure D-9, Enter the file name - QDDSSRC, and enter the library name - HELLO, then press ENTER. If the library HELLO is not built yet, then you can create it by typing **CRTLIB HELLO,** on a command line and pressing ENTER. If QDDSSRC is not in HELLO, you can create it by typing **CRTSRCPF HELLO/QDDSSRC** on a command line and pressing ENTER.

If you must create the file, restart with STRPDM in step 1 above, and your panel will again look like the panel in Figure D-9. When you get the panel in Figure D9 completed properly, press ENTER and you will be taken to Figure D-11.

Specify QDDSSRC and HELLO

Figure D-9   Specify Members to Work With.

```
                    Specify Members to Work With

  Type choices, press Enter.

    File  . . . . . . . . .    QDDSSRC      Name, F4 for list

      Library . . . . . . .    HELLO        *LIBL, *CURLIB, name

    Member:
      Name  . . . . . . . .    *ALL         *ALL, name, *generic*
      Type  . . . . . . . .    *ALL         *ALL, type, *generic*, *BLANK


  F3=Exit      F4=Prompt      F5=Refresh     F12=Cancel
```

☺Note: Figure D-10 has been intentionally skipped.

Add VENDSELECT Member

3. Press F6 from the panel in Figure D-11 for the SEU ADD member
function to add source program (member) VENDSELECT to the Source
File. The next panel you see is the START SEU panel in Figure D-12. In
this panel, you provide the name (VENDSELECT), then type (DSPF for
display file), and the text (to describe the object). In Figure D-13, type in
your DDS (covered in QuikCourse G).

Figure D-11 Work With Members

```
                    Work with Members Using PDM              HELLO

  File  . . . . . .    QDDSSRC
    Library . . . .    HELLO             Position to  . . . . .

  Type options, press Enter.
    2=Edit          3=Copy  4=Delete 5=Display      6=Print     7=Rename
    8=Display description  9=Save 13=Change text  14=Compile  15=Create
  module...

  Opt  Member     Type        Text

    (No members in file)



  Parameters or command
  ===>
  F3=Exit            F4=Prompt              F5=Refresh           F6=Create
  F9=Retrieve        F10=Command entry      F23=More options     F24=More keys
```

Figure D-12 Work With Members

```
                    Start Source Entry Utility (STRSEU)

Type choices, press Enter.

Source file  . . . . . . . . . > QDDSSRC     Name, *PRV
   Library  . . . . . . . . . . >   HELLO     Name, *LIBL, *CURLIB, *PRV
Source member  . . . . . . . . > VENDSELECT  Name, *PRV, *SELECT
Source type  . . . . . . . . . > DSPF        Name, *SAME, BAS, BASP...
Text 'description' . . . . . . . Vendor Selection Display File


Bottom
F3=Exit    F4=Prompt    F5=Refresh    F12=Cancel    F13=How to use this display
F24=More keys
```

Figure D-13 SEU Edit Panel

```
Columns . . . :    1  71              Edit
HELLO/QDDSSRC
SEU==>
VENDSELECT
FMT DP
.....AAN01N02N03T.Name++++++RLen++TDpBLinPosFunctions++++++++++++++++++
         ************** Beginning of data
***************************************
 ''''''

 . . . .
 ''''''
         ***************** End of data
*****************************************

F3=Exit    F4=Prompt    F5=Refresh    F9=Retrieve    F10=Cursor    F11=Toggle
F16=Repeat find        F17=Repeat change              F24=More keys
Member VENDSELECT added to file HELLO/QDDSSRC.
+
```

Figure D-14 SEU Edit Panel With DDS

```
   Columns . . . :   6  76          Browse
 HELLO/QDDSSRC
   SEU==>
 VENDSELECT
   FMT DP
 AAN01N02N03T.Name++++++RLen++TDpBLinPosFunctions+++++++++++++++++++++++++
           *************** Beginning of data
 **************************************
 0001.00 A                              PRINT CF03(99)
 0002.00 A         R VENDREC            BLINK OVERLAY
 0003.00 A                           6 34'VENDOR SELECTION'
 0004.00 A                           7  2'Select one of the following:'
 0005.00 A                           9  4'1.   ' DSPATR(HI)
 0006.00 A                           9  9'DISPLAY MESSAGES'
 0007.00 A                          10  4'2.   ' DSPATR(HI)
 0008.00 A                          10  9'DISPLAY LIBRARY LIST'
 0009.00 A                          11  4'3.   ' DSPATR(HI)
 0010.00 A                          11  9'WORK WITH ALL OUTPUT QUEUES'
 0011.00 A                          12  4'4.   ' DSPATR(HI)
 0012.00 A                          12  9'CALL RPG/400 VENDOR INQUIRY +
 0013.00 A                              PROGRAM'
 0014.00 A                          13  4'5.   ' DSPATR(HI)
 0015.00 A                          13  9'SIGNOFF'
 0016.00 A                          23  2'OPTION:   '
 F3=Exit    F5=Refresh    F9=Retrieve  F10=Cursor   F11=Toggle    F12=Cancel
   F16=Repeat find        F24=More keys
```

Type DDS, Save Work, Exit

4. When you have keyed the VENDSELECT Display File DDS in
Figure D-14, take F3 to end the job and save your work. This will
bring you to the SEU Exit panel shown in Figure D-15. The options
should be already filled in as seen in the panel. Press ENTER and
you will return to the PDM member selection menu as shown in
Figure D-16.

Figure D-15 SEU Exit Panel

```
                              Exit

  Type choices, press Enter.

      Change/create member  . . . . . . .  Y           Y=Yes, N=No
        Member   . . . . . . . . . . . .  VENDSELECT  Name, F4 for list
        File  . . . . . . . . . . . . .   QDDSSRC     Name, F4 for list
          Library . . . . . . . . . . .   HELLO       Name
        Text  . . . . . . . . . . . . .   Vendor Selection Display File

      Resequence member . . . . . . . .   Y           Y=Yes, N=No
        Start . . . . . . . . . . . . .   0001.00     0000.01-9999.99
        Increment . . . . . . . . . . .   01.00       00.01-99.99

      Print member  . . . . . . . . . .   N           Y=Yes, N=No

      Return to editing . . . . . . . .   N           Y=Yes, N=No

      Go to member list . . . . . . . .   N           Y=Yes, N=No

  F3=Exit    F4=Prompt   F5=Refresh   F12 Cancel
```

Figure D-16 PDM Member Selection Menu

```
                Work with Members Using PDM               HELLO

  File  . . . . . .   QDDSSR
    Library . . . .   HELLO              Position to  . . . . .

  Type options, press Enter.
   2=Edit         3=Copy  4=Delete 5=Display      6=Print      7=Rename
   8=Display description  9=Save 13=Change text  14=Compile 15=Create
  module...

  Opt  Member      Type     Text
   14  VENDSELECT  DSPF         Vendor Selection Display File


  Bottom
  Parameters or command
  ===>
  F3=Exit         F4=Prompt        F5=Refresh        F6=Create
  F9=Retrieve     F10=Command entry F23=More options F24=More Keys
```

Create Display File for CL Program

5. Place a 14 next to VENDSELECT in Figure D-16 to create the display file for the CL program. Press F4 after typing 14 to prompt for the create command. You want to be assured that the display file will compile to the HELLO library. See Figure D-17 for an example of how this should look. If it is not set to compile to HELLO, change it accordingly and press ENTER. This will compile the display file

named VENDSELECT, and place the display file object in the
HELLO library.

Figure D-17 Create Display File

```
                    Create Display File (CRTDSPF)

Type choices, press Enter.

File . . . . . . . . . . . . . . > VENDSELECT   Name
  Library  . . . . . . . . . . . >   HELLO      Name, *CURLIB
Source file  . . . . . . . . . . > QDDSSRC      Name, *NONE
  Library  . . . . . . . . . . . >   HELLO      Name, *LIBL, *CURLIB
Source member  . . . . . . . . . > VENDSELECT   Name, *FILE
Generation severity level  . . .   20           0-30
Flagging severity level  . . . .   0            0-30
Display device . . . . . . . . .   *REQUESTER   Name, *NONE, *REQUESTER
              + for more values
Text 'description' . . . . . . .   *SRCMBRTXT


                    Additional Parameters

Replace file . . . . . . . . . > *NO            *YES, *NO


Bottom
F3=Exit    F4=Prompt    F5=Refresh   F10=Additional parameters   F12=Cancel
F13=How to use this display          F24=More keys
```

After you hit ENTER on the panel in D-17, if you have done your
homework well, you will receive the following message at the bottom
of the panel:

File VENDSELECT created in library HELLO.

You will return to the panel as shown in Figure D-18.

6. From the PDM Work With Members panel, in Figure D-18,
change the source file name from QDDSSRC in the top left corner to
QCLSRC, and assure the library name continues to be HELLO.
Then press ENTER. This should place your PDM session into the
QCLSRC file in the HELLO library as shown in Figure D-19.

Figure D-18 Changing Source File in PDM

```
                      Work with Members Using PDM                    HELLO

File  . . . . . .    QCLSRC___     <<<<
   Library . . . .   HELLO___                Position to  . . . . .

Type options, press Enter.
  2=Edit          3=Copy  4=Delete 5=Display      6=Print     7=Rename
  8=Display description  9=Save 13=Change text  14=Compile  15=Create
module...

Opt  Member      Type        Text
  _  VENDSELECT  DSPF        Vendor Selection Display File


Bottom
 Parameters or command
 ===>
 F3=Exit          F4=Prompt          F5=Refresh          F6=Create
 F9=Retrieve      F10=Command entry  F23=More options    F24=More keys
 File VENDSELECT created in library HELLO.
```

Work With QCLSRC File

If QCLSRC (the source file for CL) does not exist, then create it with
the following command: **CRTSRCPF HELLO/QDDSSRC.** After
typing this, press ENTER to create the source file. When the
QCLSRC file is created, repeat this full step**.**

Your display will now look like the panel in Figure D-19.

Figure D-19 Member List of QCLSRC

```
                    Work with Members Using PDM                      HELLO
File  . . . . . .   QCLSRC
  Library . . . .     HELLO               Position to  . . . . .
Type options, press Enter.
  2=Edit          3=Copy  4=Delete 5=Display      6=Print      7=Rename
  8=Display description  9=Save  13=Change text  14=Compile  15=Create
module...


Opt  Member       Type         Text

   (No members in file)
Parameters or command
===>
F3=Exit          F4=Prompt           F5=Refresh          F6=Create
F9=Retrieve      F10=Command entry   F23=More options    F24=More keys
```

Add VENDSELECT CL Member to QCLSRC

7. Press F6 from the panel in Figure D-19 for the SEU ADD member function to add   VENDSELECT to the Source File. The next panel you see is the START SEU panel in Figure D-20 in which you provide the name (VENDSELECT), the type CLP (for CL Program) and the text (to describe the object).

Figure D-20 Start SEU

```
                 Start Source Entry Utility (STRSEU)
Type choices, press Enter.
Source file  . . . . . . . . . > QCLSRC        Name, *PRV
  Library  . . . . . . . . . . >   HELLO        Name, *LIBL, *CURLIB, *PRV
Source member  . . . . . . . . > VENDSELECT     Name, *PRV, *SELECT
Source type  . . . . . . . . . > CLP            Name, *SAME, BAS, BASP...
Text 'description' . . . . . .   Vendor Selection CL Program


Bottom
F3=Exit    F4=Prompt   F5=Refresh   F12=Cancel   F13=How to use this display
F24=More keys
```

Figure D-21 Edit Panel

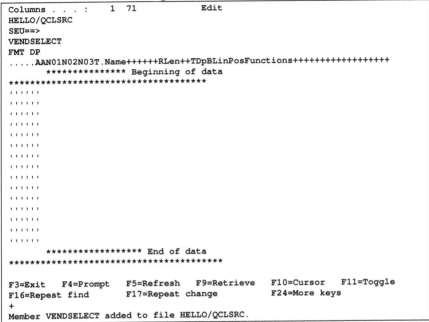

```
Columns . . . :    1  71              Edit
HELLO/QCLSRC
SEU==>
VENDSELECT
FMT DP
.....AAN01N02N03T.Name++++++RLen++TDpBLinPosFunctions+++++++++++++++++
       ************** Beginning of data
*************************************
 ''''''
 ''''''
 ''''''
 ''''''
 ''''''
 ''''''
 ''''''
 ''''''
 ''''''
 ''''''
 ''''''
 ''''''
 ''''''
 ''''''
       ***************** End of data
*****************************************

F3=Exit   F4=Prompt   F5=Refresh   F9=Retrieve   F10=Cursor   F11=Toggle
F16=Repeat find        F17=Repeat change         F24=More keys
+
Member VENDSELECT added to file HELLO/QCLSRC.
```

Type Your CL Program VENDSELECT

8.In Figure D-21, type in your CL program. When you have keyed the VENDSELECT CL Program as shown in Figure D-22, take F3 to end the job and save your work. This will bring you to the SEU Exit panel shown in Figure D-23. The options should be already filled in as seen in the panel. Press ENTER, and you will return to the PDM member selection menu as shown in Figure D-24.

Figure D-22 SEU Edit Panel With CL Program

```
  Columns . . . :   1  71              Edit
HELLO/QCLSRC
  SEU==>
VENDSELECT
  FMT **  ...+... 1 ...+... 2 ...+... 3 ...+... 4 ...+... 5 ...+... 6 ...+...
7
        *************** Beginning of data
***************************************
0001.00            PGM
0002.00            DCLF      FILE(VENDSELECT)
0003.00   START:   SNDRCVF   RCDFMT(VENDREC)
0004.00            IF        COND(&IN99) THEN(GOTO CMDLBL(END))
0005.00            IF        COND(&OPTION = '1') THEN(DSPMSG)
0006.00            IF        COND(&OPTION = '2') THEN(DSPLIBL)
0007.00            IF        COND(&OPTION = '3') THEN(WRKOUTQ)
0008.00            IF        COND(&OPTION = '4') THEN(CALL VENDINQ)
0009.00            IF        COND(&OPTION = '5') THEN(SIGNOFF)
0010.00            GOTO      START
0011.00   END:     ENDPGM
        ***************** End of data
*******************************************

  F3=Exit   F4=Prompt   F5=Refresh   F9=Retrieve   F10=Cursor   F11=Toggle
  F16=Repeat find        F17=Repeat change          F24=More keys
                                  ©) COPYRIGHT IBM CORP. 1981, 2000.
```

Figure D-23 SEU Exit Panel

```
                          Exit

Type choices, press Enter.

        Change/create member . . . . . . .   Y            Y=Yes, N=No
          Member . . . . . . . . . . . . .   VENDSELECT   Name, F4 for list
          File . . . . . . . . . . . . . .   QCLSRC       Name, F4 for list
            Library . . . . . . . . . . .    HELLO        Name
          Text . . . . . . . . . . . . . .   Vendor Selection CL Program

        Resequence member . . . . . . . .    Y            Y=Yes, N=No
          Start . . . . . . . . . . . . .    0001.00      0000.01-9999.99
          Increment . . . . . . . . . . .    01.00        00.01-99.99

        Print member . . . . . . . . . .     N            Y=Yes, N=No

        Return to editing . . . . . . . .    N            Y=Yes, N=No

        Go to member list . . . . . . . .    N            Y=Yes, N=No

  F3=Exit   F4=Prompt   F5=Refresh   F12-Cancel
```

Figure D-24 PDM Member Selection Menu

```
                    Work with Members Using PDM                HELLO

File . . . . . .   QCLSRC
  Library . . . .    HELLO                  Position to  . . . . .

Type options, press Enter.
  2=Edit           3=Copy  4=Delete 5=Display      6=Print     7=Rename
  8=Display description 9=Save 13=Change text  14=Compile 15=Create
module...

Opt  Member       Type        Text
 14  VENDSELECT   CLP         Vendor Selection CL Program

Bottom
Parameters or command
===>
F3=Exit          F4=Prompt          F5=Refresh          F6=Create
F9=Retrieve      F10=Command entry  F23=More options    F24=More keys
Member VENDSELECT added to file HELLO/QCLSRC.
+
```

Creating the CL Program

9. Place a 14 next to VENDSELECT in Figure D-24, to create the CL program. Press F4 after typing 14 for the prompt panel so that you can assure yourself that this CL Program will compile to the HELLO library. See Figure D-17 for an example of how this should look. If it is not set to compile to HELLO, change it accordingly, and press ENTER. This will compile the display file named VENDSELECT, and place the display file object in the HELLO library.

Figure D-25 Create the CL Program

```
                    Create CL Program (CRTCLPGM)
Type choices, press Enter.

Program  . . . . . . . . . . . > VENDSELECT    Name
  Library  . . . . . . . . . . >    HELLO      Name, *CURLIB
Source file  . . . . . . . . . > QCLSRC        Name
  Library  . . . . . . . . . . >    HELLO      Name, *LIBL, *CURLIB
Source member  . . . . . . . . > VENDSELECT    Name, *PGM
Text 'description'  . . . . . .   *SRCMBRTXT
                    Additional Parameters

Replace program  . . . . . . . > *NO           *YES, *NO

Bottom
F3=Exit    F4=Prompt   F5=Refresh   F10=Additional parameters   F12=Cancel
F13=How to use this display        F24=More keys
```

After you hit ENTER on the panel in D-25, again if you have done your homework well, you will receive the following message at the bottom of the Work With Members panel:

Program VENDSELECT created in library HELLO.

You will return to the panel as shown in Figure D-24.

10. From the panel in Figure D-24, Call the VENDSELECT program to execution   by typing CALL VENDSELECT on your command line and pressing ENTER. You will get the panel as shown in Figure D-26.

Figure D-26 Vendor Selection Program Operational

```
                         VENDOR  SELECTION
   Select one of the following:

      1.   DISPLAY MESSAGES
      2.   DISPLAY LIBRARY LIST
      3.   WORK WITH ALL OUTPUT QUEUES
      4.   CALL RPG/400 VENDOR INQUIRY PROGRAM
      5.   SIGN OFF
   Option:    ___
                    F3   END OF JOB
```

Take each of the options in sequence from the menu in Figure D-26. Since we have not built an RPG program for this menu, you will get a function check. Ignore it and come back to the menu. Then take option 5 to sign off. You have now completed the CL QuikCourse Mini Lab. Nice Job!

More Exercises Pardner?

No, every CL program is not as easy as VENDSELECT. You can do lots of interesting things with CL. As a compilable control language, it also serves a job control function. Batch job strings and startup job strings are built with CL and other high level languages on AS/400 and IBM i. So that we don't leave you thinking that menu programs are it for CL, we have two more example programs which we will dissect to help make your CL experience more complete.

Batch CL Program Examples

The first program is IBM's startup program (QSTRUP), which is shipped with every system, and its serves as the system startup program. The other is a homemade batch job stream which has a number of CL operations worth exploring.

First we will show the programs in their entirety. Then, we will take each program, piece by piece, section by section and explain the function and the purpose of the code.

In a short QuikCourse such as this, our objectives are not to create a crackerjack CL coder in just a few hours. Instead, we hope to make CL appear to be as easy as possible, so that you can use the system's documentation and help text to find any command you need. Then, you can be in a position to prepare the parameters necessary for that command to perform your will. This exercise should help you get there!

The startup program is shown in Figure D-27 and the homemade batch program is in Figure D-28.

```
0001.00    PGM
0002.00    DCL VAR(&STRWTRS) TYPE(*CHAR) LEN(1)
0003.00    DCL VAR(&CTLSBSD) TYPE(*CHAR) LEN(20)
0004.00    DCL VAR(&CPYR) TYPE(*CHAR) LEN(120) +
               VALUE('5722-SS1 © COPYRIGHT- +
               IBM CORP 1980, 2000. LICENSED +
               MATERIAL - PROGRAM PROPERTY OF IBM')
0006.00    QSYS/STRSBS SBSD(QSPL)
0007.00    MONMSG MSGID(CPF0000)
0008.00    QSYS/STRSBS SBSD(QSERVER)
0009.00    MONMSG MSGID(CPF0000)
0010.00    QSYS/STRSBS SBSD(QUSRWRK)
0011.00    MONMSG MSGID(CPF0000)
0012.00    QSYS/RLSJOBQ JOBQ(QGPL/QS36MRT)
0013.00    MONMSG MSGID(CPF0000)
0014.00    QSYS/RLSJOBQ JOBQ(QGPL/QS36EVOKE)
0015.00    MONMSG MSGID(CPF0000)
0016.00    QSYS/STRCLNUP
0017.00    MONMSG MSGID(CPF0000)
0018.00    QSYS/RTVSYSVAL SYSVAL(QCTLSBSD)- RTNVAR(&CTLSBSD)
0019.00  IF COND((&CTLSBSD *NE 'QCTL    QSYS     ')+                    *AND
         (&CTLSBSD *NE + 'QCTL    QGPL     '))
             THEN(GOTO     +CMDLBL(DONE))
0021.00    QSYS/STRSBS SBSD(QINTER)                  0022.00    MONMSG
MSGID(CPF0000)
0023.00    QSYS/STRSBS SBSD(QBATCH)
0024.00    MONMSG MSGID(CPF0000)
0025.00    QSYS/STRSBS SBSD(QCMN)
0026.00    MONMSG MSGID(CPF0000)
0027.00 DONE:
0028.00    QSYS/RTVSYSVAL SYSVAL(QSTRPRTWTR)-
RTNVAR(&STRWTRS)
0029.00    IF COND(&STRWTRS = '0') THEN(GOTO -
               CMDLBL(NOWTRS))
0030.00    CALL PGM(QSYS/QWCSWTRS)
0031.00    MONMSG MSGID(CPF0000)
0032.00 NOWTRS:
0033.00    RETURN
0034.00       CHGVAR VAR(&CPYR) VALUE(&CPYR)
0035.00       ENDPGM
```

Command Continuation

Before we dip into the programs, we need to discuss an important factor about CL syntax. In the two examples we are about to dissect, you will find that certain commands and parameters cannot fit on one statement. They are continued. In both examples, there are a number of statements which need several lines to complete. As you can see in the Figures, in addition to using the continuation characters (+ and -), we eliminated the line number from the continuation lines, so that we show that all of the continued lines were related.

Commands are most often entered in free format. A command does not have to begin in a specific location on a statement line. Most commands are contained entirely in one statement. However, as we have been discussing, commands can be continued on several lines, or in several statements.

Whether continued or not, the total command length cannot exceed 20,000 characters. Either of the two special characters noted above, the plus sign (+) or the minus sign (-), can be entered as the last nonblank character on the line to indicate that a command is continued. Blanks immediately preceding a + or - sign are always included. Blanks immediately following a + or - in the same statement are ignored.

Blanks in the next line (the continued line), however, that precede the first nonblank character are ignored when "+" is specified. They are included   when "-" is specified. The "+" is most often used useful between parameters or values. At least one blank must precede the sign to make it effective when it is used between separate parameters or values.

The difference between the plus and minus sign usage is particularly important when continuation occurs inside a quoted character string. Assuming that there are three blanks preceding the continued "ITH" of Smith, the following example shows the difference:

CRTLIB LIB(SMITH) TEXT('This is SM+
   ITH')
CRTLIB LIB(SMITH) TEXT('This is SM-
   ITH')

These statements materialize as the following:

For + :
CRTLIB LIB(SMITH) TEXT('This is SMITH')

For - :
CRTLIB LIB(SMITH) TEXT('This is SM   ITH')

QSTRUP Program Dissection

Now, let's look at different groups of Cl statements in the QSTRUP CL program and we'll explain them as we go.

```
0001.00    PGM
```

All Cl programs begin with the PGM Statement. When the program has a parameter passed, the PARM parameter is used to catch it.

```
0002.00    DCL VAR(&STRWTRS) TYPE(*CHAR) LEN(1)
0003.00    DCL VAR(&CTLSBSD) TYPE(*CHAR)LEN(20)
0004.00    DCL VAR(&CPYR) TYPE(*CHAR) LEN(120) +
                        VALUE('5722-SS1 ©) COPYRIGHT- +
                        IBM CORP 1980, 2000. LICENSED +
                  MATERIAL - PROGRAM PROPERTY OF IBM')
```

This program has three variables declared (defined). As you can see the first two variables are to store the results of RTVSYSVAL (Retrieve System Value). These will be tested, and the program will take different branches depending on their values. The third variable is a convention which IBM uses to store its copyright information within the running program.

```
0006.00    QSYS/STRSBS SBSD(QSPL)
0007.00    MONMSG MSGID(CPF0000)
0008.00    QSYS/STRSBS SBSD(QSERVER)
0009.00    MONMSG MSGID(CPF0000)
0010.00    QSYS/STRSBS SBSD(QUSRWRK)
0011.00    MONMSG MSGID(CPF0000)
```

This next block of code uses three STRSBS commands to get three IBM subsystems started - QSPL, QSERVER, QUSRWRK. Each of these is followed by a generic MONMSG command, which assures that the program will continue if an unexpected condition has occurred in the STRSBS commands. Unmonitored messages cause function checks which are typically very disruptive to CL programs.

The Monitor Message (MONMSG) command is used to monitor escape, notify, and status messages sent to the program message queue of the program in which the command is used. As a point of note, completion and diagnostic message types cannot be monitored.

When the MONMSG command is compiled in a control language (CL) program, such as this (QSTRUP), it establishes a monitor for the arrival of the specified messages. The command monitors the messages. It can also monitor for any special conditions when the comparison data parameter is used in the command. If a message, meeting the conditions, arrives on the message queue, the CL command specified on the MONMSG command is processed.

In the three monitor messages above, there is no EXEC clause to call another program. The sole purpose of these monitors is to assure that if the subsystems are already up and alive, and this program tries to start them, the STRSBS commands will not cause the program to terminate with a function check.

```
0012.00    QSYS/RLSJOBQ JOBQ(QGPL/QS36MRT)
0013.00    MONMSG MSGID(CPF0000)
0014.00    QSYS/RLSJOBQ JOBQ(QGPL/QS36EVOKE)
0015.00    MONMSG MSGID(CPF0000)
```

This block of code releases special System/36-related job queues and avoids a function check by monitoring for the generic CPF0000 message.

```
0016.00    QSYS/STRCLNUP
0017.00    MONMSG MSGID(CPF0000)
```

Statements 16 and 17 calls the cleanup program, which is an IBM facility that cleans up various logs and queues and reclaims otherwise wasted space.

```
0018.00    QSYS/RTVSYSVAL SYSVAL(QCTLSBSD)+
           RTNVAR(&CTLSBSD)
0019.00    IF COND((&CTLSBSD *NE 'QCTL        QSYS        ') +
           *AND (&CTLSBSD *NE +
           'QCTL        QGPL        ')) THEN(GOTO +
           CMDLBL(DONE))
```

Statement 18, which just like 19, is continued with a "+" sign, goes to the system value area in the operating system and extracts the

QCTLSBSD value. This is where the name of the controlling subsystem is stored. (Work Management is covered in QuikCourse B.)

Once the system value for the controlling subsystem is stored in the program defined CL variable, &CTLSBSD, it is compared in statement 18 to the subsystem named QCTL. If the QCTL subsystem is not the controlling subsystem, regardless of whether its description is stored in library QSYS (system library or library QGPL– IBM's general purpose library), the program branches to the label "DONE" at statement 27. Otherwise, if QCTL is the controlling subsystem, it executes the code from statements 21 through 26.

```
0021.00    QSYS/STRSBS SBSD(QINTER)
0022.00    MONMSG MSGID(CPF0000)
0023.00    QSYS/STRSBS SBSD(QBATCH)
0024.00    MONMSG MSGID(CPF0000)
0025.00    QSYS/STRSBS SBSD(QCMN)
0026.00    MONMSG MSGID(CPF0000)
```

The above block of code starts the subsystems QINTER, QBATCH, and QCMN, which are typically associated with a "System/38-like" or "native-like" system execution environment. Notice that the monitors are in place to prevent an error which would cause program termination.

```
0027.00 DONE:
0028.00    QSYS/RTVSYSVAL SYSVAL(QSTRPRTWTR)+
           RTNVAR(&STRWTRS)
0029.00    IF COND(&STRWTRS = '0') THEN(GOTO +
           CMDLBL(NOWTRS))
0030.00    CALL PGM(QSYS/QWCSWTRS)
0031.00    MONMSG MSGID(CPF0000)
```

The above block of code executes, regardless of the controlling subsystem. The QSTRPRTWTR system value is fetched, stored in the CL variable &STRWTRS, and compared to "0." If this value is set to zero, your system is set to start no print writers (printers) at startup. If you want them started later, you will have to start them manually with STRPRTWTR commands. In the value is "0," the program bypasses statement 30, which calls the system program to start the printers (QWCSWTRS). Instead, as shown in statement 29, the program branches to the NOWTRS label at statement 32.

```
0032.00 NOWTRS:
0033.00    RETURN
0034.00       CHGVAR VAR(&CPYR) VALUE(&CPYR)
0035.00       ENDPGM
```

This block of code (32 to 35) provides a branch spot for the print writer test, and it is also executed if the print writers are started. The program returns to its caller at statement 33. So that the variable &CPYR, which is a mechanism for IBM's copyright message to exist, is not unused, line 34 is added as a bogus line to use the &CPYR variable to avoid a program compilation error. It is never executed. The program ends and goes away at line 35.

You might be wondering what gets called if the QCTL environment does not get started. The answer is that regardless of the startup program, the system automatically starts the controlling subsystem. You can create your own controlling subsystem or you can use one of IBM's. You can use QCTL for a System/38 or a native AS/400-like environment or you can choose the System/36-like environment called QBASE. This subsystem handles interactive, batch, and communications within the one QBASE subsystem, rather than the more flexible QCTL, QCMN, QBATCH. and QINTER.

Now, take a look at the home grown application code in Figure D-28 which we are about to highlight in much the same way as program QSTRUP.

Figure D-28 Homemade Example Batch Program CL01

```
0001.00   PGM         PARM(&LOADPAR)
0002.00   DCL         VAR(&WRK01) TYPE(*CHAR)
0003.00   DCL         VAR(&WRK02) TYPE(*CHAR)
0004.00   DCL         VAR(&LOADPAR) TYPE(*CHAR) LEN(10)
0005.00   DCL         VAR(&PARM1) TYPE(*DEC) LEN(1)
0006.00   DCL         VAR(&PARM2) TYPE(*CHAR) LEN(10)
0007.00   /* Retrieve LDA values.            */
0008.00   CALL        PGM(LDALOAD) PARM(B LDALST 2)    0009.00   CHGVAR
VAR(&PARM1) -
VALUE(%SST(*LDA 301 1))
0010.00   CHGVAR      VAR(&PARM2) -
VALUE(%SST(*LDA 302 10))
0011.00
0012.00   CHGVAR &WRK01 -
VALUE('S' *CAT %SST(&LOADPAR 1 9))
0013.00   DLTF FILE(QTEMP/&WRK01)
0014.00   MONMSG MSGID(CPF2105)
0015.00   CRTPF FILE(QTEMP/&WRK01)
RCDLEN(1726) OPTION(*NOSRC +
                 *NOLIST) FILETYPE(*DATA) +
SIZE(*NOMAX)


0017.00   /*                           */
0018.00   OVRDBF FILE(R020) TOFILE(CUSTMST)
0019.00   OVRDBF FILE(ORD) TOFILE(ORDERS)
0020.00   OVRDBF FILE(PAR) TOFILE(QTEMP/&LOADPAR)
0021.00   OVRDBF FILE(SUM1) TOFILE(QTEMP/&WRK01)
0022.00   CALL        PGM(ROUTESHEC)
0023.00   DLTOVR FILE(*ALL)
0024.00   /*                           */
0025.00   CHGVAR &WRK02 +
VALUE('T' *CAT %SST(&LOADPAR 1 9))
0026.00   DLTF FILE(QTEMP/&WRK02)
0027.00   MONMSG MSGID(CPF2105)
0028.00   CRTPF FILE(QTEMP/&WRK02) RCDLEN(1726) +
              OPTION(*NOSRC +
*NOLIST) FILETYPE(*DATA) +
              SIZE(*NOMAX)
0030.00   /*                           */
0031.00   FMTDTA INFILE(QTEMP/&WRK01) +
              OUTFILE(QTEMP/&WRK02) +
SRCFILE(QFMTSRC) SRCMBR(SRTLOAD) +  OPTION(*NOCHK *NOPRT *NODUMP)
0034.00   /*                 */
0035.00   /* ROUTEPRT PROGRAM          */
0036.00   CHGJOB SWS(00000000)
0037.00   /* RETRIEVE LDA values.      */
0038.00   CALL        PGM(LDALOAD) PARM(B LOADRPT 1)
0039.00   OVRDBF FILE(S010) TOFILE(CONFIG)
0040.00   OVRDBF FILE(PAR) TOFILE(QTEMP/&LOADPAR)    0041.00   OVRDBF
FILE(SUM1) TOFILE(QTEMP/&WRK02)
0042.00   OVRDBF FILE(R020) TOFILE(CUSTMST)
0043.00   OVRPRTF      FILE(RPT) TOFILE(QSYSPRT) +
              OUTQ(&PARM2)  COPIES(&PARM1)
0045.00   CALL        PGM(ROUTEPRTC)
0046.00   DLTOVR FILE(*ALL)
0047.00   DLTF FILE(QTEMP/&WRK01)
0048.00   DLTF FILE(QTEMP/&WRK02)
0049.00   RETURN
0050.00   ENDPGM
```

Homemade Batch Dissection

```
0001.00    PGM          PARM(&LOADPAR)
```

This program accepts a ten-character parameter from the calling program, when called, and stores it in a character variable of ten spaces, called &LOADPAR.

```
0002.00    DCL          VAR(&WRK01) TYPE(*CHAR)
0003.00    DCL          VAR(&WRK02) TYPE(*CHAR)
0004.00    DCL          VAR(&LOADPAR) TYPE(*CHAR)
LEN(10)
0005.00    DCL          VAR(&PARM1) TYPE(*DEC) LEN(1)
0006.00    DCL          VAR(&PARM2) TYPE(*CHAR) LEN(10)
```

The above block of code defines the five variables used in this program. Four are defined as character and one is defined as decimal.

```
0007.00    /* Retrieve LDA values.          */
```

The /*   */ combination is used to sandwich CL comments.

```
0008.00    CALL         PGM(LDALOAD) PARM(B LDALST 2)
```

A program called LDALOAD is used to load specific values to the local data area. Each job has a local data area LDA (like a one record file) associated with it. In this case, the CL01 program is calling LDALOAD and instructing LDALOAD to load specific values to the LDA.

```
0009.00 CHGVAR VAR(&PARM1) VALUE(%SST(*LDA 301 1))
0010.00 CHGVAR VAR(&PARM2) VALUE(%SST(*LDA 302 10))
```

In statements 9 & 10, PARM1 and PARM2, locally defined variables are primed with the newly loaded contents of very specific sub-stringed areas of the LDA. Parm1 gets what is in position 301. Parm2 gets what is in positions 302 to 311.

The CHGVAR (change variable) command is the only CL command which cam make assignments. In my opinion, it is one of the ugliest CL commands. In a normal programming language, for example, you would say PARM1 = VALUE(%SST(*LDA 301 1)), rather than be saddled with a command. I suspect that since every CL statement is a CL command, this is the problem with the language.

CHGVAR is also used to perform addition and subtraction, multiplication and division. To add 5 to a variable, for example, you would say:

```
CHGVAR &RESULT (&VAL1 + 5)
```

or the prompted form:

```
CHGVAR      VAR(&RESULT) VALUE(&VAL1 + 5)
```

```
0012.00   CHGVAR &WRK01 +
VALUE('S' *CAT %SST(&LOADPAR 1 9))
```

Statement 12 is another assignment statement in which an "S" is concatenated to the sub-stringed positions, 1 through 9, of the LOADPAR variable, which was passed to the program. Variable &WORK01 contains the result of the concatenation of the S to the substring. This is a valuable CL statement for you to save in your CL arsenal.

```
0013.00   DLTF FILE(QTEMP/&WRK01)
0014.00   MONMSG MSGID(CPF2105)
0015.00   CRTPF FILE(QTEMP/&WRK01)
          RCDLEN(1726) OPTION(*NOSRC +
          *NOLIST) FILETYPE(*DATA) +
          SIZE(*NOMAX)
```

In the next block of code shown above, the newly changed field &WORK01 apparently contains the name of a file, which this program uses as a work file. Statement 13 deletes the file from the QTEMP library. Statement 14 monitors the existence of the file (CPF2105), so that the program does not function check if the file is not there when it is asked to be deleted.

QTEMP is a special temporary library that gets built for every job that starts on the system. When you access QTEMP, for example, it is your own QTEMP that you are accessing, though QTEMP can exist more than a thousand times in one system. When your job ends, your QTEMP disappears.

Once the file is deleted, or is definitely not there, the program recreates it again with the CRTPF command shown in statement 15. Sometimes, rather than delete files and have to recreate them (an expensive operation) programs are written which clear files (CLRPFM), or remove the data member (RMVM), and then add the member back in, rather than delete and recreate. It is much easier on the machine than the deletion and recompilation of a database file.

```
0017.00    /*                              */
0018.00    OVRDBF  FILE(FILE1)  TOFILE(CUSTMST)
0019.00    OVRDBF  FILE(FILE2)  TOFILE(ORDERS)
0020.00    OVRDBF  FILE(FILE3)  TOFILE(QTEMP/&LOADPAR)
0021.00    OVRDBF  FILE(FILE4)  TOFILE(QTEMP/&WRK01)
0022.00    CALL         PGM(ROUTE)
0023.00    DLTOVR FILE(*ALL)
```

In this next block of code, 17 to 23, we find several files being overridden, a program being called (22), and the file overrides being deleted (23), so they do not apply again in this same job.

The *override with database file* command is one of the most powerful and most common statements in CL programs which drive batch work. In the four overrides above, it is clear that the ROUTE program uses four files named FILE1, through FILE4.

This is a technique from the 1970's used by batch programmers to write generic programs that did not need a specific file to compile. The file information could be provided when the program actually ran. In mainframe systems, the DLAB or DLBL statements provided the information at execution time. On System/3, 34, and 36, the file "Label" parameter gave the information at execution time. In CL, this is provided by the OVRDBF, again at execution time. As you begin to write CL, when you prompt for the OVRDBF command, you will learn that it has substantially more facility than just overriding a file name. Yet, in the four examples above, that is all that is being done.

```
0024.00    /*                                */
0025.00    CHGVAR &WRK02 +
VALUE('T' *CAT %SST(&LOADPAR 1 9))
0026.00    DLTF FILE(QTEMP/&WRK02)
0027.00    MONMSG MSGID(CPF2105)
0028.00    CRTPF FILE(QTEMP/&WRK02) RCDLEN(1726) +
       OPTION(*NOSRC +
*NOLIST) FILETYPE(*DATA) +
       SIZE(*NOMAX)
0030.00    /*                                */
```

In lines 24 to 30, a new file name is being built for variable &WRK02 to hold, the file is deleted, monitored, and then when it is definitely gone, it is recreated fresh at statement 28.

```
0031.00    FMTDTA INFILE(QTEMP/&WRK01) +
       OUTFILE(QTEMP/&WRK02) +
       SRCFILE(QFMTSRC) SRCMBR(SRTLOAD) +
       OPTION(*NOCHK *NOPRT *NODUMP)
```

Yes, Virginia, there is a SORT on the AS/400. However, it is called Format Data (FMTDTA). In line 31, The file whose name is in variable &WRK01 in QTEMP, is the input to the sort. The output is the newly created file whose name is contained in variable &WRK02. The sort specifications are stored in a file called QFMTSRC, in a member called SRTLOAD. Three specific options are invoked so that there is no major checking of the sort specs, no specs are printed, and no dump is to be taken if there is an issue.

QFMTSRC is a file referenced in the library list. Every job has a library search list associated with it. When you ask for an object and you do not qualify it by library name, the system searches your library list to find the object. If it cannot find it, the job bombs (function check). Originally, jobs were allowed to have 10 libraries in the list. This was then raised to 25, which seemed immense. Now it has been jacked up even further to 250 libraries in a library list.

```
0034.00  /*                          */
0035.00 /* ROUTEPRT PROGRAM           */
0036.00   CHGJOB SWS(00000000)
```

The CHGJOB command can change the attributes of executing jobs on the fly. It is a powerful CL command. This particular change sets off all of the eight job switches. A program can test the job switches and make branching decisions depending on their values. They can be set on and off with a CHGJOB command.

As with all CL commands, even those which can only be used in a CL program, such as CHGVAR, you can prompt the command from a command line by typing it and hitting F4. You can then hit HELP or F1 on any and all parameters. You get a ton of information to help you make the right selections for your purposes.

Using F4 regularly gives you a lifelong method for learning about commands which you do not need today. If you have no idea as to which command, you might want to use, hit F4 with nothing on the command line. You'll get access to lists of all the IBM commands on the system. You better have a few spare days or more because that's how much help there is on the hundreds of AS/400 and IBM i commands which IBM has given us.

```
0037.00 /* RETRIEVE LDA values.            */
0038.00     CALL          PGM(LDALOAD) PARM(B LDARPT 1)
0039.00     OVRDBF FILE(FILE1) TOFILE(CONFIG)
0040.00     OVRDBF FILE(FILE2) TOFILE(QTEMP/&LOADPAR)
0041.00     OVRDBF FILE(FILE3) TOFILE(QTEMP/&WRK02)
0042.00     OVRDBF FILE(FILE4) TOFILE(CUSTMST)
0043.00     OVRPRTF    FILE(REPORT) TOFILE(QSYSPRT) +
              OUTQ(&PARM2)  COPIES(&PARM1)
0045.00     CALL         PGM(PRTREPORT)
0046.00     DLTOVR FILE(*ALL)
0047.00     DLTF FILE(QTEMP/&WRK01)
0048.00     DLTF FILE(QTEMP/&WRK02)
0049.00     RETURN
0050.00     ENDPGM
```

Now, we are at the final code block shown in statements 37 to 50. This loads a new block of values into the LDA using the trusty LDALOAD program, overrides four files, and then overrides the printer file for the job.

We have not seen the OVRPRTF command before in this QuikCourse. This command references a printer file called REPORT, which is in program PRTREPORT. The printer file this points to is an IBM standard named QSYSPRT, a generic printer file. (Printer files hold rules, such as lines per inch, etc. for how printer output should be formatted). This override does not change many of those rules, but it does change the default output queue and the number of copies.

After the report program is run with the five file overrides, the overrides are deleted from the job structure, the work files are deleted, and the program returns and ends.

Summary and Conclusions

CL Commands can be entered from command-capable menus and the command entry screen as well as within utility programs, such as SEU or PDM.   The system assists in the command entry process by providing menu displays and prompt displays. Extensive help can be obtained for the Command itself or for command options. Commands entered via any of these displays are syntax-checked for validity and conformity to syntax rules.

You have learned the rudiments of CL, how it is structured, and how to structure it for your objectives. The CL manual on the System/38 was so big, that a normal human being could not carry it. On the AS/400 it was made into five books by splitting the commands along alphabetic boundaries. Besides the huge CL reference manuals, there is also a CL programming book, plus the ton of HELP text right in the operating system.

IBM has always offered a course in CL that was at least four full days, and perhaps five days long. There is no question that CL is an exhausting topic, and no QuikCourse could treat it exhaustively. However, this course is designed to give you the ability to get up, and move on your own. From building simple programs to dissecting the programming work of others, this little CL course has been your first stop to a comprehensive understanding of CL, how it works, what it can do for you, and how you can make it do what you want.

In your CL travels, don't forget that the prompter is just an F4 away.

Best wishes in your further CL endeavors.

QuikCourse E.   AS/400 and IBM i Programming Development Manager (PDM)

Program Development Manager (PDM) Features

PDM is part of the Application Development Tool Set (ADTS) which had been a staple for application development on the AS/400 since 1988, when they were announced. Recently, the whole ADTS has been repackaged and is now part of the WebSphere Development Studio for IBM i. PDM is, therefore, not an island.   It works with all of the other tools in the tool set including the following:

1.   **Source Entry Utility (SEU)**
2.   **Screen Design Aid (SDA)**
3.   **Data File Utility (DFU)**
4.   **Advanced Printer Function (APF)**
5.   **Report Layout Utility (RLU)**

PDM is the cornerstone for a highly integrated set of development tools. It supports all AS/400 environments (S/38, S/36 and native). It is the consummate AS/400 development tool in that it enables programmers to create, test and maintain an array of AS/400 objects, from programs, to screens, to reports, and also to data files.

Better than the Programmer's Menu

Prior to PDM, my favorite development tool on the AS/400 was the old ported Programmer's Menu from System/38 days. I know a number of folks who still use the Programmer's Menu. In fact, it took me about two years to embrace it.

I first talked it down. From my eyes, it was more difficult than the Programmer's Menu, though it is not. I did not want to learn it. I did not understand it. As an IBM SE, eventually I saw my peers embrace PDM as if it were as good as the Programmer's Menu. Since I knew they were wrong, I learned PDM. They were right. Since I did not want to be a doofus using the Programmer's Menu after I knew PDM was superior, I switched. Over time, I took a lot of folks with me.

PDM provides a focal point and an integrated environment for using the development tools available to the programmer on the AS/400. It works with lists of items to be developed or maintained. Virtually all types of objects can be accessed using PDM interfaces, though it is most commonly used for programs, display files (or screens), and data base objects (or files).

PDM: the List Manager

Libraries, objects, and members can be selected easily from lists provided by PDM. Option numbers are provided for the most commonly used functions, to save keystrokes for the programmer. PDM is smart enough, that if you have not filled in required parameters, it automatically invokes a prompting facility to get that done. Additionally, developers can build their own options that can be used in standard PDM panels and they can change PDM's default values.

For example, on development-only machines, the "Compile in batch?" option of PDM invoked via the Change Defaults option (F18) may be set to "N," so the developer can more productively work with PDM members. This can also be done on production machines, but the users may very well complain about its impact on their performance. Overall, the major benefit of this PDM option is that it makes programmers more productive.

What Does PDM Do?

There are three main functions as displayed on the PDM main menu.
These are as follows:

```
1. Work with libraries
2. Work with objects in libraries
3. Work with members in a source file
```

For each option, the user is prompted for the specific library list,
library or source file to be used. A list will then be displayed, from
which the programmer can select objects and options for those
objects to be executed. The programmer has the option of seeing the
items in a single column with more information or a multiple column
format in much the same way the S/36 POP program presented the
lists.

Whether you are working with libraries, objects, or members, from
the list provided, PDM enables you to place an option number next
to the library, object, or member. The option number corresponds to
a function such as copy, move, rename, delete, view, change,
execute, compile, save, or restore. Based on the option number, and
the type of object being operated upon, PDM will ask you for
additional information to complete the operation, and then it will go
ahead and apply the function to the library, object, or member as
requested.

Of course, only those functions that can be provided for the object
type selected will be allowed. For example, the "Compile" option is
not available, unless you are working with source members. Likewise
the execute (or RUN) option is not available unless the selected
object is an executable program. Multiple options can be selected for
multiple objects at a time. PDM will group all like functions (e.g., all
"copy" functions) for all objects together and prompt for necessary
details (e.g., for the new name and/or location of the copy). This is
certainly a part of the utility that makes it a very effective and
productive tool.

Starting PDM

Let's start PDM so that we know what it looks like. You do this by
typing STRPDM and pressing ENTER. The panel in Figure E-1A
appears.

Figure E-1A, The PDM Main Menu

```
                         PDM MAIN Menu                      HELLO
             AS/400 Programming Development Manager (PDM)

    Select one of the following:

          1. Work with libraries
          2. Work with objects
          3. Work with members

          9. Work with user-defined options
       Selection or command
       ===> 1
    F3=Exit      F4=Prompt  F9=Retrieve  F10=Command Entry
     F12=Cancel  F18=Change defaults
```

From this panel in Figure E-1A, we will first select work with
libraries, option 1. Before you press ENTER here, there's a little
more to know.

PDM Main Panel

Figure E-1A shows the main menu used to begin working with PDM.
There are also menu bypass options which permit a PDM user to
ignore the menus and go directly to the functional areas. For
example, Figure E-1A can be bypassed by using the fast path method
to get into one of the specific options of PDM.

The commands to get to the options directly are:

WRKLIBPDM

WRKOBJPDM

WRKMBRPDM.

When the user or a programmer takes one of the first three options, he or she will be prompted for the libraries, objects, or members desired as in Figure E-1B. When you specify the library or *ALL for all libraries on the system, you get a panel similar to that in Figure E-2.

Figure E-1B, Specify Libraries to Work With

```
                        Specify Libraries to Work With

Type choice, press Enter.

   Library  . . . . . . . . . .     *ALL          *LIBL, name,
*generic*, *ALL,
                                                  *ALLUSR, *USRLIBL,
*CURLIB


F3=Exit      F5=Refresh      F12=Cancel
```

Work with Libraries Using PDM

This panel in Figure E-2, is an example of a typical list of libraries that would appear if one took option 1 from the menu "Work with Libraries," shown in Figure E-1B.

Notice the layout of the PDM screens. F2 is representative of PDM's list screens. They all follow this same list panel standard format. Information concerning what list you are looking at is at the top. Next is a list of options that can be entered in any of the option fields next to the items listed.   The list of items (in this case, libraries) is in the middle of the screen. Near the bottom of the screen is a command line on which AS/400 commands or parameters for the option specified above for a library can be entered.

Figure E-2, Work With Libraries Using PDM

```
                     Work with Libraries Using PDM                    HELLO

  List type  . . . . . . .   *LIBL_____

  Type options, press Enter.
    2=Change                  3=Copy      5=Display      7=Rename
    8=Display description      9=Save     10=Restore     12=Work with ...

  Opt  Library    Type      Text
   __  FROMDEBS   *PROD
   __  GENERAL    *PROD     General Query Library for Helpdesk
   __  GL02       *PROD     GL02 REL. 9.9
   __  GRIMEDEN   *PROD     COLLECTION - created by SQL
   __  GUEST      *PROD
   __  GUITEST    *PROD     Test Lib for Web GUI
   __  HAWKEYE    *PROD     PATHFINDER - CALL HAWKEYE/HAWKEYE for main menu
    7  HELLO      *PROD
    7  HELLOA     *PROD
                                                                   More...
  Parameters or command
  ===>  _____
  F3=Exit              F4=Prompt           F5=Refresh        F6=Add to list
  F9=Retrieve          F10=Command Entry   F23=More options  F24=More keys
```

Notice in Figure B-2, that we have marked two libraries for rename. If we hit ENTER with the 7's in place, we will be prompted to enter the name to which we would like to change them.

Library Options and Function Keys

At the bottom of the screen are the function keys available. Notice the eight options listed at the top of the screen. Any of these options may be entered into the "Opt"   field next to any of the library names to perform functions. (Copy, display etc.) Prompting will occur where necessary. For example, if you were to place a 7 (rename option) beside library HELLO, as shown in Figure E-2, you would be prompted to fill in the new name for the library.

Several libraries could be renamed at a time by placing 7s next to several libraries as we have done. All new name prompts would appear together on a screen making it convenient to perform multiple renames. Likewise, if one entered other options, such as 3 (copy) and 9 (save) next to library names, the proper prompting would occur for each option separately on the panel following the list selection.

Additional Options & Keys

By pressing F23, additional options appear on the bottom of the screen, as shown in Figure E-3. By pressing F24, additional Function keys appear on the bottom of the panel, as shown in both Figure E-4, and E-5.

Figure E-3, Additional Options

13=Change text 20=Move within list   21=Move before
22=Move after   23=Remove from list ...

The screen picture in Figure E-3 shows the additional options available that would appear if the   user were to press F23.

Figure E-4, Additional Function Keys Part I

F11=Display names and types   F12=Cancel
F13=Repeat F16=User options   F23=More options
F24=More keys

Figure E-5, Additional Function Keys Part I

F18=Change defaults   F21=Print List
F23=More options   F24=More keys

The panel in Figure E4 appears when you hit the F24 key for the first time. The panel in Figure E5 appears when you hit the F24 key a second time. Figure E-6 is the next slide that we would see if we pressed the ENTER key with the two option 7's filled in on Figure E-3.

Figure E-6 Rename Libraries

```
                      Rename Libraries

To rename library, type New Name, press Enter.

Library              New Name
HELLO                HELLOX1____
HELLOA               HELLOAX1___
                     Bottom
F3=Exit         F5=Refresh        F12=Cancel        F19=Submit
to batch
```

To rename libraries, you place a 7 (rename) next to the library in the opt field of the *Work with Libraries Using PDM* screen (Figure E-2) and press ENTER. You will then be prompted to provide the new name for each library as in Figure E-6. This rename action could take place interactively, or could be submitted to a batch job by pressing F19.

Change Defaults

Now, Press F18 for the *"Change Defaults"* screen from any of the "*Work With*" screens in PDM. You will see the panel as shown on Figure E-7A.

Figure E-7A Change PDM Defaults.

```
                        PDM Defaults Display

                         Change Defaults

   Type choices, press Enter.

       Object library . . . . . . .    *SRCLIB____   Name, *CURLIB, *SRCLIB
       Replace object . . . . . . .    N_            Y=Yes, N=No

       Compile in batch . . . . . .    Y_            Y=Yes, N=No
       Run in batch . . . . . . . .    N_            Y=Yes, N=No
       Job description  . . . . . .    QBATCH____    Name, *USRPRF, F4 for list
          Library  . . . . . . . . .   *LIBL_____   Name, *CURLIB, *LIBL

       Change type and text . . . .    Y_            Y=Yes, N=No

       Option file  . . . . . . . .    QAUOOPT____   Name
          Library  . . . . . . . . .   QGPL_____    Name, *CURLIB, *LIBL
       Member . . . . . . . . . . .    QAUOOPT____   Name

       Full screen mode . . . . . .    N_            Y=Yes, N=No

    F3=Exit       F4=Prompt       F5=Refresh        F12=Cancel
```

In Figure E-7A, a PDM user can tailor his or her PDM environment. The Object library is where you want objects to go when they are compiled using option 14 of the Work with Members Using PDM screen. (The user may choose to always use F4 for prompting to override these defaults, if desired.)

"Y" for Replace object will cause the new object to replace the old one if it exists in the library. "N" will cause PDM to prompt the user for permission to delete the old object first.

A"Y" for Compile in batch will submit a batch job for each compile option (opt 14) requested from the "Working with Members Using PDM" screen. The job description specified on the next line will be used to define the batch job's environment

A "Y" to Run in batch will submit a batch job for each   run option (opt 16) requested from the "Working with Objects Using PDM" screen.

The option for "change type and text" refers to the Work with members using PDM screen.   A "Y" response makes the type and text fields input-capable on the screen. An "N" response makes them display only.

Work With Objects

Now that we have set our defaults, and examined how to work with libraries, let's go through the other options on the PDM main menu as shown in Figure E1A. Instead of working with libraries, this time, let's pick option 2, *Work with objects*.

For this PDM exercise, there should be a small library called HELLO prebuilt, so that when you get the *Specify Objects to Work With* Panel, as shown in Figure E-7B, you would choose the HELLO library and let the rest default to *ALL. Before you press ENTER on the *Specify Objects to Work With* Panel, take a look at the other options.

Figure E-7B Specify Objects to Work With Panel

```
                    Specify Objects to Work With
Type choices, press Enter.

    Library  . . . . . . . . .    HELLO      *CURLIB, name
    Object:
      Name . . . . . . . . . .    *ALL       *ALL, name, *generic*
      Type . . . . . . . . . .    *ALL       *ALL, *type
      Attribute  . . . . . . .    *ALL       *ALL, attribute, *generic*,
                                             *BLANK


F3=Exit      F5=Refresh      F12=Cancel
```

Typically, the only option that is filled in is the *library name*
(contains the objects to be worked with). However, the PDM user
could also fill in *Object Type* (e.g., PGM, USRPRF, FILE, etc.), and
Object Attribute (e.g., CLP, CBL, PF-SRC, etc.). This limits (subsets)
the resulting list of objects to those types/attributes.

A user could also enter a name or a generic name (Burge*, SA*,
SA, *SA) which also limits the list to those beginning with,
containing, or ending with certain characters. As your development
efforts produce fruits, the number of objects to maintain grows
quickly, and these filtering techniques help you in finding the items
you want posthaste.

The default library for this option is always the job's current library.
For your information, the current library can be specified in the user
profile, can be overridden at sign-on, or can be changed using the
CHGCURLIB command. You can, of course type in the library name
in Figure E-7B as is shown.

After you go through the selection process described above, and you
press ENTER with just the library HELLO typed in, you would see
the *"Work with Objects Using PDM"* panel such as that in Figure E-8.

Figure E-8 *Work with Objects Using PDM*

```
                Work with Objects Using PDM                    HELLO

Library . . . . .   HELLO         Position to . . . . . . . .   _____
                                  Position to type  . . . . .   _____
Type options, press Enter.
  2=Change       3=Copy         4=Delete      5=Display      7=Rename
  8=Display description          9=Save      10=Restore     11=Move ...
Opt  Object      Type      Attribute  Text
 __  HELLOAC001  *PGM      CBL        Advanced Hello World, CBL/400
 __  HELLOAR001  *PGM      RPG        Advanced Hello World, RPG/400, Pgm1,
 __  LANGUAGE    *FILE     PF-DTA     LANGUAGE File For Hello World
 __  PANEL       *FILE     DSPF       Display FIle Panel For Advanced Hello
 __  QCBLLESRC   *FILE     PF-SRC     FILE FOR ILE COBOL SOURCE
 __  QCLSRC      *FILE     PF-SRC     CL Source FIle
 12  QDDSSRC     *FILE     PF-SRC     dds source
 __  QRPGLESRC   *FILE     PF-SRC     RPGIV Source File
                                                                   More...
Parameters or command
===>
F3=Exit          F4=Prompt         F5=Refresh          F6=Create
F9=Retrieve      F10=Command entry F23=More options    F24=More keys
```

Work With & Other Options

Option 12, as shown in Figure E9, and visible when you hit F23, is used frequently to work with a selected object. This can come in really handily if you are working with objects and then, for example you want to work with members of the QDDSSRC source file. If the QDDSSRC source file is on your screen as in Figure E-8, just take option 12 on that line and you will be taken to a *Work with members* panel for the members in QDDSSRC. It's a handy trick!

If you want to perform an action, such as option 12, but you cannot see it, it helps to remember that there are a number of command keys and options that are not visible from all views. To change your view, press F23 or F24. Figure E-9 shows the additional options, and Figures   E10 and E11 show the additional command keys, available to the PDM user with the *Work With Objects* panel.

Figure E-9   Additional options (F23)

12=Work with 13=Change text	15=Copy file
16=Run 18=Change using DFU	25=Find string

Figure E-10   Additional keys (F24)First Time

F11=Display names and types	F12=Cancel F13=Repeat	
F16=User options	F23=More options	F24=More keys

Figure E-11   Additional keys (F24) Second Time

F17=Subset	F18=Change defaults	F21=Print List	F23=More
options	F24=More keys		

After selecting the objects to work as we did with HELLO library, the *Work with Objects using PDM* screen appears. You can see in Figure E-8 that the format of the screen is just like the *"Work With Libraries Using PDM"* screen. However, the options available for working with objects,   and the function keys available are somewhat different.

For example, you can still rename and save objects, plus you can **Move** (to another library), **Run** (if it is a PGM), **Change** using DFU (if it is a data file) etc.

Notice also in the top right corner of the panel in Figure E-8 that you can position your list of objects using an object name, as well as an object type. For example, if you wanted to position the list to all files beginning with "Q," you could put   "Q" in the *"position to"* field and *"*FILE"* in the *"Position to type"* field.

Find String Function

Another powerful PDM facility, which operates at the object level, and is worth highlighting, is the *"Find String"* Function

Figure E12 Find String

```
                         Find String

Type choices, press Enter.
    Find  . . . . . . . . . MyString
        From column number. .  1_____     1 - *RCDLEN
        To column number. . .  *RCDLEN      1 - *RCDLEN
        Kind of match . . . .  2            1=Same case, 2=Ignore case

    Option  . . . . . . . .  5_____      *NONE, Valid option
        Prompt  . . . . . . .  N            Y=Yes, N=No
    Print List  . . . . . .  N            Y=Yes, N=No
    Print records . . . . .  N            Y=Yes, N=No
        Number to find  . . .  *ALL_        *ALL, number
        Print format  . . . .  *CHAR__      *CHAR, *HEX, *ALTHEX
        Mark record . . . . .  Y            Y=Yes, N=No
        Record overflow . . .  1            1=Fold, 2=Truncate
    Find string in batch. .  N            Y=Yes, N=No
    Parameters  . . . . . .  _____


F3=Exit    F5=Refresh    F12=Cancel    F16=User Options
F18=Change Defaults
```

Find String allows the PDM user to search an entire source file (or a specific member) for a string of characters. The search can be executed interactively or in batch mode. Parameters can be entered on the parameter line as necessary. You have several options to take when the string is found. The choices actually are the options that are available on the *"Working with Members Using PDM"* screen. These include:

1. Display or edit the member (using SEU),
2. Compile the member,
3. Delete the member,
4. Execute a user-defined option.

If the "Edit" option is used, for example, the programmer can use the SEU Find/Change Services function to change the string to a different string. The advantage is that this change will be remembered for all subsequent members where the string is found.

Work With Members

Now that we have set our defaults, worked through Objects, and used the FIND facility, let's go through the last major option on the PDM main menu as shown in Figure E1A. Instead of working with Objects, this time, let's pick option 3, *Work with Members.*

If you took the option from the main menu to Work With Members, you would then get a screen requesting which source file to use. For this example, pick QDDSSRC in HELLO for this example. On this same panel, you could request a sub-setting of the member list by generic name and/or source type (e.g., PF, CBL, RPG38, etc.) This helps filter the list to meaningful items. To get to the member list panel, you have to fill in the panel answering the requests. Then press ENTER to get to the *"Work with Members using PDM"* screen, as shown in Figure E-14.

Figure E-14 Work With Members

```
                       Work with Members Using PDM              HELLO

File  . . . . . .    QDDSSRC
   Library . . . .      HELLO                 Position to  . . . . .

Type options, press Enter.
   2=Edit            3=Copy  4=Delete 5=Display       6=Print     7=Rename
   8=Display description  9=Save 13=Change text  14=Compile  15=Create module...

Opt  Member      Type       Text
  2  JOBINFO     PF         Job Information File For SBMJOB
  _  LANGUAGE    PF         LANGUAGE File For Hello World
  _  LOGICINF    PF         Job Information File For EOFDLY Receive LOGIC
  _  MASTER      PF         Master Payroll File
  _  PANEL       DSPF       Display FIle Panel For Advanced Hello World
  _  TESTFILE    PF         Testing File
  _  UIINF       PF         Job Information File For EOFDLY Send UI

                                                                 Bottom
Parameters or command
===>
F3=Exit           F4=Prompt           F5=Refresh         F6=Create
F9=Retrieve       F10=Command entry   F23=More options   F24=More keys
```

Hitting F23 and F24 gives you even more options and more command keys as shown in Figures E-15 through E-17.

Figure E-15   Additional Options (F23)

14=Compile	16=Run procedure	17=Change using SDA
19=Change using RLU	25=Find string ...	

Figure E-16 Additional keys (F24)

F11=Display names and types F12=Cancel   F13=Repeat

F14=Display date   F15=Sort date

F23=More options   F24=More keys

Figure E-17 Additional keys (F24)

F16=User options F17=Subset   F18=Change defaults   F21=Print list

F23=More options   F24=More keys

As you can see, the *"Work with Members Using PDM"* panel looks like the other PDM "work with" screens. However, there are more options than the libraries and objects panels. For example, there are a number of functions that apply only to members only, such as those in the following list:

Edit (SEU).)   Edit any type of source code- RPG, COBOL, database)

Compile.   Compile any type of program - RPG, COBOL, DB

SDA   This option works only if the type is a display file.

RLU   This option works only if the type is a printer file.

The *"Work with members"* screen, as shown in Figure E-14, is affected by the *"Change type and text"* option on the *"Change Defaults"* screen shown in the panel in Figure E-7. You may recall that there was an option for this that enabled you to indicate whether   you wanted to allow the *Type* and *Text* prompts to be changed by typing over them on *the "Work with Members Using PDM"* display as in Figure E-14.

"Type" and "Text"

If you would now look at the "*Type*" and "*Text*" columns in the middle of the panel in Figure E-14, you will have a better appreciation for what can be changed here. Notice the underlines in the panel indicating "changeable." When you change the text on any of the members in this panel, you are, in fact, changing the source text within the member itself.

This data is not stored in PDM. It is actually stored within the source member sub-object. In fact, changing via PDM is the same as doing a *Change Physical File Member* (*CHGPFM*) and changing the source text of the member. The same applies to the "*Type*" parameter, though this has more implications than documentation.

Editing Source Members

When a developer places an option 2 for Edit with *SEU* next to a member, such as JOBINFO, as shown in the example in Figure E-14, the *SEU* brings a syntax checker with its editor to match the *Type* parameter. If the Type is *RPG*, the *RPG* syntax checker examines every statement that is keyed and forces you to correct those in error during your editing session. If the *C* language type is used, then *C* is what checks the member syntax during the *SEU* keying process. The same syntax examines the source during editing as during the compilation process.

To learn more about the editing process, be sure to take QuikCourse G, the Source Entry Utility.

Compiling (Creating Objects from Members) with PDM

Speaking of compilation, this happens to be *PDM* member option 14. In Figure E-14, you are dealing with source in the *Work with Members Using PDM* panel. This is the panel in which option 14 (compile) comes in to play. You cannot compile objects and you cannot compile libraries but you certainly can compile source members into objects.

By placing a 14 next to the object you want to be compiled, *PDM* invokes the proper compiler based on the "type" parameter. If, for example, you coded an *RPG* program as a *CBL* type, then *PDM* would invoke the *COBOL* compiler to compile your RPG source.

This situation would not be good, and of course, would not work. That is why the *PDM* permits you to change the source type so easily on this panel. If you want the *RPG* compiler, just make sure that the Type" says *RPG*, or type over whatever it says, and make it *RPG*. Then invoke option 14 again. If you do as prescribed in this example, the *RPG* compiler will be invoked to compile your source into an *RPG *PGM* object.

Member Source Types

A sampling of valid source types which you can use is shown in Figure E-18. The Type column in Figure E-14 is where a developer can key in a valid source type, to identify the specific type of source which is what the member should contain. This "type" attribute, just as the "text" attribute is stored in the member and is changeable with the *CHGPFM* command or, again, by typing over the "type" in the *PDM* display.

Figure E-18 Sampling of Source Types

Type	Description
BAS	Basic
C	C Language
CBL	COBOL
CBLLE	ILE COBOL for AS/400
CBL36	COBOL System/36
CBL38	COBOL System/38
CLLE	ILE Control Language
CLP	Control Language
CLP38	System/38 Control Language
CMD	Command
DSPF	Display File
DSPF36	Display File System/36
etc.	

So, again I remind you that when you hit F18 to change the options panel (Figure E-7A), remember that the "*Type*" and" *Text*" parameter enables or disables your ability to change the type or the text of a member. You can choose from the following options:

Y=Yes: You would type "Y" to indicate that you can change the Type and Text prompts on the Work with Members Using PDM display if you have the authority to do so.
N=No: You would type "N" to indicate that you cannot change the Type and Text prompts on the Work with Members Using PDM display above. For now, this is enough about type and text.

Not only does PDM invoke the editor quite well. It enables common functions such as COPY and DELETE to be performed almost as quickly as the click of a mouse. Who said that? Let's use the panel in Figure E-14 as a basis to perform a copy. Let's copy a member to another member, thereby creating a new member.

COPY Members with PDM

In fact, let's copy 3 members. To do this, enter a   "3" for COPY next to 3 members in the list in E-14 and press ENTER. The panel is Figure E-19 appears.

Figure E-19 Copy Members using PDM

```
                              Copy Members
  From file . . . . . . . :     QDDSSRC
    From library  . . . . :     HELLO

  Type the file name and library name to receive the copied members.

    To file . . . . . . .     QDDSSRC____  Name, F4 for list
      To library  . . . . .   QGPL_____

  To rename copied member, type New Name, press Enter.

  Member          New Name
  JOBINFO         JOB2INF_
  MASTER          MASTERP_
  PANEL           PANELA__

                                                        Bottom
  F3=Exit         F4=Prompt      F5=Refresh     F12=Cancel
  F19=Submit to batch
```

The PDM gives lots of prompting opportunities such as those in Figure E-19. This panel is prompting the user to input more information about the members that we asked to copy from the previous screen. The three members that you asked to copy are shown with the COPY option given. To make this work, you fill in the file and library to which you want to copy these members. You can add a new name for each new member as you see fit.

As you can see in Figure E-19, we have already filled in the new names for our to-be-copied members. Since you are copying them to a different QDDSSRC source file in a different library (QGPL), you could have let the names remain the same since this would not have created any duplicates in the originating library.

When you hit the ENTER key on this panel, the three members are copied to QDDSSRC in QGPL as fast as a cat swoops down on a nice piece of chicken.   Summary and Conclusions

In this brief QuikCourse, we introduced PDM and much of its splendor. Hopefully, by showing this small subset of PDM facilities, you now can see the capabilities and productivity benefits which PDM can provide in an AD environment. I hope you enjoyed this and the QuikCourse modules.

Addendum

This QuikCourse E addendum contains a layout of the VENDORP physical file which is used extensively in many QuikCourses. Over the course of moving from one QuikCourse to another in this book, you may find it handy to have a picture of one of the files frequently used as a reference. If you forget where it is, it is included below.

Figure E-20, Sample DDS For VENDORP File

```
"R" means that this is a Record Format
 |
 |   Names of Fields or Record Formats
 |   |
 |   |          Data type and length
 |   |              |
 |   |              |   Number of decimal positions
 |   |              |   |
 |   |              |   |       Keywords
 |   |              |   |       |
 v   v              v   v       v
                              TEXT('FIELDREF')(either or  )
                              TEXT('Vendor Master File)
     R  VNDMSTR               TEXT('VENDOR DB FORMAT')
        VNDNBR      5S  0     COLHDG('VENDOR' 'NUMBER')
                              ALIAS(VENDOR_NUMBER)
        NAME        25        COLHDG('NAME')
        ADDR1       25        COLHDG('ADRRESS LINE 1')
                              ALIAS(ADDRESS_LINE_1)
        CITY        15        COLHDG('CITY')
        STATE       2         COLHDG('STATE')
        ZIPCD       5   0     COLHDG('ZIP' 'CODE')
                              ALIAS(ZIP_CODE)
        VNDCLS      2   0     COLHDG('VENDOR' 'CLASS')
        VNDSTS      1         TEXT('A=ACTIVE, D=DELETE, S=SUSPEN')
        BALOWE      9   2     COLHDG('BALANCE' 'OWED')
        SRVRTG      1         COLHDG('Service' 'Rating')
                              TEXT('G=GOOD, A=AVERAGE,
B=BADP=POOR'
```

QuikCourse F Source Entry Utility (SEU) For AS/400 and IBM i Application Development

Part I: Introduction to SEU

In this QuikCourse, we study SEU. However, in the process, we lightly review AS/400 database technology, including physical and logical files, since the examples for SEU are all database examples. At the end of this QuikCourse, we also take a very brief look at DFU as seen through option 18 of PDM. DFU is also covered formally within this book. See QuikCourse I.

The format of the course will be to present the facts about SEU first in lecture format, followed by a tutorial-type machine exercise segment in which databases are created with SEU and data is entered with DFU. This hands-on approach can be effective whether you are following along step-by-step at the office with your AS/400 or just reading the material for self edification.

As a major source of documentation for your SEU efforts, the SEU manual is available in IBM's documentation library from the www.as400.ibm.com website. The SEU manual you would look for is known formally as Application Development Tool Set for AS/400 Source Entry Utility Version 4 – SC09-2605-00. As of 5.1, the IBM i name was not used for this manual, giving the proper impression that SEU has not been changed by IBM for quite some time. "Get used to it!"

AS/400 Database

In the Architecture and Environment QuikCourses, we described the generic attributes of the AS/400 and IBM i database. In this mini course, we will reexamine a few of the constructs which make up the database. Using SEU as the tool, we will present ways in which you can develop simple AS/400 native database facilities in your own shop. Let's now begin by taking a close look at the power of one of a developer's favorite traditional tools, the Source Entry Utility.

There Are Lots of Editors

Every machine has an editor which is recognized as the tool by which programmers get their source programs keyed into the system. On mainframes, for example, a favorite tool is called ISPF. On Microsoft PCs, there is the old standby DOS EDIT. On IBM PCs, after the breakup of the Microsoft and IBM friendship, the editor provided simply "e." It is similar to DOS EDIT.

On AS/400 and IBM i, the most used editor is the Source Entry Utility or SEU. To get the taste of using your AS/400 for SEU, we are first going to go through a few different exercises in which the objective is to bring up the Source Entry Utility. Following this we will have a break in the action to explain SEU and then we'll pick it up with a nice and easy SEU Case Study.

SEU Features Overview

SEU is packed with editing power. Most SEU users have little idea as to just how powerful this editor actually is. Full screen editing with prompts and formats, syntax checks, as well as move, copy and delete commands, are about all you typically need to be a proficient SEU user. Yet, there is lots more! AND I MEAN LOTS!

I know that you are anxious to touch your keyboards and get on this ride. We'll do that in just a minute. But, first, let's prepare ourselves by filling our tanks with an overview of the many SEU features that you will be able to use. Some of these will require plenty of example time within the lecture / tutorial, and the Case Study. Others are discussed in this section for your awareness, and will not be covered in detail elsewhere in this QuikCourse.

Please note that this is not the SEU manual. This is an SEU QuikCourse. Each time we add a feature to the QuikCourse, it slows it down. Therefore, we have tried to be both comprehensive, yet frugal in the treatment of the cavalcade of SEU features. In the features overview immediately below, we show the feature grouping, and then describe what that feature is, what it does, and briefly, how you might use it. Many of these features are described in detail in other sections of this QuikCourse

SEU Features:

Commands:
You can use SEU commands to work with the SEU environment, members, and records. You can tailor your edit sessions, hide records shown on the display, and save, file, or cancel changes to a member.

Format Lines:
You can use format lines to verify the position of statements in high-level language source statements. SEU provides predefined format lines for high level languages and for AS/400 control language (CL) commands. When you invoke a format with an "F" line command, a template appears on top of the text you are keying to help guide your positioning.

Full Screen Mode:
SEU is equipped with a full screen editor. In normal "full" screen the reminders for the command keys are placed at the bottom of the screen. You can hide these and use a real full screen mode on the Edit and Browse displays. You select to remove function keys from the SEU display, providing four more lines of source.

Function Keys:
Each SEU display supports a set of function keys at the bottom of each panel, when the display is not in full-screen mode. You use these keys as shortcuts to perform specific tasks. For example, you can press F12 (Cancel) to cancel the current operation, and return to the previous display.

If F24 (More keys) is shown, you can press this key to see additional function keys for the display. Except for F1 (Help), which is not displayed at the bottom, but is always valid, a function key is valid on a specific display only if it is listed at the bottom of the display. A function key may perform differently, depending on the operation you are doing.

If you are using SEU in full screen mode, you can use all of the function keys for that display, even though they are not shown. Detailed information on function keys is provided later in this QuikCourse, as well as in the online help information for the AS/400 system. If you place the cursor on the function keys section of any display, and press Help or F1, detailed information appears.

Language and Command Prompts:
You can use the SEU high-level-language or command prompts to create mostly error-free records. When you request a language or command prompt, you can type the data for a record, one field at a time. It makes it so much easier that way, especially for beginners. You can use the SEU-supplied prompts, or define your own.

Line Commands:
You can use line commands in SEU to do many operations, such as insert blank records, copy records, and request language and command prompts. You can create your own line commands (user-defined) to add to those provided by the standard SEU line commands.

List Displays:
You can use SEU list displays to view different types of lists, as follows:

1. Member list shows all members in a specified file. Use the member list to select a member to edit, browse, print, or delete.

2. File list shows all files in a specified library. Use the file list to select a file with members that you want to edit, browse, print, or delete.

3. Spooled file list shows all spooled files for a specified user. Use the spooled file list to select a spooled file that you want to browse or copy.

4. User list shows all jobs running under all IDs. Use the user list to select the user ID from which you want to browse or copy a job. You can only access the spooled files, and you may require authorization.

Maximum Number and Length of Records:
SEU allows a maximum number of 32,764 records (source statements) in a source member. The maximum record length SEU allows is 240 characters, which includes six characters for the sequence number and six characters for the date. To use files with record lengths of sizes larger than 92 (the standard on the CRTSRCPF command), you would need to specify the record length when you create the source file.

Options Displays:
You can use options displays to control the SEU environment and do operations on file members and spooled files. The following options displays are used frequently in SEU:

1. Change Session Defaults: Use the Change Session Defaults display to specify the characteristics of your edit or browse session.

2. Browse/Copy Options: Use the Browse/Copy Options display while editing a member to look at another member or spooled file, copy another member or spooled file into the member you are editing, or copy specific records from another member or spooled file into the member you are editing.

3. Find/Change Options: Use the Find/Change Options display to search for a specified string in some or all records, change a specified string in some or all records, or search for records that contain syntax errors.

Split Session Editing and Browsing:
You can use split session editing and browsing to edit one member and browse another on the work display at the same time. You can also browse two members at the same time, but you cannot edit two members on the work display at the same time. If you access the Browse/Copy Options display from a split session, you can copy records from one of the members shown on the display to another member that you are editing.

Syntax Checking:
You can use SEU syntax checking to verify the source statements for several high-level languages, including BASIC, PL/I, COBOL, FORTRAN, and RPG, as well as AS/400 CL programs.

System Command Window:
You can conveniently enter AS/400 system commands, while working on the SEU Edit display. To get the System Command window, press F21 (System command).

The System Command window avoids overlaying the cursor, so depending on the cursor location, the System Command window may appear in the top portion or in the bottom portion of the display. If you have used this feature, you may have wondered for years why the window shows up differently at different times. Now, you know!

You cannot enter data on the SEU Edit display while the System Command window is displayed. You can only use the command window. It is as if the rest of the panel is inoperative. You cannot enter any System/36 and System/38 commands in the System Command window. However, you can access the Command Entry display through the Attention key, though this proves to be quite inconvenient.

> ☺ **Hint: System commands such as SIGNOFF (in the AS/400 system) or ENDS36 (in the System/36 environment) end the SEU session abnormally. When you re-access the member that you were editing, the Recover SEU Member display appears**

Getting SEU Started

SEU can be invoked in any one of three ways, and actually a few more. The three popular methods of invocation are as follows:

1. STRSEU (Start SEU) Command
2. PDM Work with members panel
3. OS/400 Main Menu

To use any of the three methods above, you must first be signed onto your AS/400 or IBM i. When you sit down at an AS/400 terminal, or when you are working with PC/400, Client Excess 5250 emulation, TN5250, or Rumba, and you are in green screen session with the system, you first get a Signon screen as shown in Figure G-1.

Figure F-1 OS/400 Signon Panel

```
                              Sign on
                                      System  . . . . .:    HELLO
                                      Subsystem. . . . :    QUIKCOURSE
                                      Display . . . . .:    COURSE1

            Users  . . . . . . . . . . . . .    SEU1_____
            Password . . . . . . . . . . . .    _____
            Program/procedure . . . . . . .     _____
            Menu. . . . . . . . . . . . . .     _____
            A current library . . . . . . . .   _____



  ...


                        ©) COPYRIGHT IBM CORP. 1980, 2000.
```

Figure F-2 OS/400 Main Menu Panel

```
MAIN                         OS/400 Main Menu
                                                        System:   HELLO
  Select one of the following:

      1. User tasks
      2. Office tasks
      3. General system tasks
      4. Files, libraries, and folders
      5. Programming
      6. Communications
      7. Define or change the system
      8. Problem handling
      9. Display a menu
     10. Information Assistant options
     11. Client Access/400 tasks

     90. Sign off

  Selection or command
  ===>  5                                                         ____

  F3=Exit    F4=Prompt    F9=Retrieve    F12=Cancel    F13=Information Assistant
  F23=Set initial menu
  ©) COPYRIGHT IBM CORP. 1980, 2000.
```

From the signon panel, you enter your user ID and your password and press ENTER. Notice in Figure F-1 that there is apparently nothing keyed in the password field. On the AS/400, as you may already know, a person wanting to steal your password must watch your fingers as you type because the password does not display as you type it. When you have filled in the signon panel, press ENTER, and more than likely you will see the OS/400 Main Menu panel as shown in Figure F-2. If your system administrator has set you up differently, ask her to set you up so you can have the Main Menu appear from your user profile.

Using STRSEU to Start SEU

This is the main menu on the AS/400. From here, you can type STRSEU as one way of starting SEU and press F4 for prompting. Then, you will get the panel as shown on Figure F-5. To continue with this method, go ahead several pages, to the section titled *Start SEU Panel*.

Using PDM To Start SEU

Many developers like to use the Program Development manager to invoke SEU. PDM is fully explained in QuikCourse E in this book. To start PDM, issue the STRPDM command and press ENTER. Take option 3 to *Work with Members*. Then, type QDDSSRC as the source file and HELLO as the library. After filling in the panel, press ENTER. You will be taken to the Work with Members Using PDM screen. From here, press F6 to create a new member. At this point, you will be taken to the panel as shown in Figure F-5. If this is the method you select to invoke SEU, continue at the heading a few pages from here titled *Start SEU Panel*.

If you have not taken any other QuikCourses, for any of the methods to get into SEU, you may have to create both of the necessary objects (library and source file). You can use the following commands to accomplish this:

CRTLIB HELLO TEXT('HELLO library for QuikCourses')

CRTSRCPF HELLO/QDDSSRC TEXT('Source File for DDS')

Using the Main Menu to Start SEU

The Menu structure of OS/400 enables you to navigate quite easily. Using this path, it will take longer to explain how to start SEU than for you to actually do it. From the panel in Figure F-2, type a "5" and press ENTER. You will get the Programming Menu as shown in Figure F-3.

Figure F-3 Programming Menu

```
PROGRAM                        Programming
                                             System:    HELLO
Select one of the following:

     1. Programmer menu
     2. Programming Development Manager (PDM)
     3. Utilities
     4. Programming language debug
     5. Structured Query Language (SQL) pre-compiler
     6. Question and answer

     8. Copy screen image
     9. Cross System Product/Application Execution (CSP/AE)

    50. System/36 programming

    70. Related commands

Selection or command
===> 3

F3=Exit    F4=Prompt    F9=Retrieve    F12=Cancel    F13=Information Assistant
F16=AS/400 Main menu
©) COPYRIGHT IBM CORP. 1980, 2000.
```

There are a number of ways to get to SEU from here. Options 1, 2, and 3 will all get you there. For this example, choose option 3, since SEU is a Utility Program. You will then see the first page of a 119-option menu which is the OS/400 command grouping menu for all commands beginning with start (STR). This is shown in Figure F-4.

Figure F-4 SEU Utilities Menu (STR Menu)

```
CMDSTR                        Start Commands

Select one of the following:

    79. Start QSH                                    STRQSH
    80. Start Question and Answer                    STRQST
    81. Start REXX Procedure                         STRREXPRC

    86. Start Report Layout Utility                  STRRLU
    87. Start Remote Support                         STRRMTSPT
    88. Start Remote Writer                          STRRMTWTR

    90. Start Subsystem                              STRSBS
    91. Start Search Index                           STRSCHIDX
    92. Start Screen Design Aid                      STRSDA
    93. Start Source Entry Utility                   STRSEU
    94. Start Support Network                        STRSPTN
    95. Start SQL Interactive Session                STRSQL

More...
Selection or command
===> 93


    F3=Exit    F4=Prompt    F9=Retrieve    F12=Cancel    F16=Major menu
```

You can either ROLL until you see option 93 "*Start Source Entry Utility,*" type "93," and press ENTER, or you can take it on faith and type it in on the first page of the *Start Commands* menu and press ENTER. In either case, you will be taken to the Start SEU panel in Figure F-5.

Figure F-5 Start SEU Panel

```
                    Start Source Entry Utility (STRSEU)
Type choices, press Enter.
Source file  . . . . . . . . .    QDDSSRC       Name, *PRV
  Library  . . . . . . . . . .      HELLO       Name, *LIBL, *CURLIB, *PRV
Source member  . . . . . . . .    *PRV          Name, *PRV, *SELECT
Source type  . . . . . . . . .    *SAME         Name, *SAME, BAS, BASP...
Option . . . . . . . . . . . .    *BLANK        *BLANK, ' ', 2, 5, 6
Text 'description' . . . . . .    *BLANK

Bottom F3=Exit    F4=Prompt    F5=Refresh    F12=Cancel    F13=How to use this
display    F24=More keys
```

Start SEU Panel

No matter how you got here, from STRSEU, STRPDM or from the Main menu, the Stat SEU panel is where you are at. From the STRSEU panel as shown in Figure F-5, type in your source file

(QDDSSRC) and your library (HELLO), and press the ENTER key
to continue. You will be taken to the *Work With Members Using SEU*
panel as shown in Figure F-6.

Figure F-6 Work With Members Using SEU Panel

```
                          Work with Members Using SEU

  Source file . . . . . .   QDDSSRC                 Library . . . . .   HELLO
  Position to . . . . . . . . . . . . . . . . . . . . . . . . . . . .
  New member  . . . . . . . . . . . . . . . . . . . . . . . . . . . .  VENDORP
    Type for new member . . . . . . . . . . . . . . . . . . . . . . .  TXT
    Text  . . . . . . . . .

  Type options, press Enter.
    2=Edit     4=Delete      5=Browse          6=Print

  Opt Member        Type       Text
     (No members in the file)



   F3=Exit            F5=Refresh          F12=Cancel          F14=Display date

   F15=Sort by date                       F17=Subset
```

Notice that there are no source members in the file. To create the new
source member, which will be needed in our examples, type the file
name VENDORP for the new member. You will then get a new SEU
work panel which is shown in Figure F-7.

What is SEU?

On the System/38, System/36, AS/400, and now the IBM i, the
native source editing tool is called the Source Entry Utility or *SEU*. It
is a very nice, full screen editor with some very powerful features. It
is shipped by IBM as part of the WebSphere Development Studio for
IBM i in the Application Development Tool Set (ADTS)category.
It is full of nice features including the following:

1. Full screen editor
2. Built-in syntax checker for CL/ CLP, DDS, RPGII/ RPGIII/ RPGIV, COBOL, BASIC, PL/I, C, C++, Java, Commands etc.
3. Language prompt lines
4. Language format lines to place formats on line preceding lines being edited.
5. Full variety of line commands - COPY, MOVE, INSERT, DELETE, etc.
6. Variety of SEU commands - TOP, Bottom, Find, etc.
7. Pop-up system command line - command functions without leaving SEU.

SEU the Editor

SEU is a full screen editor, which enables a programmer to type anywhere on the screen. Once SEU is invoked for example, and you have typed your source into the system, a panel, such as that shown in G-7, can be modified by typing over any of the lines.

In the panel shown in Figure F-7 for example, suppose you had originally misspelled the two highlighted fields at statements 6 and 10. As you can see, you need only type over these fields to change them. Multiple lines may be changed at once. All changes are reflected in the SEU session with the depression of the ENTER key. To write the changed file back, you would need to issue a SAVE command or exit SEU. These are demonstrated in the CASE Study.

Figure F-7 SEU Full Screen Main Edit Panel

```
SEU Edit screen

  Columns . . . .:   1  71              Edit            HELLO/QDDSSRC
  SEU==> _____      VENDORP
  FMT A* .....A*. 1 ...+... 2 ...+... 3 ...+... 4 ...+... 5 ...+... 6 ...+... 7
         *************** Beginning of data *********************************
  0001.00        A*  VENDOR MASTER PHYSICAL FILE
  0002.00        A                                    REF(FIELDREF)
  0003.00        A         R VNDMSTR                   TEXT('VENDMAST DB FORMAT')
  0004.00        A           VNDNBR      R
  0005.00        A           NAME        R
  0006.00        A           ADDR1       R
  0007.00        A           CITY        R
  0008.00        A           STATE       R
  0009.00        A           ZIPCD       R
  0010.00        A           VNDCLS      R
  0011.00        A           VNDSTS      R
  0012.00        A           BALOWE      R
  0013.00        A           SRVRTG      R
         ***************** End of data *********************************

  F3=Exit      F4=Prompt     F5=Refresh     F9=Retrieve   F10=Cursor
  F16=Repeat find           F17=Repeat change            F24=More keys
```

Syntax Checking

One of the most powerful features of SEU is its syntax checker. SEU provides extensive syntax checking of source statements. The syntax checker uses the same rules as the compiler. This can save you many compiles trying to catch syntax errors.

There is a syntax checker for all languages within SEU. The languages include CL and the S/36 and S/38 versions of RPG and COBOL and others. The syntax checking rules to be applied are determined by the SEU source type. It's that easy to get a syntax-checked, clean source.

You can see in the example shown in Figure F-8 how the syntax checker does its work. If, for example, you free-form typed line 8 and you were off by just one position, the syntax checker would stop you dead in your tracks and make you change the line before continuing. As you can see in Figure F-8, the error line is highlighted, and a message describing the error is displayed at the bottom of the panel.

Figure F-8 SEU Syntax Checking

```
Columns . . . :    1  71              Edit                HELLO/QDDSSRC
SEU==>                                                         VENDORP
FMT PF  .....A..........T.Name+++++RLen++TDpB......Functions++++++++++++++++++++
        ************** Beginning of data ***************************************
0001.00   A                                     REF (HELLO/VENDORPA)
0002.00   A         R VNDMSTR                    TEXT('VENDMAST DB FORMAT')
F003.00   A           VNDNBR     R
0004.00   A           NAME       R
0005.00   A           ADDR1      R
P006.00   A           CITY       R
0007.00   A           STATE      R
0008.00   A           ZIPCD     R
0009.00   A           VNDCLS     R
0010.00   A           VNDSTS     R
0011.00   A           BALOWE     R
0012.00   A           SRVRTG     R
        **************** End of data ***************************************
 F3=Exit    F4=Prompt    F5=Refresh    F9=Retrieve    F10=Cursor   F11=Toggle
 F16=Repeat find       F17=Repeat change           F24=More keys
 Position 18 must be blank.
 +
```

Prompting and Formatting

SEU provides prompting and format lines for the different types of source on the system.   Prompts for different languages and types of source allow the programmer to key column-sensitive source code without trying to align columns. SEU provides labeled spaces for keying in the data and aligns it into the correct columns after entry.

In Figure F-8, you may have noticed that we slipped in two line commands without describing line commands at all as of yet. They are coming up next. The command "F" typed on statement 3 of Figure F-8 is the Format command and the command "P," which is typed on statement 6, is the Prompt command. When you repair the statement caught by the syntax checker and you press ENTER, you will get the panel as shown in Figure F-9.

As you can see in Figure F-9, immediately above line 3, the editor has placed a Format line. This line provides hints for column placement, and is a favorite of those who like to use the full screen capabilities of the editor. You can place as many format lines as you like in your source. To get rid of one, place a "D" over the "F" and press ENTER. The line command DELETE (D) causes the format line or any other line to be deleted.

Near the bottom of the screen, you can notice that line 6 has been brought down for some fully prompted editing. In this example, for demonstration purposes, we change the length from 20, to 30, and remove the "R," so that the field no longer is defined by a reference field. This is further explained in the case study. After we change the field as shown in Figure F-9, we changed it back as to not affect the case study results.

Figure F-9 SEU Formatting and Prompting

```
 Columns . . . :     1  71          Edit             HELLO/QDDSSRC
 SEU==>                                                      VENDORP
 FMT PF  .....A.........T.Name++++++RLen++TDpB......Functions++++++++++++++++++
         ************** Beginning of data ********************************
 W23 .00    A                              REF(HELLO/VENDORPA)
 0002.00    A         R VNDMSTR            TEXT('VENDMAST DB FORMAT')
 FMT PF  .....A.........T.Name++++++RLen++TDpB......Functions++++++++++++++++++
 0003.00    A           VNDNBR    R
 0004.00    A           NAME      R
 0005.00    A           ADDR1     R
 0006.00    A           CITY      R
 0007.00    A           STATE     R
 0008.00    A           ZIPCD     R
 Prompt type . . .  PF     Sequence number  . . .  0006.00

 Name                              Data    Decimal
 Type      Name        Ref    Length Type  Positions   Use
           CITY         _       30     _      _         _
 Functions


 F3=Exit    F4=Prompt   F5=Refresh      F11=Previous record
 F12=Cancel             F23=Select prompt  F24=More keys
```

Not only does this help you remember the layout of the form and prevent you from field misalignments, it also provides context-sensitive help. When working in a prompted field, press the Help key or F1. SEU will give you information about the type of data you should be entering in that particular area of the form. It is extremely helpful and saves lots of manual lookup time. For example, if you position your cursor to the REF field and hit F1, you will see the following text:

Type R in this field to use the reference function to copy attributes of a previously defined named field to the field you are now defining.   That's quite nice!

QuikCourse G   SEU Commands and Functions

Line Editing Commands

There is a comprehensive set of line commands provided to do such functions for copying, moving, inserting and deleting lines. Some of the more commonly used line commands are shown below.

Why Line Commands?

Because SEU is a full screen editor, you may be asking why line commands are needed. With a full-screen editor, you can change any line on the screen. If you can see it, you can change it. However, the nature of programming languages is statement-at-a time functionality. SEU's line commands add powerful individual line and block line command functions to help the programmer work naturally with source.

List of Line Commands

When you open up an SEU session, you will note a sequence number on the left side of the screen. Line commands are typed right over the sequence numbers. The whole bevy of powerful SEU line commands are shown in the list below:

1.   Vertical positioning: +n, -n, absolute (n.n)
2.   Skeleton: S, IS, ISn
3.   Tabs line: TABS
4.   Columns scale: COLS
5.   Insert lines: I, In
6.   Delete lines: D, Dn, DD
7.   Repeat lines: RP, RPn, RPP, RRPn
8.   Copy lines: C, Cn, CC, CR, CRn, CCR
9.   Move lines: M, Mn, MM
10.   Destinations: A, An, B, Bn, O, On, OO
11.   Horizontal positioning: W, Wn
12.   Shift right: R, Rn, RR, RRn, RT, RTn, RRT,   RRTn
13.   Shift left: L, Ln, LL, LLn, LT, LTn, LLT, LLTn
14.   Exclude: X, Xn, XX
15.   Show: SF, SFn, SL, SLn
16.   Prompt: P, Pxx, IP, IPxx, IP?
17.   Format: F, Fxx, F?, IF, IFn, IFxx, IFxxnn,
18.   IF?, IF?nn

Types of Line Commands

The above list contains most of the line commands available in SEU. The most commonly used are versions of the copy, move, insert, delete, and prompting commands. Let's take an example of the copy line command to describe the different variations of using line commands.   A single "C" copies a single line from one place to another.   The destination of the copied line is designated by either an "A" for after, "B" for before, "O" for an overlay.

"C5" copies the current line and the four following lines to the destination. "CC" copies the current line through the line containing the next "CC" in a block to the destination.   A "CR" (and its number and block versions) copies the line(s) to multiple destinations and leaves the CR line command in place so that it can be copied again. It always helps to remember that PF5 removes the outstanding (incomplete) line commands.

Most of these line commands with AS/400 were available in S/38 SEU. There have been no new commands added with IBM i. The line commands that are not available on S/38 include the following:

A. TABS (any char. on the TABS line becomes a tab location)
B. RP (repeat a line or lines immediately following this line)
C. O (overlay destination line command)
D. X (exclude line or lines from viewing in SEU)
E. Sx (shows the lines excluded using the exclude command)

Window Line Command

We have already shown you a few line commands such as FORMAT and PROMPT, and we discussed how to delete a format line. Now, let's use a different command which comes in very handy when you want to look at parts of a statement that do not fit in the 80 character window. In Figure G-9, you may have noticed that we slipped in a "W20" line command at statement 1.00. When you hit ENTER with this command on any line, you get a panel such as that shown in Figure G-10.

Figure G-10 Windowing At Column Position 23

```
Columns . . . :   23  80              Edit                    HELLO/QDDSSRC
SEU==>  SAVE                                                           VENDORP
FMT PF  ++++++RLen++TDpB......Functions++++++++++++++++++++++++++++++
        ************** Beginning of data **********************************
0001.00                         REF(HELLO/VENDORPA)                    020505
0002.00 STR                     TEXT('VENDMAST DB FORMAT')             020505
FMT PF  ++++++RLen++TDpB......Functions++++++++++++++++++++++++++++++
0003.00 BR      R                                                      020505
0004.00         R                                                      020505
0005.00 1       R                                                      020505
0006.00         R                                                      020505
0007.00 E       R                                                      020505
0008.00 D       R                                                      020614
Prompt type . . .   PF      Sequence number . . .  0006.00

Name                                Data      Decimal
Type            Name        Ref     Length    Type      Positions    Use
 _       CITY               R        30        _          _           _
Functions
_____

F3=Exit   F4=Prompt    F5=Refresh         F11=Previous record
F12=Cancel             F23=Select prompt  F24=More keys
```

You may notice that the text now starts at position 20 of the statement. This lets you see the far right side of the record. In SEU, this area stores the date of change for a given line. In this case, the code was built on February 5, 2002. I bet it was cold that day in the Northeast!

SEU Top-Line Commands

Beginning with V1 R3 (some may think of this time frame - late 1980's and early 1990's as the Dark Ages), SEU was enhanced with a command line at the top of each screen. The special SEU commands that can be entered on this command line, provide a shortcut to the functions found on the Change Session Defaults, Find/Change options, Find options and Exit screens. The beauty is that you can do more things without ever leaving the work screen.

To run an SEU command, type it on the command line. Later we will further discuss SEU commands. As of V1 R3, function key F21 provides a pop-up window for entering system commands directly while browsing or editing SEU source.

The following is a list of SEU commands which can be entered in the top input line above the text which is being edited:

1. FIND - "F" searches for character strings
2. CHANGE - "C"   change character strings
3. SAVE   - save without exit
4. CANCEL - "CAN" exit immediately without save
5. FILE - exit and save
6. TOP - go to top of source member
7. BOTTOM - go to bottom of source member
8. SET - changes editing environment -"S" to set tabs on, set roll key operation, set full screen mode on/off, set caps on/off, etc.

To use an SEU command, type it on the command line. Command parameters are either required, positional, or optional. The help key can be pressed after keying a command to get a list of the parameters. To quickly jump from the body of the Edit panel to the command line, press F10. It is almost faster than a mouse click.

Once again we slipped in something on a panel to help us describe a function we were about to describe. If you would be so kind as to check back to Figure G-10, you can see the "SAVE" command on the SEU Command Line. Notice that it does not have to be typed on the far left. It can be placed anywhere on the line. When you hit ENTER with SAVE on the command line, if you are very quick, you will see a message flash at the bottom of the screen which says the following:

Member is being saved

The SEU Main Edit Panel

Let's keep our keyboards and mouse still for a while as we take a more detailed look at the SEU main editing screen in Figure G-11A.

Figure G-11A SEU Main Edit Panel

```
Columns . . . :    1  71                   Edit                          HELLO/QDDSSRC
   SEU==> _____
   FMT A*  .....A*. 1 ...+... 2 ...+... 3 ...+... 4 ...+... 5 ...+... 6 ...+... 7
           *************** Beginning of data ********************************************
   0001.00      A*   VENDOR MASTER PHYSICAL FILE
   0002.00      A                                       REF(FIELDREF)
   0003.00      A          R VNDMSTR                     TEXT('VENDMAST DB FORMAT')
   0004.00      A            VNDNBR      R
   0005.00      A            NAME        R
   0006.00      A            ADDR1       R
   0007.00      A            CITY        R
   0008.00      A            STATE       R
   0009.00      A            ZIPCD       R
   0010.00      A            VNDCLS      R
   0011.00      A            VNDSTS      R
   0012.00      A            BALOWE      R
   0013.00      A            SRVRTG      R
           **************** End of data *************************************************

F3=Exit    F4=Prompt    F5=Refresh    F9=Retrieve    F10=Cursor    F11=Toggle
F16=Repeat find          F17=Repeat change           F24=More keys
```

As you can see in Figure G-11A, at the very top center of the screen, is the Screen Title "Edit." This is the SEU Main Edit panel. To the left in this 80-column SEU Window is an indication that columns 1 to 71 are displayed. To the right is the name of the library and source file of the source member being edited.

On line 2, from left to right, you see the prompt for the SEU Command Line followed by 60 spaces in which to place the SEU command. To the right is the source member name being edited.

On the third line, SEU provides a format line for physical file "PF" DDS to help display the code in a meaningful fashion. On the fourth line the body begins with a begin data marker, followed by 13 lines of DDS statements, and the end data marker.

As you will see, these data markers can be used as targets for copy and move commands. For example, you can place an "A" on the begin data marker and copy or moved data will flow following the marker. You can also place a "B" on the End Data marker and copied or moved text will flow above it.

SEU Command Keys

Now, we have progressed to the bottom of Figure G-11A. Here we see the command key prompts. There are really more command keys than those displayed in Figure G-11A. To get a look at more of them, press F24.   The bottom 2 lines of the panel, after F24 is depressed once, appears as follows:

F13=Change session defaults	F14=Find/Change options
F15=Browse/Copy options	F24=More keys

The bottom 2 lines after F24 is pressed again with the above functions displayed, looks as follows:

F19=Left F20=Right	F21=System command	
F23=Select prompt	F24=More keys	

As noted above, Figure G-11A shows the main SEU edit screen. The function keys listed at the bottom of the screen change as F24 is depressed. The extra function keys are shown above. The second set is from pressing F24 two times.

The meanings of most of the command keys may be self-evident. However, we present the following list and short description to help you understand what command key functions are available within the SEU environment:

Command Key	Description
F1=Help	Show SEU Main Help panel.
F3=Exit	Exit SEU.
F4=Prompt	Invoke line prompter at bottom
F5=Refresh	Redisplay the current display.
F9=Retrieve	Bring back the last command

F10=Cursor	Move cursor to command line
F11=Toggle	Toggle left and right to show the source field on the left side and the comment field on the right side.
F13=Change defaults.	Set SEU envi. values such as roll amt.
F14=Find/Change opt.	Set Find and Replace options.
F15=Browse/Copy opt.	Set Browse and Copy options
F16=Repeat find	Perform last Find again.
F17=Repeat change	Perform last F & Replace again.
F19=Left	View the info to left of current display.
F20=Right	View the info to right
F21=System command	Display window for IBM i commands
F23=Select prompt	

Go to the Select Prompt display.   After you select a prompt, such as PF for database physical or I for RPG input SEU returns to the Edit session and displays the new prompt.

F24= More keys	Displays two additional sets of command key prompts at bottom of screen as shown above.

Special Panels: Defaults, Find/Change, Browse/Copy

SEU has a few special panels which you can evoke as you can see by reading the list of command keys above. These are (1) the Session Defaults panel, (2) The Find/Replace options panel, and the Browse/Copy options panel. Because these can come in quite handy in your productive use of SEU, we provide details on each below:

Figure G-11B   SEU Change Defaults Panel - Roll Amalgamation

```
                        Change Session Defaults

Type choices, press Enter.

    Amount to roll . . . . . . . . . . .    15           H=Half, F=Full
                                                         C=Cursor, D=Data
                                                         1-999
    Uppercase input only . . . . . . . .    Y            Y=Yes, N=No
    Tabs on  . . . . . . . . . . . . . .    N            Y=Yes, N=No
    Increment of insert record . . . . .    0.01         0.01-999.99
    Full screen mode . . . . . . . . . .    N            Y=Yes, N=No

    Source type  . . . . . . . . . . . .    PF
    Syntax checking:
        When added/modified  . . . . . .    Y            Y=Yes, N=No
        From sequence number . . . . . .                 0000.00-9999.99
        To sequence number . . . . . . .                 0000.00-9999.99


    Set records to date  . . . . . . . .       / /       YY/MM/DD or YYMMDD
                                                                   More...
    Resequence member default  . . . . .    P            Y=Yes, N=No
                                                         P=Previous
    Default to uppercase input
        for this source type . . . . . .    Y            Y=Yes, N=No

    User exit program  . . . . . . . . .    *REGFAC      *REGFAC, *NONE, Name


        Program selection filter . . . . .    *ALL          *ALL, *USRPRF, String



    F3=Exit        F5=Refresh      F12=Cancel

    F14=Find/Change options     F15=Browse/Copy options
```

SEU Defaults (F13)

There are lots of SEU defaults which you can change. These defaults
are like the system values in OS/400. They control your editing
environment. If you look at the panel in Figure G-11B, which is all of
the SEU defaults, including the defaults after one roll, you can see the
many values that can be set. As soon as you get to an SEU Edit panel
in this QuikCourse, don't forget to hit F13 so you can set your default
sessions to those which are right for you. The default values as set in
Figure G-11B are as follows:

Value   **Meaning**

Amt to roll   How many lines to roll when roll key is pressed. Can be set to 15 as in this example, or other numeric values. Can also be set to half, full, from the cursor, or all the data on a screen minus the last line.

Upper input only Y or N determines whether you can type lower case or not.

Tabs on   Determines whether tabs you set with the TABS line are operative or not.

Incr. of insert Controls how the statements are numbered - Default is 0.01. Range is 0.01-999.99

Full screen mode Determines whether the command key prompts are displayed at the bottom. Gives a chance for four more lines in the edit window.

Source type   Prompt type which SEU is currently using to syntax check. In this example we are using a PF (Physical file)

Syntax checking Determines when, what and whether syntax checking is done. The default is as follows:
When added/modified . . . .   Y
        From sequence number . . . . __
            To sequence number . . . .

(Not specified)

Set records to date   Type the date you want all records to be reset to.

Re-sequence member Determines whether you want members re-sequenced when saved.

Default to uppercase Specify a value for the default case setting used for source members with the same source type that are edited in subsequent sessions.

User exit program   Used for user defined line commands

Prog. selection filter   Helps determine which exit program gets picked for user command keys.

To move back and forth between the first and second pages (more) of the defaults panels, use the roll key. When you have your defaults set correctly, press ENTER to continue.

SEU Find/Change Options (F14)

During an edit session, you can look for (FIND) a string of characters in a source member which you are editing. You can also optionally change that string to a new string, by using the Find/Change Options display as shown in Figure G-11C.

To get the Find/Change Options display, press F14 while on the main SEU Edit display. You can do the following on the Find/Change Options display as shown in Figure G-XB:

1. Find a specified string
2. Change a specified string
3. Find records with a specified date
4. Find syntax errors

Figure G-11C   SEU Find/Change Options

```
                        Find/Change Options
Type choices, press Enter.

   Find . . . . . . . . . . . .   Catnip
   Change . . . . . . . . . . .   catnip for the cat
   From column number . . . . .   1        1-80
   To column number . . . . . .   80       1-80 or blank
   Occurrences to process . . . . 1        1=Next, 2=All, 3=Previous
                                           4=First, 5=Last
   Records to search . . . . . .  1        1=All, 2=Excluded
                                           3=Non-excluded
   Kind of match . . . . . . . .  2        1=Same case
                                           2=Ignore case
   Allow data shift . . . . . . . Y        Y=Yes, N=No

   Search for date . . . . . . .  02/06/16  YY/MM/DD or YYMMDD
       Compare . . . . . . . . . .          1=Less than
                                            2=Equal to
                                            3=Greater than

 F3=Exit    F5=Refresh        F12=Cancel    F13=Change session defaults
 F15=Browse/Copy options      F16=Find      F17=Change
                              ©) COPYRIGHT IBM CORP. 1981, 2000.
```

As you can see in the sample in Figure G-11C, we have typed a "find" string of "Catnip," ignoring the case. When the Change option is invoked (F17), this string will be replaced by "catnip for the cat." The other Find/Change parameter options in Figure G-11C are self-explanatory, except for the second to last - "allow days shift." This parameter defaults to "NO." With it set to yes, as we have changed it, the 19-character string is inserted wherever the 6-character string exists. The other data on the line is shifted accordingly to accommodate the larger replacement string.

Finding and Changing Strings

To "find" a string of characters in an SEU source member, perform the following tasks:

1. Type the character string you want to locate in the "*Find*" prompt of the *Find Options* display or the *Find/Change Options* display.

2. Change any of the other parameter prompts, as necessary.

3. Press F16 (Find). The string is found if it exists in the member.

4. To find a character string and replace it with a different string, perform the following tasks:

5. Type the string you want to change in the "Find" prompt of the *Find/Change Options* display.

6. Type the string you want to replace it with into the *Change* prompt display.

7. Change any of the other parameter prompts, as necessary.

8. Press F17 (*Change*). Each time the string is found, the occurrence of the string that you specified is replaced with the string you typed in the *Change* prompt.

> ☺ Hint: For help on any of the prompts on the display, press F1 (Help) to display the online help information. If the string, you type for the Find or Change prompt, is enclosed in quotation marks or apostrophes, the quotation marks and apostrophes are ignored for the search. Otherwise, the string begins in the first position and includes all characters up to and including the last nonblank character. Enclose the string in quotation marks or apostrophes to include beginning and ending quotation marks, apostrophes, and trailing blanks. Two quotation marks adjacently to each other define the null string.

Finding Records by Date

To find a source statement line last changed on a specified date, perform the following tasks:

1. Press F14 (Find options) to access the Find Options display (Figure G-11C).

2.   Specify the date in the Search, using the date prompt.

3.   Specify 1, 2, or 3 in the Compare prompt based upon (LT GT EQ).

4.   Press F16 (Find). The record with the specified date is found. Use F16 (Repeat Find) to find the next record with the specified date. Searching for a date and searching for the "find" string are mutually exclusive.

The Compare prompt determines which type of find is performed when you press F16 (Find). If the Compare prompt is blank, SEU searches for the "find" string. If the compare prompt is not blank, SEU searches for the date.

Browse / Copy Options (F15)

Use the Browse/Copy display as in Figure G-11D to select another member or even a spooled file to be shown on the bottom portion of your display in split screen mode. You get there by pressing F15 from the Edit display.

Figure G-11D   SEU Browse /Copy Options

```
                         Browse/Copy Options

Type choices, press Enter.

    Selection . . . . . . . . . .     1          1=Member
                                                 2=Spool file
                                                 3=Output queue
    Copy all records  . . . . . .     N          Y=Yes, N=No
    Browse/copy member  . . . . .     VENDORPA     Name, F4 for list
        File  . . . . . . . . . . .     QDDSSRC      Name, F4 for list
        Library . . . . . . . . . .     HELLO        Name, *CURLIB, *LIBL

    Browse/copy spool file  . . . .   VENDORP      Name, F4 for list
        Job . . . . . . . . . . . .     VENDORP      Name
        User  . . . . . . . . . . .     BKELLY       Name, F4 for list
        Job number  . . . . . . . .     *LAST        Number, *LAST
        Spool number  . . . . . . .     *LAST        Number, *LAST, *ONLY

    Display output queue  . . . . .   QPRINT       Name, *ALL
        Library . . . . . . . . . .     *LIBL        Name, *CURLIB, *LIBL

F3=Exit       F4=Prompt        F5=Refresh      F12=Cancel
F13=Change session defaults    F14=Find/Change options
```

Split Screen Mode

Split Screen mode is a very powerful feature of SEU. You fill in the options and bring in the member or spool file that you want to view or copy. This comes in handy, especially when typing in programs with externally described files. You can edit a program in the main edit window, for example, and you can be checking out the DDS with the field names you need in the program in the lower window.

Another popular use of the split screen is, to copy code into your member from another member you bring into the bottom of the screen. For example, you may be working on a source member, which needs code from other modules. Once the source is brought to the bottom of your edit screen, you can use line commands to selectively copy   the statements that you want into the module you are editing.

One of the most powerful uses of the Browse/Copy feature is that you can place a spool file listing in the bottom display window. Consider the typical development cycle of edit, compile, and error review. You can review the latest compile on the bottom of your screen, while you are making the changes to the source at the top of the screen. You get to make the changes that reflect the corrections needed by the compile listing – without having to leave your session or get a printout.

Member / Spool File Options

The first three choices on the panel in Figure G-11D are Member, Spool file, or Output queue, respectively. Here you decide whether you want a source member (option 1) , or a spool file (option 2) brought into the bottom panel. If you feel you really want a full screen look at the output queue, you can also pick the output queue (option 3) with this selection.

The next set of options pertains just to members, and is ignored for spool files. The first parameter asks whether you want all of the records from the member copied into your edit window. If so, SEU copies all records at once into the source member being edited. In the next three parameters, you tell SEU in which Library / File / Member to get the new source.

The next set of options has to do with spool files. In this section, you give the job information about the spool file so that SEU can locate the printout. For recent compiles, as you can see in Figure F-11D, SEU very nicely copies most of the information into this area for you from your current job. The last two lines of the panel are where you specify the output queue you want displayed if you have selected option 3 at the top.

On the panel in Figure G-11D, we selected the member VENDORPA, which is the field reference file for VENDORP. We might do this in a real development mode so we could be assured that all of the field definitions are proper, and we can also copy any information we choose into the edit session. After you fill in the panel as in Figure G-11D, Press ENTER, and the EDIT panel splits to look like the screen shown in Figure G-11E.

Figure G-11E Split Screen Copy Block

```
 Columns . . . :    1  71            Edit              HELLO/QDDSSRC
 SEU==>                                                        VENDORP
 FMT A*  .....A*. 1 ...+... 2 ...+... 3 ...+... 4 ...+... 5 ...+... 6 ...+... 7
        ************** Beginning of data **************************************
 0001.00     A*   VENDOR MASTER PHYSICAL FILE
 A 02.00     A                                   REF (HELLO/VENDORPA)
 0003.00     A          R VNDMSTR                TEXT('VENDMAST DB FORMAT')
 0004.00     A            VNDNBR      R
 0005.00     A            NAME        R
 0006.00     A            ADDR1       R
 ────────────────────────────────────────────────────────────────────────────
 Columns . . . :    1  71            Browse            HELLO/QDDSSRC
 SEU==>                                                        VENDORPA
        ************** Beginning of data **************************************
 CC 1.00     A          R VNDMSTR                TEXT('VENDORP  DB FORMAT')
 0002.00     A            VNDNBR      5S 0        COLHDG('VENDOR' 'NUMBER')
 CC 3.00     A                                    ALIAS(VENDOR_NUMBER)
 0004.00     A            NAME        25          COLHDG('NAME')
 0005.00     A            ADDR1       25          COLHDG('ADDRESS LINE 1')
 0006.00     A                                    ALIAS(ADDRESS_LINE_1)

 F3=Exit    F4=Prompt    F5=Refresh   F9=Retrieve   F11=Toggle    F12=Cancel
 F16=Repeat find         F17=Repeat change         F24=More keys
```

When you get to the panel in Figure G-11E, press F24 until you see the option for F6. This option lets you change the split line. Position your cursor on the line at which you want the split to occur and press F6. This changes the split line accordingly.

As you can see in the panel in Figure G-11E, we primed the panel with a block copy. When you hit ENTER, after typing the block copy command, SEU will copy the blocked statements from one member to the other. As you would expect, this feature really comes in handy when you are trying to get work done in a productive fashion - by stealing from your past work, or that of a colleague.

Line Command Exercises

Before we wrap up this primer on SEU with a comprehensive summary of line commands, and we move on to the Case Study, let's do a few COPY / DELETE / MOVE line command exercises.

Copy One Line

Take a look at Figure G-12A. In this figure, we demonstrate the use of the COPY line command as representative of SEU line commands. When you want to copy just one line of code, as in Figure 12-A and Figure 12-B (before and after), place a "C" next to the line you want to copy. Place an "A" for **After** or a "B" for **Before,** or an "O" for **Overlay,** on the line to which you want to begin to place the copy.

Figure G-12A SEU Copy Line Command - Before

```
  Columns . . . .:   1  71                 Edit                   HELLO/QDDSSRC
  SEU==> _____          VENDORP
  FMT A* .....A*. 1 ...+... 2 ...+... 3 ...+... 4 ...+... 5 ...+... 6 ...+... 7
         *************** Beginning of data *********************************
>C           A*  VENDOR MASTER PHYSICAL FILE
  0002.00    A                                     REF(FIELDREF)
  0003.00    A          R VNDMSTR                   TEXT('VENDMAST DB FORMAT')
  0004.00    A            VNDNBR    R
  0005.00    A            NAME      R
  0006.00    A            ADDR1     R
  0007.00    A            CITY      R
  0008.00    A            STATE     R
  0009.00    A            ZIPCD     R
  0010.00    A            VNDCLS    R
  0011.00    A            VNDSTS    R
  0012.00    A            BALOWE    R
>A           A            SRVRTG    R
         ***************** End of data *****************************************

  F3=Exit    F4=Prompt    F5=Refresh    F9=Retrieve   F10=Cursor
  F16=Repeat find          F17=Repeat change          F24=More keys
```

Figure G-12B SEU Copy Line Command - After

```
Columns . . . .:   1  71                    Edit                HELLO/QDDSSRC
SEU==>                                                              VENDORP
FMT A*  .....A*. 1 ...+... 2 ...+... 3 ...+... 4 ...+... 5 ...+... 6 ...+... 7
       *************** Beginning of data *******************************************
0001.00     A*  VENDOR MASTER PHYSICAL FILE
0002.00     A                              REF(FIELDREF)
0003.00     A          R VNDMSTR           TEXT('VENDMAST DB FORMAT')
0004.00     A            VNDNBR      R
0005.00     A            NAME        R
0006.00     A            ADDR1       R
0007.00     A            CITY        R
0008.00     A            STATE       R
0009.00     A            ZIPCD       R
0010.00     A            VNDCLS      R
0011.00     A            VNDSTS      R
0012.00     A            BALOWE      R
0013.00     A            SRVRTG      R
0014.00     A*  VENDOR MASTER PHYSICAL FILE
       ***************** End of data *******************************************
  F3=Exit      F4=Prompt     F5=Refresh     F9=Retrieve    F10=Cursor
  F16=Repeat find           F17=Repeat change            F24=More keys
```

The COPY Results

As you can see in Figure G-12B, there is a definite difference between the FROM-panel (Figure G-12A) and the TO-panel (Figure G-12B). There is an extra line – # Fourteen in Figure G-12B. It was copied right where we said to copy it. If we had executed a move command (M, MM), the FROM lines would have been deleted during the move to the new location.

Delete Operations

Before we issue the block copy commands, let's delete one line from the source member. The first line is just a comment and removing it will give more room to manipulate the member as shown in Figures G12B through G12D. The delete is simple. Place a single "D" on the line as in Figure G-12C and press Enter. You will then see a panel similar to that in Figure G-12D (without the already typed block copy commands).

The member in Figure 12-D, of course, has already been renumbered. Therefore, to get these results, the SEU session would have ended and was restarted.

Figure G-12C SEU Delete Line Command

```
Columns . . . :    1  71              Edit
HELLO/QDDSSRC
 SEU==>
VENDORP
 FMT A*  .....A*. 1 ...+... 2 ...+... 3 ...+... 4 ...+... 5 ...+... 6 ...+...
7
        *************** Beginning of data
 *************************************
D  1.00      A*  VENDOR MASTER PHYSICAL FILE
0002.00      A                              REF(HELLO/VENDORPA)
0003.00      A        R VNDMSTR             TEXT('VENDMAST DB
FORMAT')
0004.00      A          VNDNBR    R
0005.00      A          NAME      R
0006.00      A          ADDR1     R
0007.00      A          CITY      R
0008.00      A          STATE     R
0009.00      A          ZIPCD     R
0010.00      A          VNDCLS    R
0011.00      A          VNDSTS    R
0012.00      A          BALOWE    R
0013.00      A          SRVRTG    R
        **************** End of data
 *************************************
 F3=Exit    F4=Prompt   F5=Refresh   F9=Retrieve   F10=Cursor   F11=Toggle
 F16=Repeat find        F17=Repeat change          F24=More
```

If you want to delete a number of lines, you can use the Dn form in which you specify "n" as the number of lines to delete. If you had more than one line to delete, you could use the block delete "DD" command in the first line and another "DD" block command in the last line to be deleted.

When you press ENTER with these commands in place, SEU gets rid of the deleted statements. Poof! They are gone. There is no UNDO. Thus there is risk in all forms of the DELETE line commands. While you are in an SEU session it is good to save your work regularly, so that, by mistake, you do not make it disappear.

> ☺ **Hint: Your SEU editing is done in a work file so if you don't really want what you have done since the last save, you can theoretically undo it. Here's how: If you would like to revert to the saved version after you mistakenly delete good statements, you can exit SEU and choose not to update the member. Then you can start SEU again and the old form of the source member will be brought to your edit window.**

Copy Blocks

To copy blocks of lines, as in Figures G-12D and G-12E (before and after), place "CC" on the lowest sequence # of the from-block and place another "CC" on the highest sequence number of the from-block. For the receiving (target) location, position yourself to the line that you have selected (to-location). On that line, type an "A," a "B," or an "O" (for **write over blanks**) to tell SEU where to put the copied text. The "O" says not to destroy the existing text but instead to copy the characters in the "from" area to blank positions in the "to" area. The "A" or "B" says to create a new area for the copied text. It is very powerful.

Figure G-12D SEU Post Delete Pre Block Copy

```
Columns  . . . :    1  71              Edit                HELLO/QDDSSRC
SEU==>                                                         VENDORP
FMT PF
.....A..........T.Name++++++RLen++TDpB......Functions+++++++++++++++++++
      *************** Beginning of data *********************************
B 01.00      A                              REF(HELLO/VENDORPA)
0002.00      A         R VNDMSTR            TEXT('VENDMAST DB
FORMAT')
0003.00      A           VNDNBR    R
0004.00      A           NAME      R
0005.00      A           ADDR1     R
0006.00      A           CITY      R
0007.00      A           STATE     R
0008.00      A           ZIPCD     R
0009.00      A           VNDCLS    R
CC 0.00      A           VNDSTS    R
0011.00      A           BALOWE    R
CC 2.00      A           SRVRTG    R
      ***************** End of data
****************************************
F3=Exit    F4=Prompt   F5=Refresh   F9=Retrieve   F10=Cursor   F11=Toggle
F16=Repeat find        F17=Repeat change          F24=More keys
                                       ©) COPYRIGHT IBM CORP. 1981, 2000.
```

Figure G-12E SEU Block Copy Line Command - After

```
Columns . . . :    1  71              Edit                    HELLO/QDDSSRC
SEU==>                                                            VENDORP
FMT PF  .....A..........T.Name++++++RLen++TDpB......Functions++++++++++++++++++++
        *************** Beginning of data ****************************************
DD 0.01        A              VNDSTS      R
0000.02        A              BALOWE      R
DD 0.03        A              SRVRTG      R
0001.00        A                                      REF (HELLO/VENDORPA)
0002.00        A          R VNDMSTR                   TEXT('VENDMAST DB FORMAT')
0003.00        A              VNDNBR      R
0004.00        A              NAME        R
0005.00        A              ADDR1       R
0006.00        A              CITY        R
0007.00        A              STATE       R
0008.00        A              ZIPCD       R
0009.00        A              VNDCLS      R
0010.00        A              VNDSTS      R
0011.00        A              BALOWE      R
0012.00        A              SRVRTG      R
        ***************** End of data ****************************************

 F3=Exit    F4=Prompt    F5=Refresh   F9=Retrieve   F10=Cursor   F11=Toggle
 F16=Repeat find         F17=Repeat change           F24=More keys
```

As you can see in Figure G-12E, the block COPY was completed successfully. It is probably a good idea to delete the copied lines as we do in this display (Block Delete), since they are of no value and will cause an error. When you press ENTER after the block delete, you will no longer have the lines before line 1 of Figure G-12E.

The line commands "C" and "A" are in action in Figure G-12A and G-12B. The block line commands "CC" and "B" are in action in Figures G-12D and G-12E, as you can see. The single line Delete is shown in Figure G-12C, and the block Delete (DD) is shown in Figure G-12E..

More Command Line Tricks -Move, Insert, and Repeat

We outdid ourselves with the example panels shown in Figures G-13A (Before) and G-13B(After). Yet, this is very valid. It demonstrates how you can supply multiple line commands to SEU, at the same time, and it will get them all done with just one ENTER Key.

In Figure G-13A, we start with a block move of lines 1 to 3 to the line after line 12. At line 6, we then ask for two lines to open up (I Command) so we can insert some code. The last command is to repeat line 8 (RP Command) and make a duplicate of it as the following statement. When you press ENTER on the panel in Figure G-13A, you will see the changes reflected in the panel in Figure G-13B.

Figure G-13A   SEU Combination Line Command Panel - Before

```
 Columns . . . :   1  71             Edit                 HELLO/QDDSSRC
 SEU==>                                                           VENDORP
 FMT PF  .....A..........T.Name++++++RLen++TDpB......Functions++++++++++++++++++
         ************** Beginning of data *********************************
 MM 1.00       A                                    REF(HELLO/VENDORPA)
 0002.00       A          R VNDMSTR                 TEXT('VENDMAST DB FORMAT')
 MM 3.00       A            VNDNBR     R
 0004.00       A            NAME       R
 0005.00       A            ADDR1      R
 I2 6.00       A            CITY       R
 0007.00       A            STATE      R
 RP 8.00       A            ZIPCD      R
 0009.00       A            VNDCLS     R
 0010.00       A            VNDSTS     R
 0011.00       A            BALOWE     R
 A 12.00       A            SRVRTG     R
         ***************** End of data *********************************

 F3=Exit    F4=Prompt    F5=Refresh    F9=Retrieve    F10=Cursor    F11=Toggle
 F16=Repeat find         F17=Repeat change           F24=More keys
                        ©) COPYRIGHT IBM CORP. 1981, 2000.
```

Figure G-13B SEU Combination Line Command Panel - After

```
 Columns . . . :   1  71             Edit                 HELLO/QDDSSRC
 SEU==>                                                           VENDORP
 FMT PF  .....A..........T.Name++++++RLen++TDpB......Functions++++++++++++++++++
         ************** Beginning of data *********************************
 0004.00       A            NAME       R
 0005.00       A            ADDR1      R
 0006.00       A            CITY       R
 '''''''
 '''''''
 0007.00       A            STATE      R
 0008.00       A            ZIPCD      R
 0008.01       A            ZIPCD      R
 0009.00       A            VNDCLS     R
 0010.00       A            VNDSTS     R
 0011.00       A            BALOWE     R
 0012.00       A            SRVRTG     R
 0013.00       A                                    REF(HELLO/VENDORPA)
 0014.00       A          R VNDMSTR                 TEXT('VENDMAST DB FORMAT')
 0015.00       A            VNDNBR     R
         ***************** End of data *********************************

 F3=Exit    F4=Prompt    F5=Refresh    F9=Retrieve    F10=Cursor    F11=Toggle
 F16=Repeat find         F17=Repeat change           F24=More keys
```

Operation Results

As you can see, there is a definite difference between the FROM-panel (Figure G-13A) and the TO-panel (Figure G-13B). For one thing, lines 1 to 3 have been moved and now appear as lines 13 to 15. Lines 1 to 3, their prior location, have been deleted. and are no longer visible in the panel. Additionally, two insertion lines have been added between statements 6 and 7. The last notable accomplishment is that statement 8 has been repeated and its clone now appears at statement 8.01.

The intention of this little SEU primer in this QuikCourse is to give you a good-enough feeling about SEU to go out and try it. The Help text is very good, and the IBM SEU manual is also very comprehensive. Both can help advance your SEU studies even further.

This next last segment, before we get into the SEU Case Study section, is a rehash of line commands, which we have already demonstrated. Additionally, this segment contains information about a number of line commands which are not covered elsewhere   in this QuikCourse.

Line Command Summary

To copy, delete, insert, move, or print records from the SEU main edit panel, use the following line commands:

Command	Description
A, B, O	After, Before, and Overlay (target commands)
C, CC	Copy, Copy block
CR	Copy Repeat
D, DD	Delete, Delete block
I	Insert
M, MM	Move, Move block
R	Repeat
LP	Line Print

Target Command Summary

As noted above, the After (A), Before (B), and Overlay (O) commands are the target commands you use to tell SEU where to copy the identified lines. You are specifying the to-area which you can also think of as the receiving area.

How to Specify the Target Area

You specify either an After (A) , Before (B), or Overlay (O, OO) command as a target for a Copy ©), Copy Repeat (CR), or move Move (M) command. The block versions of these commands - CC, CCR, and MM, also work with the same target commands - A, B, O, or OO. For the target line, you select a statement (line) representing the receiving line for the command, and you place the target command on that line, to the left side, over the numbers.

The Overlay command replaces blank data in the selected line with nonblank data from another line. It will not wipe out any text in the target area. The Overlay command selects the target, or the line whose blanks are replaced. The Copy, Copy Repeat, and Move commands select the line that replaces the blanks.

You can use any of the following line commands to specify a target:

Command	Description
A	Place the specified records after this record.
A n	Place the specified records after this record and repeat the lines –1 times.
B	Place the specified records before this record.
B n	Place the specified records before this record and repeat the lines –1 times.
O	Overlay this record with the first record specified by the Copy, Copy Repeat, or Move line command.
O n	Overlay this record and the next –1 lines with the records specified by the Copy, Copy Repeat, or Move line command.
OO	Overlay all records in this block (defined by a set of
OO commands	One for *overlay block begin* and one for *overlay block end*) with the records defined by the Copy, Copy Repeat, or Move line commands.

☺ **Hint: Using Overlay lines is really tricky. I have found little use for them over the years. When you use the Overlay line commands, you should keep the following in mind:**

1. If you specify more records to overlay than you are copying or moving, SEU reuses the moved or copied records to complete the overlay.

2. The records to be moved (not copied) are deleted from their original location after the overlay is performed, unless one of the following is true:
A. There are more records to overlay than to move.
B. Not all nonblank characters from the move records are copied to the overlay records.
In either situation, SEU retains the records in their original position and issues a message.

Copy Command Summary

You can copy a record or block of records to another location in a member or to another member using the following line commands:

Command	Description
C	Copy this record to the target specified by A, B, O, or OO.
CC	Copy this block of records (defined by a pair of CC commands - once for *copy block begin* and one for *copy block end*) to the target specified by A, B, O, or OO.
C n	Copy n records, starting with this record, to the target specified by A, B, O, or OO.

When typing COPY commands, you can type the line commands in any sequence you choose. For example, you can type the target (A, B, or O) line command before or after typing the CC and CC line commands that identify the block of records to be copied. In all cases, as you would expect, the target must be outside the range of the block command.

Copying Records Repeatedly Summary

You can repeatedly copy a line or block of lines to one or more locations by using the powerful Copy Repeat (CR) command. This command is used with the target commands (A, B, O), in much the same way you use the Copy command. After processing the command, SEU removes the target commands, but keeps the CR command on the display, right where you had specified them. To do the COPY again, you do not have to specify the from-location. Just enter the new target for the records to repeat the copy operation as many times as you need.

Of course, the CR command will hang around forever unless you get rid of it from the SEU work screen. To cancel the command, type over it or press F5 (Refresh).

The following line commands can be used to repeatedly copy the same records:

Command	Description
CR	Copy this record to the targets specified by A, B, O, or OO, and retain this command.
CR n	Copy n records, starting with this record, to the targets specified by A, B, O, or OO, and retain this command.
CCR	Copy this block of records (defined by a pair of CCR commands - one for *copy block repeated begin* and one for *copy block repeated end*) to the targets specified by A, B, O, or OO, and retain these commands.

☺ **Hint: There are always little things to consider when using these powerful operators, For the Copy Repeat commands, you should keep the following in mind: 1. Do not use the Copy Repeat line command in conjunction with the Copy or Move line commands. If you do, SEU issues an error message. 2. Specify just one block of records to be copied. If you specify more than one block of records, SEU issues an error message.**

Deleting Records Summary

You can delete a line, or a block of lines, from a source member, by using any of the following Delete line commands:

Command	Description
D	Delete this record.
DD	Delete this block of lines (defined by a set of DD commands).
D n	Delete n lines, starting with this record.

☺ **Hint: There are a few caveats when using the DELETE command. When you are using DELETE, keep the following in mind: 1. To delete all the records following (and including) the record where the D n line command is typed, use a large value for n in a D n line command. 2. You can process more than one Delete line command at the same time.**

Inserting Blank Records Summary

The primary way of getting new lines into a source member is the insert command.   You can insert blank lines in a member to add new records. You can add one or more blank lines by using the following line commands:

Command   Description

I   Place a blank line below this record. Each time you type data on the blank line and press Enter, SEU adds another blank line.
I n   Place n blank lines below this record. When you type data on the last inserted line and press Enter, SEU adds another blank line.

☺ **Hint: The Prompt command (P) can also be used with the insert command to designate a type of prompt to display for the inserted record. For example, suppose you were typing an RPG program, and you were working on File Descriptions. If you wanted to insert a calculation specification with a prompt, you would type a command such as IPC (insert with calculation prompt). The line would open up, and a calculation prompt would appear at the bottom of the screen.**

☺ **Hint: When you use the Insert commands, be sure to keep the following in mind:**
1. The I line commands are repeating commands. Each time you type data including a blank, on the blank line of an I line command, or the last blank line of an I n command, and press Enter, SEU inserts another blank line. This continues until you:
A. Press F5 (Refresh).
B. Press Enter without changing the newly inserted   line.
C. Move the cursor off the line.
2. If the value of n in an I n line command is greater than the number of spaces below the I n line command, SEU supplies only the number of blank lines that can fit on the display.

3. If you press F19 (Left) or F20 (Right), SEU shifts the display left or right, but does not insert a new line until you press ENTER.

Moving Records Summary

If you can copy, you should be able to Move. A Move is a copy in which the "from" line(s) are deleted. You can move a record or block of records, to another location in a member, or to another member by using the following line commands:

Command	Description
M OO.	Move this record to the target specified by A, B, O, or
MM	Move this block of records (defined by a pair of MM commands - one for *begin move block* and the other for *end move block*) to the target specified by A, B, O, or OO.
Mn	Move n records, starting with this record, to the target specified by A, B, O, or OO.

Just as with a COPY, you can type the line commands for a MOVE operation in any order. For example, you can type the target (A, B, O, or OO) line command before or after typing the MM (begin block) and MM (end block) line commands that identify the records to be moved.

Repeating Records Summary

The SEU REPEAT command is a more productive, special purpose version of the COPY command. It is a COPY without a target. Actually, it is a COPY with an implied target. It saves lots of keying if it fits. You can repeat a record or block of records on the display one or more times. Again, the REPEAT command is similar to the Copy command, but does not require a target command (A, B, O, or OO). The Repeat command automatically repeats the line or block of lines immediately below the specified line or lines.

You can use the following line commands to repeat a record on the display:

Command	Description
RP	Repeat this record immediately below the current record.
RP n	Repeat this record immediately below the current record n times.
RPP	Repeat a block of records (defined by a pair of RPP commands) immediately below the current block.
RPP n	Repeat a block of records (defined by a pair of RPP commands) n times immediately below the current block.

Printing Records Summary

The last line command we discuss in this QuikCourse is the PRINT command. You can use a line command to print records during an edit session or a full-display browse session by using the following Line Print commands:

Command	Description
LP	Prints one record.
LP n	Prints the next n records, starting with this record.
LLP	Prints a block of records (defined by a pair of LLP commands).

> ☺ **Hint: When you use the Line Print command, you should keep the following in mind: 1. Lines already selected with the Exclude command are not printed, but remain in the member as a special record. The special record prints with a message stating how many records are excluded. 2. Lines already selected with the *Hide* command are not printed in the full screen browse session.**

QuikCourse H. SEU Case Study Lab

Making SEU Work for You

In the rest of this QuikCourse, you will enter the DDS source statements necessary to create a physical file, VENDORP, and a logical file, VENDMST. It would be helpful to the learning process for you to examine the IBM AS/400 database manuals, as well the SEU, DFU, and PDM manuals referenced in the Appendix. Another tool is the LETS GO PUBLISH The IBM i Pocket Database Guide. Moreover, The other QuikCourses in this Pocket Developer's Guide should also come in handy. Having said that, there is a tremendous amount of SEU knowledge and even some database knowledge that can be gained if you just follow along in the text and you choose to do none of the above

We certainly do not purport that you can learn all there is to know about these topics in these QuikCourses. However, you certainly can learn an awful lot. Moreover, by simplifying the initial learning process, these courses stage you for even more learning. One of the nice things about SEU is that understanding the actual source statements, which you are keying, is not a prerequisite to learning it.

> ☺**Note:** In this Lab, you will be asked to type statements which we do not explain. The whole idea of database and DDS coding is covered in a 350 page LETS GO Publish IBM i Pocket Database Guide.

> Even though we tell you that we cannot fully explain the statements that are being keyed, we do attempt to include enough information to give you a general idea of what you are keying. Please remember that this is an SEU exercise, not a database exercise. To make it real, we include real DDS, and we create a real file. However, if the explanations make it more difficult for you to understand the SEU concepts that

we are enforcing with this Lab, then we would suggest that
you treat each statement lightly, and do not worry about the
fact that it represents a part of something bigger.

In this QuikCourse, our objective is to teach SEU, not
database, and not anything else. To the extent that it may
help some developers, we have made our examples real. In
addition to SEU, for example, we also create the database,
and we use DFU (covered in the QuikCourse I) to enter data
into the physical file object that is created from the DDS, that
is typed using SEU. Again, we do this to help you see the
whole picture, not because it is essential for your
understanding of SEU.

The general agenda for the remainder of this QuikCourse is as
follows:

1.   Introduction to Basic database DDS
2.   Introduction to Source Entry Utility
3.   Introduction to Data File Utility
4.   Lab Exercises using the ADTS tools
5.   Start PDM (via STRPDM command or menus)
6.   Work with members in source file QDDSSRC in
       HELLO library
7.   Create a new member, VENDORP
8.   Use SEU to build source DDS
9.   Compile the DDS
10.   Work With Objects
11.   Use Option 18 for DFU to enter data into the VENDORP
       file, then VENDMST

Starting the Lab Exercises

To start this process, sign on and get to an AS/400 command line.
PDM will be your entre' to SEU in this section, though you certainly
can use the Start SEU *STRSEU* command to get there directly. From
a command line, enter the following command to begin PDM:

STRPDM

As you know from the PDM QuikCourse, the main PDM menu typically has just three main options. Regardless of how many options yours has, continue by typing a "3" –   the option number for *Work with members* as shown in Figure H-14A.

Figure H-14A Specify the members to Work With

```
                AS/400 Programming Development Manager (PDM)

Select one of the following:

     1. Work with libraries
     2. Work with objects
     3. Work with members

     9. Work with user-defined options




Selection or command
===> 3_____

F3=Exit       F4=Prompt       F9=Retrieve       F10=Command entry
F12=Cancel
```

The next panel you see will look similar to that shown in Figure H-14B.

Figure H-14B Specify the Members to Work With

```
                    Specify Members to Work With

  Type choices, press Enter.

     File  . . . . . . . . . . qddssrc___    Name, F4 for list

       Library . . . . . . . . HELLO_____   *LIBL, *CURLIB, name

     Member:
       Name  . . . . . . . . . *ALL_____    *ALL, name, *generic*
       Type  . . . . . . . . . *ALL_____    *ALL, type, *generic*,
                                             *BLANK


  F3=Exit      F4=Prompt      F5=Refresh      F12=Cancel
```

Specify File and Library

Specify source file QDDSSRC in the HELLO Library. For the member name and type, in order to get a full list of the members, use *ALL. If you want to subset your list, as your QDDSSRC file grows in members, you might want to use a generic name such as pan* or g* in the name field. Then, when you are ready to proceed, press the ENTER key. If you leave the name field as *ALL, you will see a panel similar to that in Figure H-15.

Figure H-15 Work with Members Using PDM

```
                        Work with Members Using PDM                    HELLO

File  . . . . . .   QDDSSRC
  Library . . . .     HELLO                 Position to  . . . . .

Type options, press Enter.
  2=Edit          3=Copy  4=Delete 5=Display      6=Print    7=Rename
  8=Display description 9=Save  13=Change text  14=Compile  15=Create module..

Opt  Member      Type        Text

  (No members in file)


Parameters or command
===>
F3=Exit          F4=Prompt           F5=Refresh          F6=Create
F9=Retrieve      F10=Command entry   F23=More options    F24=More keys
```

Create New Source Member

Using the *"Work with Members Using PDM:* screen in Figure H-15, create a new   member in your QDDSSRC file in library HELLO. Press F6 to create a new member.

Figure H-16 STRSEU Specify New Member to Be Created

```
                    Start Source Entry Utility (STRSEU)

   Type choices, press Enter.

   Source file  . . . . . . . . . . > QDDSSRC       Name, *PRV
     Library  . . . . . . . . . . > HELLO         Name, *LIBL, *CURLIB, *PRV
   Source member  . . . . . . . . .   *PRV          Name, *PRV, *SELECT
   Source type  . . . . . . . . . .   *SAME         Name, *SAME, BAS, BASP...
   Text 'description' . . . . . . .   *BLANK


 Bottom
  F3=Exit    F4=Prompt   F5=Refresh   F12=Cancel   F13=How to use this display
  F24=More keys
```

SEU is always primed to use the last member that you typed as the member for the current editing session (Figure H-16.) That is why it shows the term *PRV (previous) for *Source member* to start with. Type "VENDORP" for the source member and type "PF" for the *Source type*. For the *Text*, use "Vendor Master File." Text is optional in SEU, but recommended.

Figure H-17 Initial SEU Entry Screen

```
  Columns . . . :    1   71            Edit
HELLO/QDDSSRC
  SEU==>
VENDORP
  FMT PF
.....A..........T.Name++++++RLen++TDpB......Functions++++++++++++++++++
         ************** Beginning of data
**********************************
IPPF'''
,,,,,,,,
,,,,,,,,
,,,,,,,,
,,,,,,,,
,,,,,,,,
         ***************** End of data
******************************************

  F3=Exit   F4=Prompt   F5=Refresh   F9=Retrieve   F10=Cursor   F11=Toggle
  F16=Repeat find        F17=Repeat change         F24=More keys
Member VENDORP added to file HELLO/QDDSSRC.
  +
```

Insert with Prompting to Begin

This is the initial edit screen (Figure H-17.) Other than the IPPF in the left-hand area under *Beginning of data*, this is how the panel will look. You enter IP as the SEU command. It means *insert with prompt*. For the type "physical file" use "PF." Thus, the full line command is IPPF. DDS will then be prompted, and the DDS syntax checker will be invoked for physical file source statement checking.

This puts you into *insert with prompting* mode. You will remain in this mode until you press ENTER without keying any new data.

Figure H-18 Main SEU Edit Panel

```
Columns . . . :    1  71              Edit                    HELLO/QDDSSRC
SEU==>                                                              VENDORP
FMT PF  .....A..........T.Name++++++RLen++TDpB......Functions++++++++++++++++++
        ************** Beginning of data ***********************************
0001.00
''''''''

        ***************** End of data ***************************************



Prompt type . . .  PF       Sequence number . . .  '''''''

Name                                    Data      Decimal
Type        Name         Ref    Length  Type      Positions   Use
_                         -      ------  -         -           -
Functions
REF(HELLO/FIELDREF)                                        /

F3=Exit   F4=Prompt   F5=Refresh       F11=Previous record
F12=Cancel            F23=Select prompt F24=More keys
```

Using Field Reference File

If you decide to use a "data dictionary," which is called a field
reference file on an AS/400 and IBM i, the first DDS statement in
the source you are typing would be a *REF* keyword. The statement is
shown in Figure H-18. It tells the *DDS compiler* to go to the *HELLO*
library into the Field Reference File named *FIELDREF*, in order to
find the referenced fields for file *VENDORP*.   *REF* is the file level
DDS keyword specifying *FIELDREF,* as the reference file to be used
during the compilation of the DDS to create the database file object.

Figure H-19   Entering Field Definitions with Field Ref

```
Columns . . . :    1  71              Edit                    HELLO/QDDSSRC
SEU==>                                                              VENDORP
FMT PF  .....A..........T.Name++++++RLen++TDpB......Functions++++++++++++++++++
        ************** Beginning of data ***********************************
0001.00    A                                     REF(HELLO/FIELDREF)
''''''''

        ***************** End of data ***************************************



Prompt type . . .  PF       Sequence number . . .  '''''''

Name                                    Data      Decimal
Type        Name         Ref    Length  Type      Positions   Use
 R          VNDMSTR       -      ------  -         -           -
Functions
TEXT('VENDMAST DB FORMAT')

F3=Exit   F4=Prompt   F5=Refresh       F11=Previous record
F12=Cancel            F23=Select prompt F24=More keys
```

Entering DDS

The statement in Figure H-19 would be the first statement of the DB source if we were not using a field reference file. The R stands for *record format definition*. It represents the name (VNDMSTR) that we give to all of the fields in the file structure.

Figure H-20 Adding the First Field to The Database

```
Columns . . . :   1  71         Edit                    HELLO/QDDSSRC
SEU==>                                                         VENDORP
FMT PF ....A..........T.Name++++++RLen++TDpB......Functions++++++++++++++++++++
      *************** Beginning of data *************************************
0001.00    A                              REF(HELLO/FIELDREF)
0002.00    A         R VNDMSTR            TEXT('VENDMAST DB FORMAT')
' ' ' ' ' ' '
      ***************** End of data ****************************************

Prompt type . . .   PF      Sequence number . . .  ' ' ' ' ' ' '

Name                              Data     Decimal
Type       Name       Ref   Length Type    Positions    Use
 _         VNDNBR      R     _____   _        __          _
Functions

F3=Exit    F4=Prompt  F5=Refresh        F11=Previous record
F12=Cancel            F23=Select prompt  F24=More keys
```

Since we are demonstrating the way you complete DDS specifications for databases using field reference files, place an R in the REF column of the field you are defining. This tells the database compiler that the field uses the reference file, defined in the REF keyword, at the beginning of the DDS specifications.

If using the option for the field reference file, you simply place an R in the Reference column of the prompt following the field name as we have done in Figure H-20. The field attributes will then be derived from the field reference file.

To complete the description for VENDORP, continue entering the field definitions using the reference file as illustrated above. When you have completed defining all fields, you press F3 to save your work and exit SEU.

Figure H-21 Full VENDORP File With Field References

```
Columns . . . :    1  71              Edit                    HELLO/QDDSSRC
SEU==>                                                        VENDORP
FMT PF
.....A..........T.Name++++++RLen++TDpB......Functions++++++++++++++++++
 *************** Beginning of data ************************************
0001.00     A                                      REF(HELLO/FIELDREF)
0002.00     A          R VNDMSTR                    TEXT('VENDMAST DB
FORMAT')
0003.00     A            VNDNBR    R
0004.00     A            NAME      R
0005.00     A            ADDR1     R
0006.00     A            CITY      R
0007.00     A            STATE     R
0008.00     A            ZIPCD     R
0009.00     A            VNDCLS    R
0010.00     A            VNDSTS    R
0011.00     A            BALOWE    R
0012.00     A            SRVRTG    R
 ***************** End of data ************************************


    F3=Exit    F4=Prompt    F5=Refresh   F9=Retrieve   F10=Cursor   F11=Toggle
    F16=Repeat find         F17=Repeat change          F24=More keys
```

Creating a Starter Field Reference file

Figure H-24 (VENDORPA) shows the DDS for the same file, without using the field reference file (FIELDREF). However, since you have already keyed the source in Figure H-21, which depends on a field reference file, you do not have to rekey the whole member in order to create a mini field reference.

By the way, you would not build a dependent file before you built a field reference file. The Field Reference File is used as a dictionary for database files. It should be built first. By defining the words (fields) in the dictionary, you do not have to declare their lengths and attributes when you use the referenced fields in your database files. You just use the referenced information. Therefore, you would always build the dictionary first. In this case, we did it backwards using extreme educational (poetic) license.

Instead of re-keying to create the mini reference, you need only use PDM to copy the *VENDORP* member and create a new member as a base. One more thing: Since you already have a *VENDORP* member in the *QDDSSRC* source file in *HELLO*, when you copy this file, you cannot name it VENDORP, so pick a different name such as FIELDREF. We chose *VENDORPA* for this educational example.

In this example, you will learn how the *VENDORP* source   member looks without using a reference file. Additionally, by naming the member *VENDORPA*, you can compile it and use it as a database file or as a field reference file for *VENDORP*.

To make this transition, you would change statement 1 of *VENDORP* as shown in Figure F-18 to look like the following:

0001.00   A   ...   REF$\left($HELLO/VENDORPA$\right)$

There really is nothing that says that an AS/400 field reference file must be called *FIELDREF*.   Therefore, by changing the statement above in *VENDORP,* if you were to compile *VENDORPA* first, to create the reference file, and then you compiled *VENDORP* with the change as above, *VENDORP* would be the database file and would use the definition of all the fields as defined in VENDORPA. VENDORP would use the definitions just as if *VENDORPA* were a more commonly-named field reference file, such as *FIELDREF*.

Though *VENDORPA* can theoretically contain data, since it is compiled as a physical database file, it is not a good convention to have reference files used as database files. Therefore, in this case study, it remains a physical file with no data, used solely as a reference file.

You probably have guessed by now that any AS/400 file can be a reference file for any other file, as long as it has field definitions (externally described). Now let's finish up what is needed to get out of Figure H-21 and hustle us off to Figure H-24.

Copy VENDORP to VENDORPA

When you exit SEU from Figure H-21, by pressing CF03, you will come back to the Work With Members panel, such as in Figure G-22.

Figure H-22 Work with Members Using PDM

```
                        Work with Members Using PDM                    HELLO

File  . . . . . .    QDDSSRC
  Library . . . .       HELLOA                  Position to  . . . . .    _____

Type options, press Enter.
  2=Edit              3=Copy  4=Delete 5=Display      6=Print      7=Rename
  8=Display description  9=Save  13=Change text  14=Compile  15=Create module..

Opt  Member      Type        Text
  3_  VENDORP     PF          Vendor Master File

Parameters or command
===>
F3=Exit             F4=Prompt           F5=Refresh          F6=Create
F9=Retrieve         F10=Command entry   F23=More options    F24=More keys
```

To start the COPY process, place a 3 next to the VENDORP file in
the *Work With members* list in Figure H-22, then press ENTER, and
you will see a panel similar to that in Figure H-23.

Figure H-23 COPY VENDORP Source to VENDORPA   Member

```
                           Copy Members
From file . . . . . . . :    QDDSSRC
  From library  . . . . :      HELLO

Type the file name and library name to receive the copied members.
    To file . . . . . . .    QDDSSRC      Name, F4 for list
      To library  . . . . .     HELLO

To rename copied member, type New Name, press Enter.

Member          New Name
VENDORP         VENDORPA
                                                                    Bottom
F3=Exit             F4=Prompt      F5=Refresh      F12=Cancel
F19=Submit to batch
```

Type *VENDORPA* for the name of the new member as in Figure H-23,
and press the ENTER key.

Figure H-24 VENDORPA - Full Descriptions

```
Columns  . . . :    13  80           Edit                   HELLO/QDDSSRC
SEU==>                                                           VENDORPA
FMT PF  ....T.Name++++++RLen++TDpB......Functions++++++++++++++++++++++++++++
0001.00     A        R FREF                        TEXT('Field Reference File')
0002.00     A          VNDNBR      5S 0            COLHDG('VENDOR' 'NUMBER')
0003.00     A                                       ALIAS(VENDOR_NUMBER)
0004.00     A          NAME        25              COLHDG('NAME')
0005.00     A          ADDR1       25              COLHDG('ADDRESS LINE 1')
0006.00     A                                       ALIAS(ADDRESS_LINE_1)
0007.00     A          CITY        15              COLHDG('CITY')
0008.00     A          STATE        2              COLHDG('STATE')
0009.00     A          ZIPCD        5  0           COLHDG('ZIP''CODE')
0010.00     A                                       ALIAS(ZIP_CODE)
0011.00     A          VNDCLS       2  0           COLHDG('VENDOR' 'CLASS')
0012.00     A                                       ALIAS(VENDOR_CLASS)
0013.00     A          VNDSTS       1              COLHDG('ACTIVE' 'CODE')
0014.00     A                                       ALIAS(ACTIVE_CODE)
0015.00     A                                       TEXT('A=ACTIVE, D=DELETE, +
0016.00     A                                        S=SUSPEND')
0017.00     A          BALOWE       9  2           COLHDG('BALANCE' 'OWED')
0018.00     A                                       ALIAS(BALANCE_OWED)
0019.00     A          SRVRTG       1              COLHDG('SERVICE' 'RATING')
0020.00     A                                       ALIAS(SERVICE_RATING)
0021.00     A                                       TEXT('G=GOOD, A=AVERAGE, +
0022.0      A                                        B=BAD, P=PREFERRED')
 F3=Exit    F4=Prompt    F5=Refresh   F9=Retrieve   F10=Cursor    F11=Toggle
 F16=Repeat find         F17=Repeat change          F24=More keys
```

Adding Field Definitions to VENDORPA

After you copy the member, the member *VENDORPA* would appear in the PDM member list along with *VENDORP* (Similar to Figure H-26). Place a 2 next to *VENDORPA*, in the *Work With members* panel to edit it using SEU. You must add the records and the text and the column headings as shown in Figure H-24 to the member as it is shown in Figure H-11. The objective is for the new member to look like that in Figure H-24.

You will find that it sure is easier typing up a new DDS member that uses a field reference file, than it is to type up a new member without a field reference file. There would be even more detailed keying in Figure H-24 if we had not copied in the field names first.

One look at Figure H-24, which represents what *VENDORP* would look like if it were built without a field reference file, and you can see that there is a lot more work in Figure H-24, compared to Figure H-21. Most shops build a field reference file for standardization and programmer productivity. Then, when they need to define fields in a new database, they merely reference the fields from the field reference, so that the new field attributes come into each new database the same way each time without having to be remembered, and without having to be typed.

Exiting to Save

When you finish typing VENDORP and VENDORPA, you will press F3 to exit SEU. You then get the Exit SEU panel as shown in Figure H-25.

Figure H-25 Exit SEU Exit Session

```
                                    Exit

   Type choices, press Enter.

       Change/create member  . . . . . . .   Y           Y=Yes, N=No
           Member  . . . . . . . . . . . .   VENDORPA___   Name, F4 for list
           File  . . . . . . . . . . . . .   QDDSSRC___   Name, F4 for list
              Library . . . . . . . . . . .     HELLO____  Name
           Text  . . . . . . . . . . . . .   Vendor Physical File_____
           Resequence member . . . . . . .   Y           Y=Yes, N=No
              Start . . . . . . . . . . . .   0001.00     0000.01 - 9999.99
              Increment . . . . . . . . . .   01.00       00.01 - 99.99
       Print member  . . . . . . . . . . .   N           Y=Yes, N=No
       Return to editing . . . . . . . . .   N           Y=Yes, N=No
       Go to member list . . . . . . . . .   N           Y=Yes, N=No


    F3=Exit       F4=Prompt      F5=Refresh        F12=Cancel
```

On the SEU Exit panel, as in Figure H-25, you can often take the defaults and the results will be what you want. In the example in Figure H-25, SEU will update the member, with the source statements as keyed in the session, as long as there are no outstanding syntax errors. If there are no errors, SEU returns you   to the PDM member list screen. If there are errors, you would, by default, return to editing the member in SEU.

Compile Two DDS Members

Now that we have created two SEU members, let's compile them both. You must remember however, that the VENDORPA must be compiled before the VENDORP file, since it serves as its reference. To compile these members, let's back go to the *Work with Members Using PDM* panel as shown in Figure H-26.

Figure H-26 Compile the PF Objects

```
                         Work with Members Using PDM               HELLO

 File  . . . . . .    QDDSSRC
    Library . . . .     HELLO                    Position to  . . . . .

 Type options, press Enter.
   2=Edit            3=Copy  4=Delete 5=Display       6=Print     7=Rename
   8=Display description  9=Save  13=Change text  14=Compile  15=Create
 module...

 Opt  Member      Type      Text
   _  VENDORP     PF        Vendor Master File
  14  VENDORPA    PF        Vendor Master File



 Bottom
  Parameters or command
  ===>
 F3=Exit            F4=Prompt            F5=Refresh           F6=Create
 F9=Retrieve        F10=Command entry    F23=More options     F24=More keys
```

To first compile the VENDORPA file, enter the compile option (14) next to the member name as shown in Figure H-26. Depending on your PDM defaults, The compile may be submitted to run in a background job.   If you submit the job, you will need to check for completion messages after the compile, to ensure successful creation of the reference physical file, before compiling the database physical file and the logical file in subsequent steps.

Getting Batch Messages

To check for completion messages, you can press the ATTENTION key on your keyboard, to invoke Operational Assistant, as shown in Figure H-27.

Take option 3 (Work with messages) on the   Operational Assistant screen, and check for a successful completion message. You would be looking for a message such as the following:

Job 014135/BKELLY/VENDORPA completed normally on 05/05/02 at 17:15:48.

Once you get the reference file VENDORPA compiled, it is ok to compile the Vendor Master physical file - VENDORP. You do this the same exact way as you did the VENDORP file in Figures G-26 and G-27 with one exception. This time, you place the 14 next to VENDORP, not VENDORPA. When you check the messages again, you should see something similar to the message immediately below:

Job 014141/BKELLY/VENDORP completed normally on 05/05/02 at

18:12:38...

Figure H-27 Display Messages Using Operational Assistant

```
 ASSIST                    AS/400 Operational Assistant

System:   KELLY
  To select one of the following, type its number below press Enter:

       1. Work with printer output
       2. Work with jobs
       3. Work with messages
       4. Send message
       5. Change your password

      10. Manage your system, users, and devices

      75. Documentation and problem handling

      80. Temporary sign-off


  Type a menu option below
  ===> 3

  F1=Help    F3=Exit    F9=Command line    F12=Cancel
```

Data File Utility DFU Example

Now that the physical file is created, we can enter data into it using the Data File Utility. DFU can be invoked with a *STRDFU* command, or right from the *Work With Objects* **PDM** option. Let's do it the easy way with *PDM* by getting back to the *PDM* main menu, and selecting option 2, Work With Objects. Select the HELLO library, and you should see a list of objects which includes both file *VENDORP* and *VENDORPA*. Place an 18 for *STRDFU* next to *VENDORP,* and press ENTER.   You will be taken to a panel which looks very much like that in Figure H-28.

Figure H-28 DFU Default Program PDM Option 18

```
WORK WITH DATA IN A FILE                    Mode . . . . :    ENTRY
Format . . . . :    VNDMSTR                 File . . . . :    VENDORP

VENDOR NUMBER:           _____
NAME:                   _____
ADDRESS LINE 1:         _____
CITY:                   _____
STATE:                  __
ZIP'CODE        _____
VENDOR CLASS:           __
ACTIVE CODE:            _
BALANCE OWED:           _____
SERVICE RATING:         __

F3=Exit            F5=Refresh            F6=Select format
F9=Insert          F10=Entry             F11 Change
```

Entering Data with DFU

Using the DFU panel in Figure H-28, you can now enter records into
the VENDORP file. You can also recall records for update or
you can choose to just look at records. Moreover, if you get sick of
looking at them, you can delete them with impunity. Together with
DSPPFM (display physical file member), which gives a full record
look at physical data files, the option 18 DFU is a marvelous tool for
making sure your programs did the right thing, before you turn them
over to production.

It surely can't be any easier than option 18. When entering data, just
make sure that you press ENTER after entering each record. You can
recheck a few times to be sure the data is there, but once you get it
right, it's a breeze. To see your data in rapid fire, you can also roll
through the records with the ROLL and/or the PAGE keys.

Creating Logical File over VENDORP

We have just built physical file source statements with SEU,
compiled them with a field reference file (VENDORPA), creating a
database object. We have also entered data into the file (VENDORP)
with DFU. Now, let's create a Logical File (VENDMST) over this
file (VENDORP). This will help us see if we can put a few records
into the physical file through the logical file.

As with all other great source adventures, the place to start is PDM.
By now, you should be getting good at this. Select Work With

Members from the main PDM menu. Then, choose the QDDSSRC source file in the HELLO library. When you get the source member list, remember that the source has not been built yet for the logical file VENDMST. You are about to create it.

Press the F6 key to create a new member. Key the name VENDMST, and the type LF. Then, press ENTER. You should now be into SEU with a big blank screen waiting for your first keystroke.

Figure H-29 Typing in The Logical File VENDMST Panel 1

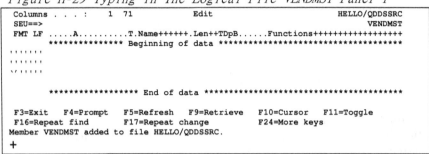

Figure H-29 is the initial edit screen. This is the same type panel we saw in Figure H-17 earlier in this Case Study. Just like then, to begin entering the source statements, it is good to start with the *Insert With Prompting* command on the top line of the panel in the sequence # area. Place the IPLF (insert with prompting for logical file) line command at the beginning line and press ENTER and you will get the panel as shown in Figure H-30.

You can follow along in the that you executed SEU from Figure G14 to G-18, when you originally entered the physical file source. Our objective is to produce a panel which looks like that in Figure H-32.

Figure H-30 Entering LF DDS Panel 2

```
  Columns . . . .:   1  71            Edit              TEAMxx/QDDSSRC
  SEU==> _____      VENDMST
  FMT LF
  .....A..........T.Name++++++.Len++TDpB......Functions++++++++++++
  ++++++
        *************** Beginning of data********************************
  .......
        ***************** End of data *********************************
  Prompt type . . .   LF      Sequence number . . .  0001.00
  Name                                Data     Decimal
  Type      Name          Length      Type     Positions    Use
  _       _____      _____       _        _____        _
  Functions
  UNIQUE_____

  F3=Exit    F4=Prompt     F5=Refresh         F11=Previous record
  F12=Cancel               F23=Select prompt  F24=More keys
```

Since you want the logical file to have unique keys (no duplicates),
type the file level keyword (UNIQUE), as shown in Figure H-30,
which instructs the database not to permit duplicates in the to-be-
created file. When you hit ENTER, the panel will look like Figure H-
31.

Figure H-31   Entering LF DDS Panel 3

```
  Columns . . . .:   1  71            Edit              TEAMxx/QDDSSRC
  SEU==> _____      VENDORPM
  FMT LF
  .....A..........T.Name++++++.Len++TDpB......Functions++++++++++++
  ++++++
        *************** Beginning of data *****************************
  0001.00    A                                   UNIQUE
  .......
        ***************** End of data *********************************
  Prompt type . . .   LF      Sequence number . . .  0002.00

  Name                                Data     Decimal
  Type      Name          Length      Type     Positions    Use
  R        VNDMSTR___      _____        _        _____        _
  Functions
  PFILE(VENDORP)_____      _____

  F3=Exit    F4=Prompt     F5=Refresh         F11=Previous
  record
  F12=Cancel               F23=Select prompt  F24=More keys
```

Staying in *Prompt* mode, in Figure H-31, now define the record
format of the logical file by giving it an "R" code and naming it,
VNDMSTR. After entering the PFILE keyword, telling the system
which physical file the logical file is based upon, and pressing

ENTER, type the other source records for the logical file . . . until the source looks like the panel as shown in Figure H-32.

Figure H-32   Logical File DDS Panel 4

```
  Columns . . . .:   1   71                Edit              TEAMxx/QDDSSRC
  SEU==>  _____            VENDORPM
  FMT LF
.....A..........T.Name++++++.Len++TDpB......Functions++++++++++++++
           *************** Beginning of data*************************
  0001.00      A                                     UNIQUE
  0002.00      A           R VNDMSTR                  PFILE(VENDORP)
  0003.00      A           K VNDNBR
           ***************** End of data****************************
  F3=Exit      F4=Prompt    F5=Refresh    F9=Retrieve    F10=Cursor
  F16=Repeat find           F17=Repeat change           F24=More keys
```

Since no data fields are specified in the DDS shown in Figure H-32, this logical file uses each and every field, from the physical file, for the logical file definition. Thus, the record layout, provided by the logical file, is the same exact layout as the physical file

As you can see in Figure H-32, after the DDS statement that we added in the panel shown in Figure H-31, there was only one additional DDS statement needed to complete the source for the logical file. It is the *key statement* as shown in statement 0003. Through this statement, the file maintains an index against the VENDORP file in vendor number sequence. It uses this index to help programs randomly access the file by vendor number, and to provide the underlying records in VNDNBR sequence to requesting programs.

Thus, this new logical file, when created, will present the records from VENDORP to a program or Query facility in VNDNBR sequence, regardless of the sequence of the underlying data. Moreover, an RPG or COBOL HLL program can randomly access the VENDORP file by key (CHAIN etc.) merely by specifying the name of this logical file in the program instead of the name of the physical file.

Exit SEU, Compile Logical File

After entering the source statement for the key by VNDNBR, your logical file source is finished. You can press F3 to exit, and assure that on the EXIT prompt you save the member as VENDMST in the QDDSSRC source file in the HELLO library.

After you exit SEU and the logical file source is complete, it is time to compile the logical file. This is done exactly the same as you would compile a physical file or a program. You place a 14 (Compile) next to member VENDMST in the member list and press ENTER.

When the file passes syntax checking, if you are compiling interactively, and you have data in the physical file, you can sometimes see the system message about building the index for the logical file. If you do not compile interactively, you can use the Operational Assistant to check the messages for successful completion as you did in Figure H-17.

Whether you compile the database interactively or in batch, you can then use DFU to enter data into the VENDORP physical file using the VENDMST logical file. You use DFU for the logical file in the same fashion as you already did for the physical file. The DFU will behave the same as when you built it for the physical file. There will be no perceptible difference.

Summary and Conclusions:

There have not been substantial SEU enhancements since Version 1, Release 3 of OS/400 back in the early 1990s. If you checked IBM's revenue stream from the green screen ADTS components, since SEU is not a separate product, you would more than likely find that SEU is extremely profitable. IBM executives joke about not enhancing SEU and other green screen tools, while those of us out where the rubber meets the road, continue to use them.

IBM thinks we are using client server tools. I guess if 5250 emulation from Client Access qualifies as a client server development tool, then IBM is probably right. As noted on the cover, however, recent published statistics show that 39 of 40 of us, continue to persist in our use of the ADTS interactive tools. These are now shipped with the WebSphere Development Studio for IBM i.

Somehow IBM has an identity crisis with its own green screen tools, yet those of us who use them regularly find them quite nice, but in need of some updates. Next chance you get, ask IBM to spend some (just a little) of the SEU proceeds on SEU and other things we use, rather than things IBM would like us to use. Enough of that!

In this QuikCourse, we studied the Source Entry Utility (SEU), the editor used by all developers on the AS/400 and IBM i. Since a developer uses SEU as a tool to enter the source for objects such as programs and data files, we chose a simple database example in the Case Study. In the process, we lightly reviewed AS/400 database technology, including physical and logical files, so that what was done in SEU made sense. Near the end of this QuikCourse, we also took a look at DFU as seen through option 18 of PDM. This helped us in seeing real data appear in the VENDORP file object whose source was originally built with SEU.

During this QuikCourse, we presented the facts about SEU first in lecture format, and then we followed this with machine exercises to augment the learning. You created source, changed defaults, copied and moved lines, created databases, entered data, displayed data, and then, again using SEU, you created a logical file as part of the learning process. Hopefully, you were able to use this hands-on approach as an effective learning tool, whether you were following along step-by-step at the office with your own AS/400, or just reading the material for self-enrichment.

There is still lots more SEU work, which you can do. For example, you may want to go back to the section on copies, moves, inserts, and deletes, and run through a few more exercises of your own against a copy of the DDS file. This can only strengthen your appreciation of the wonders of SEU. Don't forget to make syntax mistakes so that you can see how nicely SEU catches them and allows you to correct them on the spot.

Now that you have completed this QuikCourse, you are armed with the green-screen development tool of the champions, SEU. The concepts you learned here will also help you if you choose to take IBM's advice and move to the CODE/400 GUI editor. This is now included with the client portion of the AS/400 developer's package, called the WebSphere Development Studio for IBM i. The last name change for the client package announced with V5R2 was The WebSphere Development Studio Client, Version 4.0.

Regardless of your tool choice in the future, SEU can provide you with immediate benefit today. Congratulations and best wishes in all of your future editing projects.

QuikCourse™ I.   AS/400 and IBM i Screen Design Aid (SDA)

What is AS/400 SDA?

SDA allows a programmer or analyst to interactively design, create, and maintain display screen panels and menus for applications.

When designing screen panels for programs, SDA allows the user to:

1. Define fields and constants for the screen
2. Select a data base file and fields from that file
3. Change attributes (blinking, highlighted, colors, etc.) for fields and constants
4. Move, copy, or remove a field from the screen
5. Display or change the conditions that control when a field will be displayed
6. Define cursor-sensitive help areas for the screen

Menus

Menus are a tremendous aid to building applications. SDA has a powerful menu build capability which takes all of the heavy work from this important task.

AS/400 menus are very similar to a menu in a restaurant. They tell you what you can have. In essence, they present a list of options. The workstation operator can then make a selection from the available options, and the system does the work of getting that application alive and ready for the user.   Online help information can also be built for menus, making it even that much easier to navigate through the options.

Display Panels

Display panels (a.k.a screens or panels) define the screens a user works with when using interactive application programs. The display files which are produced by SDA have a natural affinity to inclusion in RPG, COBOL, and other high level language programs. Moreover, with the introduction of the WebSphere Development Studio and the Workstation Client, the DDS source produced by SDA for display files can be readily WebFaced into java server pages. This provides the same function for the web as the display file does for interactive green screen applications. Just as with SDA menus, you can also build online help information for your SDA-created displays.

In this QuikCourse, we will demonstrate that you do not need extensive knowledge of DDS coding, its forms, keywords or syntax to use SDA. In fact, with a few simple commands, You will be able to move fields and/or constants or groups of fields and/or groups of constants around on the screen to suit your end user's needs – even before even creating the screen or menu.

SDA Features

In a nutshell, SDA provides tremendous facility for programmers. Some of its major features are as follows:

1. Generate data description specifications (DDS)
2. Create menus with message files
3. Present displays in functional groups at file, record and field level
4. Test displays with data and status of condition indicators
5. See the display being designed and changes as work is being done.

Not only does SDA remove the burden of creating DDS from the back of the programmer, but it also provides a very nice testing facility. Using the test display option, a developer can test different data inputs, provide specific status conditions for   indicators, and observe the look, feel, and overall behavior of the display file object, even before linking the display with a program. This not only provides the developer with a way of quickly assuring his or her work, but it also serves as a powerful prototyping facility, permitting users to approve, disapprove, or modify panel design before programs are even written.

Getting Started

You begin using SDA by invoking the STRSDA command from an AS/400 or IBM i command line. If you press F4 with the command, you will be presented with a fill-in screen. The last option is your first major decision. Do you want to create your display panels or menus in AS/400 mode (*STD), System/38 mode (*S38), or System/36 mode (*S36)? For different reasons, you may choose any of these options. As you would probably expect, AS/400 mode is the default, and there is no IBM i mode. For IBM i systems, you can use any of the provided options . . . but there is no specific IBM i choice. The first SDA panel you see then, is shown in Figure I-1.

Figure I-1 SDA Prompt Panel

```
                        Start SDA (STRSDA)

Type choices, press Enter.

SDA option . . . . . . . . . . .   *SELECT       *SELECT, 1, 2, 3
Source file  . . . . . . . . . .   *PRV          Name, *PRV
  Library  . . . . . . . . . . .     *PRV        Name, *PRV, *LIBL, *CURLIB
Source member  . . . . . . . . .   *PRV          Name, *PRV, *SELECT
Object library . . . . . . . . .   *PRV          Name, *PRV, *CURLIB
Job description  . . . . . . . .   *PRV          Name, *PRV, *USRPRF
  Library  . . . . . . . . . . .     *PRV        Name, *PRV, *LIBL, *CURLIB
Test file  . . . . . . . . . . .   *PRV          Name, *PRV
  Library  . . . . . . . . . . .     *PRV        Name, *PRV, *LIBL, *CURLIB
Mode . . . .    . . . . . . . .    *STD          *STD, *S38, *S36


                                                                Bottom
F3=Exit   F4=Prompt   F5=Refresh   F12=Cancel   F13=How to use this display
F24=More keys
```

If you make no choices on this panel, it will be as if you just typed in STRSDA and did not hit the F4 prompter. You can see in Figure I-1 that almost all of the options are defaulted to *PRV. This specifies that SDA is to use the name of the source file and library used in your last SDA session for the AS/400 system. There is actually a little item on the AS/400 which the system keeps for each user. It is called your interactive profile, and the system uses it to remember what parameters you may have used the last time you were in an interactive session with a product. This comes in very handy. For our purposes at this time, let's assume you changed no option on the display panel selected.

Screen Design Aid Menus

When you hit ENTER on this panel or after typing STRSDA, you will see the main SDA Menu. When you examine Figure I-2, you will notice that it looks a lot like the standard PDM panel but, believe me it is much different.

Figure I-2 Main Screen Design Panel

```
                      AS/400 Screen Design Aid (SDA)

Select one of the following:

      1. Design screens
      2. Design menus
      3. Test display files




Selection or command
===>2
_____

F1=Help    F3=Exit    F4=Prompt    F9=Retrieve    F12=Cancel
                                 ©) COPYRIGHT IBM CORP. 1981, 2000.
```

Main SDA Menu

In Figure I-1, you are presented with the main SDA Menu. It is good to remember when using SDA that just as many other of the Application Development Tool Set utilities, SDA comes with significant help facilities. In fact, cursor-sensitive help is always available. This means that whatever field or option you have the cursor on, when you press the help key, detail help text will be displayed. To proceed with the next SDA menu, let's pick the option of creating a menu. I would recommend at this point that you press the help key just to display the definitions of all the function keys. This will help immensely as you begin designing menus and screen panels. For now, select option 2 and press ENTER. You will be taken to a panel similar to that in Figure I-3

Figure I-3 SDA Design Menu Initial Panel

```
                          Design Menus

   Type choices, press enter.

     Source File  . . . . . . . . . . .   QDDSSRC____   Name, F4 for list

         Library  . . . . . . . . . . .   HELLO_____   Name, *LIBL, *CURLIB

     Menu . . . . . . . . . . . . . . .   MENUX_____   Name, F4 for list


   F3=Exit    F4=Prompt    F12=Cancel
```

SDA Initiation

In Figure I-3, you specify the name of your source file, your library, and the name you want to give your menu.

SDA Build Menu Process:

The SDA Build menu process is as follows:

1. SDA looks for the name of the menu's menu source member in the file.
2. If the source is there, it brings it up for you to work with and to update.
3. If the source is not there, SDA creates it upon completion.

Note well that the member name always has the same name as the compiled *menu object as created by SDA, but they may be in different libraries. When updating a menu, and you don't know the name, press F4 with the cursor on the Menu prompt. The Select Menu Using SDA display appears. It lists all the menu image source members for the specified library.

Take the Defaults

After you hit the ENTER key from the panel in Figure I-3, you will see a panel primed with the two SDA defaults as shown in Figure I-4.

Figure I-4 Specify Menu Functions Panel

```
                         Specify Menu Functions

File  . . . . . . :    QDDSSRC                Menu  . . . . . . . :    MENUX
   Library . . . . :    HELLO

Type choices, press Enter.

  Work with menu image and commands  . . . . . .   Y_   Y=Yes, N=No

  Work with menu help  . . . . . . . . . . . . .   N_   Y=Yes, N=No

F3=Exit    F12=Cancel                   Menu MENUX is new.
```

For this introductory SDA QuikCourse, take the defaults by keeping
the "Y" selection to the   *Work with menu image and commands* option
while also keeping the "N" selection for the *Work with menu help*
option. We are not going to add help text to this menu. The
responses in Figure I-4 are completed accordingly.

Menu Design Panel

The next panel you see will be the standard *designing menus* panel as
shown in Figure I-5.

Figure I-5 Menu Design Panel

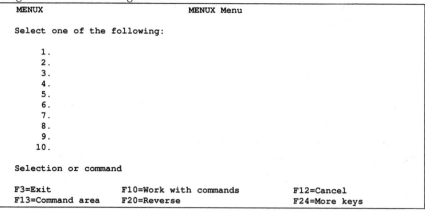

```
   MENUX                          MENUX Menu

   Select one of the following:

        1.
        2.
        3.
        4.
        5.
        6.
        7.
        8.
        9.
       10.


   Selection or command

   F3=Exit           F10=Work with commands        F12=Cancel
   F13=Command area  F20=Reverse                   F24=More keys
```

It is a good idea to press HELP early on in your session to get a list of
valid options with this panel. Before you can really deal with this
"blank" menu, you must have an appreciation for what it is supposed
to look like when completed. Go ahead and take a peak at Figure I-6
now, and then come back to this panel description. Here, in the panel
shown in Figure I-5, you actually type in those nice menu options

you saw in Figure I-6. Remember that cursor-sensitive help can be added to your menu if you choose to do so.

Let's take a hard look at the work panel in Figure I-5:

1.   Row one is for the title. (You can change the   default title.)
2.   Rows 2 through 20 are for the menu skeleton. (Can be changed or replaced.)
3.   Rows 21 and 22 are blank when you are creating a menu.
4.   If you want uppercase only, press F13.   This will only affect new input to the display, not already existing source.
5.   To find out in which areas of the display you can input text press F11 for underlining. This will really help.

Now, let's see just what our menu will look like when we finish typing in our text options. See Figure I-6.

Figure I-6 SDA Completed Menu Image

```
 MENUX                            MENUX Menu

 Select one of the following:

       1. Display messages
       2. Display library list
       3. Work with all output queues
       4. Call RPG vendor inquiry program
       5. Sign off workstation




 Selection or command _____
 F3=Exit                 F10=Work with commands      F12=Cancel
 F13=Command area        F20=Reverse                 F24=More keys
```

In Figure I-6, the example shows text description entered for options 1through 5 of the menu. We pressed the FIELD EXIT key (RIGHT ENTER in CA400) to remove the options 6 through 10, which were not used in this menu.

The nest step from here is to press F10 so that you can enter the command information for the options which you typed.

Command Source Definition Panel

For each specific menu option used, you type the command or program call you want the system to process when you select that numbered menu option.   If you have more than six or seven items on a menu, you can use page down or page up to page through the commands for your menu. The *MenuX* menu has only five visible options so paging is not an issue for this example. As you can see with option 6, you can also place commands or programs for options which are not visible on the menu (STRPDM).

Figure I-7 Define Your Menu Commands

```
                        Define Menu Commands

  Menu . . . . . . :     MENUX           Position to menu option . . . . ___

  Type commands, press Enter.

  Option    Command
    01      DSPMSG_____

    02      DSPLIBL_____

    03      WRKOUTQ_____

    04      CALL HELLO/VENDINQ_____

    05      SIGNOFF_____

    06      STRPDM_____

    07      _____

                                                                    More...
  F3=Exit      F11=Defined only options      F12=Cancel    F24=More keys
```

As you look at the executables for this menu, you will notice that the menu can also contain user programs. The whole gamut of AS/400 executable objects can be specified, from DFUs to Queries to other AS/400 commands.

When you are entering the executable information for the menu option, depending on the type, you can get a lot of help from the system. For example, commands can be prompted by pressing F4. You can also use nested prompting within commands as permitted. However, it is easy to get trapped in a "bad prompt." In these instances it is helpful to remember that you can press ENTER to exit prompting. If that is not enough for your escape, pressing ENTER returns you to the Menu Design screen. Hit F3 or F12, and, prior to the exit, you will again get the Specify Menu Functions panel, from which you can resume design or exit SDA.

Exit SDA Menu Creation

To get the SDA exit panel from here, press ENTER or F3 or F12 from the *Specify Menu Functions* panel. That should be enough to get you to the exit panel. You will then be presented with an exit screen showing options for saving the generated source code, and for creating the menu objects. You can see these in Figure I-8. From here, you should be able to get out.

In Figure I-8, select the options to create your menu. If you are replacing an existing menu of the same name, you can specify that the old menu is to be deleted. As you can see from the options, both menu source and menu objects get created in this process. You have the option of replacing one, the other, or neither. To save your source and build the SDA, press ENTER from this Exit panel. You will return to the SDA initial *Design Menus* panel from which you can specify another menu to work with.

Figure I-8 Exit SDA Menus

```
                        EXIT SDA MENUS

    File . . . . . . .   QDDSSRC          DDS Member  . . . .  MENUX
      Library  . . . . .   TEAMxx         Commands Member . . MENUXQQ

    Type choices, press Enter.

      Save new or updated menu source . . .  Y          Y=Yes, N=No
        For choice Y=Yes:
          Source File . . . . . . . . . . .  QDDSSRC___   Name
                                                          F4 for list
            Library   . . . . . . . . . . .  HELLO_____   Name, *LIBL, *CURLIB
          Text. . . . . . . . . . . . . . .  X menu _____

        Replace menu members  . . . . . .  Y          Y=Yes, N=No

      Create menu objects . . . . . . . . .  Y          Y=Yes, N=No
        For choice Y=Yes:
          Prompt for parameters . . . . . .  N          Y=Yes, N=No
          Object Library  . . . . . . . . .  HELLO_____   Name, *CURLIB
          Replace Menu Objects  . . . . . .  Y          Y=Yes, N=No

    F3=Exit    F4=Prompt    F12=Cancel
```

Do not press F3 from this panel (Figure I-8), unless you do not want to save your work, and create your menu objects. If you accidentally hit F3, the system will ask if you really meant to exit without saving (*Source not saved. Press F3 again to confirm exit*). Pressing ENTER with this message gets you back to the SDA Exit panel. Pressing F12 from the Exit panel cancels the exit and brings you back to the   *Specify Menu Functions* to permit you to make additional changes.

As noted above, the correct option from the SDA Exit panel is an ENTER key. This assumes that you are finished, and want to save your work. You will then see the *Design Menus* menu, as in Figure I-3, along with the following message at the bottom of the panel:

Menu MENUX saved in HELLO/QDDSSRC and

compiled in HELLO.

Running From the Menu

Now that you have a menu, it would be nice to execute it and then pick some options from it. To get this process going, you use the MENU command from the AS/400 command line as follows:

GO MENUX
or

GO HELLO/MENUX

This will bring you your newly created menu as shown in Figure I-9.

Figure I-9 Newly Created Menu Built by SDA

```
MENUX                          MENUX Menu

Select one of the following:

     1. Display messages
     2. Display library list
     3. Work with all output queues
     4. Call RPG vendor inquiry program
     5. Sign off workstation


Selection or command
===>
_____
F3=Exit    F4=Prompt    F9=Retrieve    F12=Cancel
F13=Information Assistant  F16=AS/400 main menu
```

Figure I-9 is your menu example. Please note that errors will occur if option 4 is selected prior to the creating and compiling of the RPG/400 VENDINQ program and display file.

Creating a Display File

Now, let's create a panel for a display file. Assume you are at the SDA main menu as seen in Figure I-2. From here, pick option 1 to design screens and press ENTER. You will then get a panel similar to that shown in Figure I-10.

Figure I-10 Design Screens Initial Panel

```
                        Design Screens
       Type choices, press Enter.

           Source file . . . . . . . .   QDDSSRC___    Name, F4 for list
             Library . . . . . . . . .   HELLO_____    Name, *LIBL, *CURLIB
           Member  . . . . . . . . . .   NEW_____    Name, F4 for list




       F3=Exit     F4=Prompt     F12 = Cancel
```

Screen Panel Exercise Objectives

In Figure I-10, specify the new   member name, source file , and library where the generated DDS resides (or will reside when generated). As you attempt to create the member named *NEW* in the QDDSSRC file in the HELLO library, let's suppose it is already there. On your systems, this will not happen to you. But, for this exercise, let's just suppose that somebody before you has created this display file object. Let's also say that later you learn that it is an unnecessary, bogus object and you are authorized to delete it. Then, you will be able to create your own version of *NEW* from scratch.

That's exactly what this coming display file exercise is all about. You are about to find (in this book exercise) that the file *NEW* already exists. Then, you will bring up the *NEW* member and take a look at it with SDA's full screen panel editor.. From here, you will try to delete it and you will discover that there is no easy way to get all the pieces. Along the way, you will be shown the tools you need to delete all of the entrails of the SDA application, and you will begin again from scratch.

Before we get into the thick of the exercise, let's review a few items that will help put display file DDS in perspective. After all, SDA creates DDS on its way to building the display file object from the DDS that it generates. Sometimes DDS operations can be designed to relate to certain portions of a display file. Some operations pertain to all the panels in a display file; some pertain to one file, while others may pertain to just one field.

The following brief section is designed to put this in perspective as well as present the nature and consistency of a display file object and its relationship to a calling program.. Then we resume the case study.

Levels: Files, Records, Fields

It is important to remember   the relationship between Files, Record Formats, and Fields. These important relationships have even more bearing in display formats than in database. This material is covered in detail, in both the IBM database manuals as well as in the new LETS GO Publish Book: The IBM i Pocket Database Guide.

Each record in the display file specifies all the characteristics of one display panel. Thus, operations occurring on one panel are known as *Record Level* operations. A record   is composed of fields, which exist within a panel and are designated as input, output or both(input and output). Operations on individual fields are known as *Field Level* operations. Operations that occur in all records within a file are referred to as *File Level* operations. The sum total of all of the screens (record formats, panels etc.), with all of the associated fields and attributes, is referred to as the *display file object.*

The name of the file is important. The HLL programs reference the display file by name. Therefore the link from program to display file is through the display file name as specified in the file section of the HLL program. In RPG for example the display file name would appear in the File Description Specifications as a WORKSTN device file.

That's it for the diversion. Now, let's get back on te case study. When you have your panel from Figure I-10 completed, press ENTER to get to the *Work with Display Records* panel as shown in Figure I-11.

Figure I-11 Work with Display Records SDA Panel

```
                         Work with Display Records

  File  . . . . . . :  QDDSSRC          Member  . . . . . . :  NEW
     Library . . . . :  HELLO           Source type . . . . :  DSPF

  Type options, press Enter.
    1=Add          2=Edit comments    3=Copy         4=Remove
    7=Rename       8=Select keywords  12=Design image

  Opt  Order  Record      Type    Related Subfile  Date      DDS Error
   __
   __    __10  VENDFMT     RECORD                   10/04/90


  F3=Exit                   F12=Cancel      F14=File-level keywords
  F15=File-level comments   F17=Subset      F24=More keys
```

Working with an Existing Source Member

The NEW member already exists. Therefore, SDA goes inside the member and picks up the information about the one record format within the DDS that has been previously built. As you can see in Figure I-11, the record format name is VENDFMT.

To add a new format (display panel), from this panel, you would specify the option(OPT) to add (1) and specify the name of the record format. If you want to update the existing format, type the appropriate option number (12) next to the record format name. For this example, upon arriving at this panel the first time, there would   not be a record format (VENDFMT). But, in this educational example, we have one.

The panel in Figure I-11demonstrates how an existing record format in a display file member would look as you enter SDA. Again, for you to add a new format, or create your first one, you would use option 1 next to the blank record format space (No Order #) and type the name of the new format (panel name), which you are about to build.

As you can see by looking at the options, including option 12, you can use this panel to change information about an existing format, add or change comments, select record level keywords (option 8), or file level keywords (F14), etc. You can also change the image itself.

Look at an Existing Screen Image

As noted above, to work with the actual screen image for the existing panel, you would use option 12. Let's take that option now to see just what the heck is already there. Press ENTER with option 12 specified and you will see the panel in Figure I-12.

Figure I-12 Screen Image Existing Format

```
... ... 1 ... ... 2 ... ... 3 ... ... 4 ... ... 5 ... ... 6 ... ... 7 ...
 2                    Vendor Inquiry
 3
 4
 5 Enter Vendor Number:
 6
 7 Name and Address                        Balance Owed
 8
 9
10
11
12
13
14
15
16
17
18
19
20                    F3    End of Job
21
22
23
24
```

In order to get your work panel to look like the panel in Figure I-12, you must press PF14. This brings up the "rule." The *ruler* will give you a numeric columnar grid on the left and top so you have an idea on which row and which column you are placing your design.

It should be no surprise that the VENDFMT panel defined in Figure I-12 looks an awful lot like the panel that we hope to build, as shown in Figure I-24. If you want to go take a peek at what the panel will ultimately look like, feel free to look at Figure I-24 right now. The image in Figure I-12, at this point is just the prompts. Regardless, of what it is, our mission is to scratch it and start over.

Cleaning Up Old Entrails

When you begin your SDA experience in designing panels, for your first screen panel, as you know by now, you will not have the luxury of already having an already-built panel in your display file. You will have to start from scratch. To start from-scratch now, you first have to delete the DDS for this panel as well as the display file which was created from this panel. To get this done, first you will try the SDA Delete.

Since you do not really care about the panel in Figure I-12, and since neither do I, let's delete it now. To delete a panel which is in your design window, you must first exit the design panel. Press F12 or F3 to return to the *Work with Display Records* screen. You will see a line in the body of the panel similar to the line below:

 ____   10   VENDFMT   RECORD

Type a "4" right next to the sequence # 10 record as above, so that the line looks like that immediately below:

 __4 10   VENDFMT   RECORD

Now, press ENTER. As soon as you press ENTER, you will see a message such as:

Record VENDFMT deleted from member NEW.

Now, the *Work with Display Records* screen has no display records. If you went through a normal exit at this point and you asked for a display file to be built, none would be built for you.

No Real Content

There is not a single record format in the NEW source file which was generated by SDA for the "panel-less" file which we left behind. We deleted the only format above. For your information, we have brought up an SEU panel in Figure I-13. This   shows the DDS for this "record-less" file. Though there are no panels defined, it is not gone. I would suggest to IBM that SDA would be better off not creating such a "nothing" member.

Figure I-13 Source for Display File NEW After Format Deletion

```
Columns . . . :    1  71              Browse                    HELLO/QDDSSRC
SEU==>                                                                   NEW
FMT A*  .....A*. 1 ...+... 2 ...+... 3 ...+... 4 ...+... 5 ...+... 6 ...+...
        ************** Beginning of data *********************************
0000.10      A*%%TS  SD  20020512  150636  BKELLY      REL-V5R1M0  5722-WDS
0000.20      A*%%EC
0000.30      A                                    DSPSIZ(24 80 *DS3)
        ***************** End of data***********************************

F3=Exit   F5=Refresh   F9=Retrieve   F10=Cursor   F11=Toggle   F12=Cancel
F16=Repeat find        F24=More keys   ©) COPYRIGHT IBM CORP. 1981,
```

For the record, the source in Figure I-13 will never compile as it exists.. There are two comments and a display size parameter. Yet, SDA saves this source anyway under the member name, NEW, which is the member we intended to create. So, SDA will not bring us back to the point of having nothing in the member. Moreover, since the new source has no record format and therefore it cannot compile, using SDA, we cannot wipe out the old display file object which existed before we began this modification process. So what do we do to delete this "crap" if SDA gives us no tools?

Deleting Bogus SDA Source

How do we get rid of the entrails of a display file object and display file member when we want to start over? There are two answers:

1. Not with SDA
2. With PDM

Both answers are equally important since, if you did not know answer one, you would not look for answer two. Use your PDM knowledge to reset the files to how they would be if a member *NEW* and a display file *NEW* never existed. From the Work with members panel for QDDSSRC in HELLO, place a *"4" for DELETE* right next to member *NEW* and press ENTER. This gets rid of the SDA-built source.

You're only half finished. The next thing to do is to get rid of the display file object. From the *Work with Objects Using PDM* panel find *NEW*, the file object. Place a *"4" for DELETE* right next to the Display File object named *NEW* and press ENTER. At this point, there would be no entrails left for the member and the file named *NEW*, so you can now build a new member and a new panel and a new object from scratch.

Building SDA Image from Scratch

Start your session by typing the start SDA command (STRSDA). The
SDA main menu would appear as in Figure I-2. Type "1" for Design
screens. The Design Screens option panel is presented as shown in
Figure I-10 and filled in as in Figure I-10. After completing the panel
in H-10 and pressing ENTER, you will see a panel as in Figure I-11
with one big difference. There is no record format in the file. In fact
when you arrive, it says very clearly, as shown near the bottom of
Figure I-14: (**No records in file**).

Figure I-14 Creating The First Display Panel for the Display File

```
              Work with Display Records

File  . . . . . . :   QDDSSRC          Member . . . . . . :   NEW
   Library . . . . :   HELLO           Source type  . . . :   DSPF
Type options, press Enter.
   1=Add            2=Edit comments      3=Copy         4=Delete
   7=Rename         8=Select keywords   12=Design image
Opt  Order   Record      Type     Related Subfile   Date  DDS Error    1   VENDFMT
   (No records in file)                                    Bottom

F3=Exit               F12=Cancel       F14=File-level keywords
F15=File-level comments  F17=Subset    F24=More keys
```

In this from-scratch effort, your mission is to create one record format
for this display file. In the end, the panel you create will look like that
in Figure I-24. To begin this process, place a "1" in the options
column and place the name of the new format (VENDFMT) in the
Record column. This is already done for you in Figure I-14. Press the
ENTER key to get the process under way. You will then be asked
what *type* of record to add to the display file. This question is shown
in Figure I-15.

You can see in Figure I-15 that we answered the question by filling in
the word RECORD for the type. There are nine choices for the
record type, from which you can choose. A normal display file is
known as a record. That's what you want to create for this case
study. That's what you pick. When you pick RECORD and hit
ENTER, SDA makes that panel image part of the display file SDA
source.

Figure I-15 Add a New Record Selection

```
                          Add New Record

File  . . . . . . . :    QDDSSRC          Member . . . . . . . :    NEW
    Library . . . . :       HELLO         Source type  . . . :    DSPF

Type choices, press Enter.

  New record  . . . . . . . . . . . . . .    VENDFMT        Name

  Type  . . . . . . . . . . . . . . . . .    RECORD         RECORD,  USRDFN
                                                            SFL,     SFLMSG
                                                            WINDOW,  WDWSFL
                                                            PULDWN,  PDNSFL
                                                            MNUBAR


F3=Exit        F5=Refresh      F12=Cancel
```

Specify Record Format Type

SDA is most helpful in being able to build most, if not all of the
powerful display facilities supported by DDS. The panel types in
Figure I-15, include record type keywords for subfiles, windows, pull-
down menus, and menu bars. We are keeping the examples simple in
this introductory QuikCourse. As noted, the correct choice for a
regular display panel, such as that, which we are selecting is
RECORD. After making this selection, press the ENTER key.

The No-Nonsense Design Image Panel

You will immediately be taken to a completely black design screen
with no hints at all as to what you should do next. The closest thing
to help you at this point is a little message at the bottom of the black
void which says:

Work screen for record VENDFMT: Press Help for function keys.

If you follow the message and hit either the Help key or the F1 (Help)
key, you will get a ton of help. Among other things, this Help text
will "help" you know what to do next. As soon as you get into the
design panel, on your own, take the Help trip and study how much
text is available. Then, when you need to get a question answered,
you know where to find the Help text. Roll through all the Help if
you can spare the time. Everything you are about to do in this
exercise is covered in the Help text after a "few" rolls.

Typing Your Screen Constants

When you are finished with the HELP text review, press F14 so that you can see the reference lines on the top and left as shown in Figure I-12. After you see the lines, type up the constant information onto the display as shown in Figure I-12.

When you have this typing done, you have one more task to do before this phase is completed. On your design panel, after it looks exactly as Figure I-12, place a single quote around (*in front of and after*) each set of constant text. Do not place quotes around each individual word. When you finish, you should have ten single quotes in total, in five pairs, surrounding the five different clumps of text on the panel. When your display looks like this, press the ENTER key.

You will notice that the quotes disappear. The purpose for the quotes is to define blocks of text to be treated in the same fashion. If, for example, you wanted to highlight just the title text, *Vendor Inquiry*, you could do so by placing the highlight (h) code immediately to the left of the text such as:

hVendor Inquiry

When you press the ENTER key from the design panel, immediately, you would see this text highlighted, such as the following:

Vendor Inquiry

Instantaneous Feedback Upon ENTER

You may also notice that after you press ENTER, any SDA commands on the design screen, such as the quotes to block text together or the "h" command to highlight a block of text, are all gone. ENTER causes a design panel interaction with SDA. SDA does its work during these interactions. The panel returns to a WYSIWYG form so that you know what the effect of your change has been immediately. For example, your highlighted field will immediately appear highlighted

If you are here with me at this point, then, you are just about done with the panel as it existed prior to deleting it and starting over. It's back! You keyed the constants at the desired locations. As you can see from your own work in getting the panel to look like that in H-12, the panel is really incomplete. It does not yet include any variable fields - either input or output. You are about to add fields from the database to this panel shortly.

Intermediate Exit and Creation

To know which command keys to hit for ending the database design session (F3 or F12) and to know the various attribute commands, such as "h" for highlight, you already toured the Help text earlier in this QuikCourse by hitting the Help key or F1. During the tour, the Help text told you about using F14 for the ruler and it also told you that the F10 key is to be used to bring in field descriptions from the data base file – for both prompt and field reference purposes.

As a final review point before moving on, we also discussed the motion of multi word constants, and we suggested enclosing them in quotes. Overall, blocking constant text in this fashion, results in fewer DDS statements, and it makes working with / examining the SDA-created DDS substantially easier.

Before we add to the display file DDS that SDA is about to create, let's exit SDA from the display panel, without adding any variables. Do this by pressing F12 twice. Then hit ENTER after reviewing the "defaults" specified on the SDA exit panel. When you get to a command line, the file NEW has been created, though it is incomplete. Moreover, SDA has created DDS specs for you in a source member. Take a look at the DDS which exists now before you proceed to complete the panel.

Figure I-16 NEW Source with Only Constant DDS

```
Columns . . . :    1  71              Edit                    HELLO/QDDSSRC
SEU==>                                                               NEW
FMT A*  .....A*. 1 ...+... 2 ...+... 3 ...+... 4 ...+... 5 ...+... 6 ...+... 7
       *************** Beginning of data ********************************
000.10      A*%%TS  SD  20020512  171200  BKELLY     REL-V5R1M0  5722-WDS
000.20      A*%%EC
000.30      A                             DSPSIZ(24 80 *DS3)
000.40      A           R VENDFMT
000.50      A*%%TS  SD  20020512  171012  BKELLY     REL-V5R1M0  5722-WDS
000.60      A                      2 24'Vendor Inquiry'
000.70      A                      5  9'Enter Vendor Number:'
000.80      A                      7  9'Name and Address'
000.90      A                      7 51'Balance Owed'
001.00      A                     20 29'F3   End of Job'
       ***************** End of data ****************************************


F3=Exit    F4=Prompt    F5=Refresh   F9=Retrieve   F10=Cursor   F11=Toggle
F16=Repeat find          F17=Repeat change          F24=More keys
                                    ©) COPYRIGHT IBM CORP. 1981, 2000.
```

Checking Intermediate DDS with SEU

The quick way to check your DDS is as follows:

Use PDM to Work with members; select QDDSSRC in the HELLO
library. Press ENTER to get the list of SDA members. Display
member NEW (PDM option 5), which is the newly created DDS
from SDA. Yes. It is incomplete, but let's see it in its incompleteness.
The source should look similar to that in Figure I-16. Notice the big
chunks of text. If you had not used the quotes around the constant
text blocks as suggested, there would be many more, but smaller
DDS statements. SDA would make each word a statement by
default.

Incremental DDS from SDA

If you contrast the source of Figure I-13, and Figure I-16, you can see
that six lines have been added. There is one line for each quoted
block of constant text and there is a record format ("R" in column 17)
statement line in which the screen panel is named. The same file level
keyword DSPSIZ which existed in the shell in Figure I-13 is recreated
and there are no other keywords. Moreover, as predicted, there are
no variable fields defined in DDS.

The numbers you see prior to the text represent the screen panel
location information for the row and column starting positions. This

is where you placed the text on the screen. These positions are determined based on where you keyed the text on the design panel.

This is one of the major timesaving benefits of SDA. Can you imagine manually coding these DDS statements in such detail, as well as having to specify the exact "from" and "to" positions? The panels would just be lovely! Wouldn't they now?

Adding Variable Fields from the Database

Let's exit SEU and PDM and bring back our SDA design panel as it was in Figure I-12. We get there by the following:

1. F3 from PDM
2. STRSDA
3. Design Screens - option 1
4. Specify QDDSSRC in HELLO, member NEW
5. Place a 12 next to New in the record list.

Adding Fields with Database References to Display File Panels

Now, let us begin to add input and output information to this panel. First press F10 to get at the database. Pick the VENDORP file created in an earlier QuikCourse. You will see a panel similar to that in Figure I-17.

Figure I-17 Select Database Files For Screen Reference

```
                        Select Database Files

   Type options and names, press Enter.
     1=Display database field list
     2=Select all fields for input (I)
     3=Select all fields for output (O)
     4=Select all fields for both (B) input and output


   Option   Database File   Library      Record
     1         VENDORP       HELLO        VNDMSTR
     —         _____      _____     _____

     —         _____      _____     _____


   F3=Exit    F4=Prompt   F12=Cancel
```

To get a look at all of the fields in the VENDORP file, which you might choose to use as input or output references, select option 1, and specify the location for the VENDORP database file as shown in

Figure I-17. In this panel, select the data base file, library and the specific record format, to serve as a reference for the fields being defined on the screen image panel.

Of course, this all depends on the VENDORP database file already having been created in a prior QuikCourse.

Figure I-17 Select Database Fields for use on Design Display

```
                        Select Data Base Fields

    Record . . . :    VNDMSTR
    Type information, press Enter.
      Number of fields to roll  . . . . . . . . . . . . . . .  __8
      Name of field to search for . . . . . . . . . . . . . .  _____

    Type options, press Enter.
      1=Display extended field description
      2=Select for input (I), 3=Select for output (O), 4=Select for both(B)

    Option  Field         Length    Type    Column Heading
       4    VNDNBR         5,0      P       VENDOR NUMBER
       3    NAME            25      A       NAME
       3    ADDR1           25      A       ADDRESS LINE 1
       3    CITY            15      A       CITY
       3    STATE            2      A       STATE
       3    ZIPCD          5,0      P       ZIP CODE
       _    VNDCLS         2,0      P       VENDOR CLASS
       _    VNDSTS           1      A       ACTIVE CODE
                                                              More...
    ...
       3    BALOWE         9,2      P       BALANCE OWED

    F3=Exit    F12=Cancel
```

Selecting Database Fields for Use

Before you see the panel in Figure I-17, you must have an idea of what you want to do. In this panel, you take what you want to do, and you ask the AS/400 database to make your job easier in defining the fields that will be on the display. Knowing what data, from what files, you need for your panel, makes it easier to select the fields. This is the right time in the process. After picking F10 from the image panel, it is time to pick the fields that should appear in the particular image panel that you are building with SDA..

As you pick the fields, you also must tell SDA to select the field for use on the panel for input, output or both purposes. Both is short for both input and output. Fore each database field that you want to be used in the panel, Enter a "2" to select it for input, a "3" for output, and a "4" for both (input and output). Notice that in the panel shown in Figure I-17, we have already selected the VNDNBR field as both (option 4), and we have selected six other fields as output only (3).

To get to see field six, BALOWE on this panel, you must hit Page down or Roll Down. Then, select the field as an output field (3). In Figure I-17, we superimposed field BALOWE at the bottom of the panel, so you could see it in better context.

The idea with this application as you may have already surmised is that this one panel is to be used to enter a vendor number. The program will then look up the vendor information, and redisplay the vendor number as an output field. Additionally, after looking up the vendor information, the program writes the data to the same display panel with the same "write" operation. Because the vendor information is sent to the screen as output, it cannot be read in. Since it cannot be read, it cannot be changed. In fact, SDA produces DDS which will send the data out, but will lock the keyboard if the user tries to change one of the output fields.

When you are done with this panel hit F3 or ENTER to return to the design panel. When you get back to the design panel, you should be pleased to see that the selected fields are displayed on the bottom row of the work screen where you design your display. Press page down (Roll on some terminals) to display more data base fields if all of them are not visible.

Exiting the Data Base Option

Press ENTER on the display shown in Figure I-17 to return to the
Select data base files display if you want to reference another file for
input, or if you are on your way to exiting. In this example, press F3
or ENTER again from the database files display, to return to the
design panel. You will see a screen similar to that shown in Figure I-
18.

Figure I-18 Vendor Inquiry Panel With Fields in On-Deck Circle

```
 ... ... 1 ... ... 2 ... ... 3 ... ... 4 ... ... 5 ... ... 6 ... ... 7 ...
 ..8
  2                      Vendor Inquiry
  3
  4
  5  Enter Vendor Number:
  6
  7  Name and Address                        Balance Owed
  8
  9
 10
 11
 12
 13
 14
 15
 16
 17
 18
 19
 20                       F3    End of Job
 21
 22
 23
  1:VNDNBR 2:NAME 3:ADDR1 4:CITY 5:STATE 6:ZIPCD 7:BALOWE
```

When you are looking for a field and it is not in the list, remember
that the bottom line holds only so many. The fields are inserted and
appear in a multiple-field mode at the bottom of the work screen as
shown in Figure I-18.   This is what we referred to as the "On-Deck
Circle." A "+" at the end of the field name list indicates there are
more field names.   Just press page down to display more field
names.

SDA Image Commands

Notice in Figure I-18 that the text fields are in tact, and the design panel is in somewhat of a wait state. It is waiting for you to do something with these fields. They don't just pop up into the screen panel. You have to place them. To do this, SDA has given some handy commands. The first command is the "&." With this command, you tell SDA to "place a database field right here!"

Following the "&" command, you then tell SDA which database field number to place. We already pre-typed the SDA database commands "&" in the panel in Figure I-19.   These reference by number the on-deck fields that SDA lsts at the bottom of the panel after you select them in the panel shown in Figure I-17. You may also notice that we did one more thing with Figure I-19.

In real life, you would not split your design by (1) implementing the constant fields, (2) saving the panel, (3) creating the file, and (4) coming back in update mode to add the variables with database fields, as we did for this training example. Thus, Figure I-19 shows how the panel as it should look when you build it with all the necessary information specified at once. In other words, the quote commands surround the text as they should have at the time we built the constants-only panel.

Figure I-19 Database Fields Selected for Action

```
... ...1 ... ...2 ... ...3 ... ...4 ... ...5 ... ...6 ... ...7 ... ..
   2                   'Vendor Inquiry'
   3
   4
   5'Enter Vendor Number:' &1
   6
   7'Name and Address'                        'Balance Owed'
   8
   9 &2                                       &7
  10 &3
  11 &4               &5 &6
  12
  13
  14
  15
  16
  17
  18
  19
  20                   'F3   End of Job'
  21
  22
  23
   1 VNDNBR 2 NAME 3 ADDR1 4 CITY 5 STATE 6 ZIPCD 7 BALOWE
```

Getting Column Headings from the Database

As you can see in Figure I-19, in addition to the blocked text shown with quotes, we have placed the "&" command plus the field number at the location desired for each field. If you want to be more productive than this, or perhaps you are feeling a little lazy during your design trip, SDA gives you a few more tools to eliminate even more keying and more guesswork.

You can ask SDA to get you the column headings from the database and you can then use them as your prompts. If you have good column headings, the idea is that there should be lots less keying and lots less opportunity for misinterpretation of field meanings. Moreover, you can tell SDA to place the prompt text to the left or to the right of the inserted database input or output field, so you have initial design flexibility. Additionally, you can tell SDA to place the column heading right on top of the field being defined.

You add the column heading and provide its placement with one-letter commands. You place the letter "L" for left, or the letter "R" for right or the letter "C" for center, along with the "&" command and the field number. This is how you tell SDA to grab the column heading, along with the field definition, and place them on your design panel – based on the specific command you used.

When you press ENTER on the display, you see how nice or how ugly the text prompts appear in the work display. If they are not so nice, without re-keying or excess typing, you can simply change them and move them accordingly.

After hitting ENTER on Figure I-19, your display panel should look similar to that in Figure I-20.

Figure I-20 The Resulting Display Panel

```
  ... ...  1 ...  ... 2 ...  ... 3 ...  ... 4 ...  ... 5 ...  ... 6 ...  ... 7 ...
 .
   2                    Vendor Inquiry
   3
   4
   5  Enter Vendor Number:*99999-
   6
   7  Name and Address                        Balance Owed
   8
   9  OOOOOOOOOOOOOOOOOOOOOOOOOO               *666666666
  10  OOOOOOOOOOOOOOOOOOOOOOOOOO
  11  OOOOOOOOOOOOOOO   OO*66666
  12
  13
  14
  15
  16
  17
  18
  19
  20                    F3   End of Job
  21
  22
  23
  24
```

The field Vendor Number, which is represented by all 99999s, is an output/input (both) field, and it is defined as numeric. The fields defined at lines 9 to 11 are a combination of alphabetic output (O) and numeric output(6). If you were not using SDA database referencing to supply the field attributes and lengths, you would have had to count field spaces and assure that your coding lined up properly.

This would be another thing you would have to do that   would not be much fun! SDA helps keep it light-hearted. The database referencing ability is just another way that SDA saves this type of drudgery, and in so doing, it saves time. Who wants to be counting O's as you are hitting the O key, hoping not to have one too many or one too few?

Adding Fields and Changing Field Attributes

Oh! It's not that you can't make a mistake with SDA. You can make as many as you please, and you can fix them just as fast – long before you'd know you'd made them if you were dealing just with DDS. You can add fields and/or change the attributes of fields after they are on your work display — years after you've first created your display file. As you can see in Figure I-20, we are doing exactly that for the vendor number field and the balance owed field.   By placing asterisks "*" next to fields to be edited for highlighting or perhaps to display their attributes. The "*" is just another tool that enables you to open the fields up for many different combinations of changes, without once having to refer to your DDS manual.

Field Manipulation Commands

There are also one-character commands which immediately highlight a field. You have already seen the highlight command. A few more examples include the "r" for reverse image, and the "u" for an underline.

Delete Field Command

Some one-character commands do more than just highlight. They are much more powerful. The "d" command, for example, is for *dangerous*.   OK, it is not.   But it is dangerous! You can place a "d" next to any field you want to delete from the panel. It's that easy. Press ENTER and it's gone.

Two Forms of Move Commands

Two other powerhouse commands are the two forms of   "move." To move fields you have two choices. And, they are both good!   To move them a little, use the symbols " >>>>" and "<<<<."   There is a one-to-one relationship between symbols used and characters moved. These field move commands move fields, and blocks of fields, to the left (<) or to the right(>) as many positions as symbols you type.

If you type four ">>>>" signs, for example,   and you place them next to the rightmost character of text to be moved, when you press ENTER, the text will be four positions over to the right. Likewise if you wanted to move to the left, you would type the "<" symbols to the left of the text to be moved.

Another tremendous tool is the "block move" operation. To move fields a lot, use this command. This move command is a simple dash "-" preceding the field or text block to be moved. Just like SEU, it needs a corresponding to-position indicator to get its job done. SDA has chosen the equal sign "=" for this. An example of the way this works is as follows: If you place a dash on text at, say line 23, and you put an equal sign in some column on say, line 5, after you hit the ENTER key, the block of text from line 23 is now on line 5, starting at your designated column position. It is no longer on line 23. The move operations make it so easy to redesign the work panel on the fly that it actually isn't any fun getting it right the first time.

Adding a New Field to Your Display

There will also be times that you must add a field to the panel which is not in a database. For example, if your program is calculating a result which goes nowhere else but the screen panel, your panel must know about that field somehow. SDA handles it. You can easily add your own fields to the work screen.   Just key a "+"   to specify a user-defined field. For numeric, "3" is input, "6" is output and "9" is both. For alphabetic, "I" is input, "O" is output,   and "B" is both. For example: +6(8,2) creates a field named FLD001 (default field name) with a length of eight, and   with two decimals for output only.

Changing Display attributes

It's been so long, we would like to remind you that, in our example panel in Figure I-20, we have placed asterisks "*" next to the vendor number field (VNDNBR), the balance owed field (BALOWE), and the zip code (ZIPCD) field . When you hit ENTER, with these asterisks positioned where they are, you will first see a panel similar to that in Figure I-21.

Figure I-21 Select Field Keywords

```
                        Select Field Keywords

 Field . . . . . :    VNDNBR          Usage . . :  B
 Length  . . . . :    5,0             Row . . . :  5    Column . . . :  31

 Type choices, press Enter.
                                   Y=Yes    For Field Type
     Display attributes  . . . . . . .    Y    All except Hidden
     Colors  . . . . . . . . . . . .     __    All except Hidden
     Keying options  . . . . . . . .     __    Hidden, Input or Both
     Validity check  . . . . . . . .     __    Input or Both, not float
     Input keywords  . . . . . . . .     __    Input or Both
     General keywords  . . . . . . .     __    All types
     Editing keywords  . . . . . . .     Y    Numeric Output or Both
     Database reference  . . . . . . .   __    Hidden, Input, Output, Both
     Error messages  . . . . . . . .     __    Input, Output, Both
     Message ID (MSGID)  . . . . . . .   __    Output or Both

     TEXT keyword  . . . . . . . . .    VENDOR NUMBER
 F3=Exit    F4=Display Selected Keywords    F12=Cancel
```

You will see a panel similar to Figure I-21 once for each of the fields
selected with the "*" command. From this panel, for VNDNBR,
change the *Display attributes* and *Editing keywords* by placing "Y"
responses in this panel. For BALOWE and ZIPCD, change just the
Editing keywords by typing a "Y."   To proceed from this panel for the
field VNDNBR, type "Y" in the appropriate columns as shown in
Figure I-21. You will first be taken to a panel similar to the *Select
Display Attributes* panel as in Figure I-22.

By placing the "*" next to the vendor number field (VNDNBR),
you first get the panel in Figure I-21. From there, you determine
which type of attribute you want to change. By selecting a "Y" for
Display Attributes, you get to work with the panel in Figure I-22. By
selecting a "Y" for editing keywords, you get to work with a panel
similar to that in Figure I-23.

Figure I-22 Select Display Attributes

```
                        Select Display Attributes

    Field . . . . . :    VNDNBR          Usage . . :  B
    Length  . . . . :     5,0            Row . . . :  5    Column . . . : 26

    Type choices, press Enter.

                                         Keyword   Y=Yes    Indicators/+
        Field conditioning . . . . . . . . . . .
        Display attributes:              DSPATR
          High intensity . . . . . . . . . . . . HI       _      ___ ___ ___
          Reverse image  . . . . . . . . . . . . RI       Y      _44 ___ ___
          Column separators  . . . . . . . . . . CS       _      ___ ___ ___
          Blink  . . . . . . . . . . . . . . . . BL       _      ___ ___ ___
          Nondisplay . . . . . . . . . . . . . . ND       _      ___ ___ ___
          Underline  . . . . . . . . . . . . . . UL       _      ___ ___ ___
          Position cursor  . . . . . . . . . . . PC       _      ___ ___ ___
          Set modified data tag  . . . . . . . . MDT      _      ___ ___ ___
          Protect field  . . . . . . . . . . . . PR       _      ___ ___ ___
          Operator ID magnetic card  . . . . . . OID      _      ___ ___ ___
          Select by light pen  . . . . . . . . . SP       _      ___ ___ ___

    F3=Exit    F12 = Cancel
```

Changing Attributes

Our display objective for the VNDNBR field is to make it a reverse-image, if a certain condition occurs in the program. To display the field in reverse-image (like a negative) under certain conditions, specify the attributes as shown in the panel in Figure I-22. When you come back to the design work panel, the field VNDNBR will show in reverse-image.

Conditional Attributes Using Indicators

However, it will not be shown in reverse-image when put out by the program unless indicator 44 is on in the controlling program at the time of the output operation. You set the condition (indicator 44 in this case) for the field to be shown in reverse-image within the high-level language program. If the indicator is on, the VNDNBR field will be lit up in reverse-image when the program sends out this screen panel. Field conditioning and un-conditioning can be achieved by entering a "Y" by the desired display attribute (DSPATR) when you select an indicator to condition the attribute.

Adding Editing Keywords

When you have changed the attributes in Figure I-22 to your satisfaction, press the ENTER key until the display changes to *Select Editing Keywords* for VNDNBR. This panel is shown in Figure I-23. Notice that we used the "3" edit-code for the field since, for this field type, we found it desirable to edit it so that zero value vendor numbers will show, and there will be no commas, and no decimals in the vendor number field.

Figure I-23 Selecting Editing Keywords or Codes.

```
                        Select Editing Keywords
 Field . . . . . :    VNDNBR          Usage . . :  B
 Length . . . . :    5,0             Row . . . :  5    Column . . . :  31


 Type choices, press Enter.
                                     Keyword
More
   Edit code  . . . . . . . . . . .  EDTCDE   3   A-D, J-Q, W, Y, Z, 1-9
      Replace leading zeros with . . . .            *, $

   Edit word  . . . . . . . . . . .  EDTWRD

   Edit mask  . . . . . . . . . . .  EDTMSK

 F3=Exit    F12=Cancel
```

After you finish with the VNDNBR field for both attributes and editing, keep pressing the ENTER key until the field name changes to BALOWE. It should be right away. By having placed the "*" next to the balance owed field, you also get a panel similar to that in Figure I-21. However, the field name is primed with BALOWE instead of VNDNBR, since that is the field you now want to adjust. Since it is a nice big numeric field, it would be nice for it to show up edited on the final display.

You do not need a Y for Display Attributes, as in VNDNBR, since the attributes are fine. However, to make the field look right, you need to do some editing of the output. If you look down, near the bottom of the panel in Figure I-21, you will notice Editing Keywords. Place your "Y" in this field. Make sure there is not a "Y" in any of the other attributes, and press ENTER. You will see a panel similar to that in Figure I-23. Instead of VNDNBR, however, the field name will be BALOWE.

If you hit Help on the Edit-codes field, it will tell you which code produces which level of editing. This is very handy. I like to show dollar fields with commas and have zero balances appear on the report rather than be hidden. Also, I like to have a minus sign show to the right of the number if the value is negative. If you hit the Help or F1 key now, you will see that the edit-code to do all of that is a "J." To select "J," type it into the Edit-code instead of the "3" as in Figure I-23 and press Enter.

You should see the panel as in Figure I-21 again, except this time, the field name should be ZIPCD. Follow the same process for editing this field as you did for VNDNBR, but leave the attributes alone. Change the edit-code to "3". When you have made all of your editing and attribute changes for the asterisked "*" fields, you should return to the SDA work panel. Your display should no longer show the "-" sign to the right of VNDNBR and ZIPCD and the BALOWE field should appear nicely edited. See Figure I-24 for the final display panel.

Figure I-24 Final Version of Display Panel

```
... ... 1 ... ... 2 ... ... 3 ... ... 4 ... ... 5 ... ... 6 ... ... 7 ... ..
 2                    Vendor Inquiry
 3
 4
 5 Enter Vendor Number: 99999
 6
 7 Name and Address                      Balance Owed
 8
 9 OOOOOOOOOOOOOOOOOOOOOOOOOOO           $6,666,666.66-
10 OOOOOOOOOOOOOOOOOOOOOOOOOOO
11 OOOOOOOOOOOOOOO  OO 66666
12
13
14
15
16
17
18
19
20                    F3   End of Job
21
22
23
24
```

The example in Figure I-24 shows the final form of the screen just
designed. This is the screen in its completed form. Remember, even
now, you can move any of the fields around, delete fields, or add
more fields and more constants.

Assigning End-of-Job Indicator

Before you close this out, there is one more job to do. You need to
enable a command key (CF03) and assign an indicator (switch) value
to the command key so that the program can get a signal from the
display panel when the operator decides that it is time to end it. Since
there is only one display panel, and since other panels, if added, may
very well want to end the program in the same fashion, add the CF03
function key at the file level.

From Figure I-24, press F24 to return to the *Work with Display Records*
panel similar to that in Figure I-14. From this screen, if you were
assigning the indicator to just this one panel design, you would type
an "8" next to the format name. You would then press ENTER, and
select *Indicator keywords* by placing a "Y," next to the prompt.   You
would then see a panel similar to Figure I-25. On this panel, you
would type *CF03* for keyword. You would pick response indicator 03.
And, you would type *"end-of-job"* for text. This would create the
indicator reference at the record format (display panel) level.

Indicator at File Level

However, you would want this command key to work for all display panels, even those not yet built. To do this, from the panel shown in Figure I-14, you would press F14 for "File-level keywords." You would then select "Indicator keywords" as above for the record level. After all that, you would get a panel, which looks the same as the panel used for record function keys, as shown in Figure F-25.

Figure I-25 Defining Command Keys and Indicators

```
                         Define Indicator Keywords

Member . . . :   NEW

Type keywords and parameters, press Enter.
   Conditioned keywords:        CFnn CAnn CLEAR PAGEDOWN/ROLLUP PAGEUP/ROLLDOWN
                                HOME HELP HLPRTN
   Unconditioned keywords:      INDTXT VLDCMDKEY

Keyword    Indicators/+ Resp Text
CF03       __ __ __     03   end-of-job_____
_____     __ __ __     ___  _____
_____     __ __ __     ___  _____
_____     __ __ __     ___  _____
_____     __ __ __     ___  _____
   . . .

Bottom
F3=Exit    F12=Cancel
```

   Press ENTER to return to the Work with Display Records panel. After defining the command keys, we have no more design work to do. From here then, it is time to compile and test your display file. Press F3 to exit. You will get the SDA exit panel similar to that in Figure I-8. Take the same options. The source will be saved and your updated file will be created. At this point of success, you now have a display file to test.

Testing Display Files

The third option from the SDA main menu is to test display files. Take option 3 and you will see a panel similar to that in Figure I-26.

Figure I-26 Testing Display Files

```
                        Test Display File

Type choices, press Enter.

   Display file . . . . . . . . . . . .    NEW          Name, F4 for list
      Library  . . . . . . . . . . . . .     HELLO      Name, *LIBL ...

   Record to be tested  . . . . . . . .    VENDFMT      Name, F4 for list

   Additional records to display  . . . .    _____  Name, F4 for list




F3=Exit     F4=Prompt     F12=Cancel
```

In Figure I-26, you put the name of the file, the library and the screen panel to be tested, and then you come to the test data panel as shown in Figure I-27.

Figure I-27 Setting Output Values for Panel Test

```
                        Set Test Output Data
Record . . . :    VENDFMT

Type indicators and output field values, press Enter.

Field           Value
*IN44           0:
VNDNBR          00028:
NAME            C ENGRAVING CO           :
BALOWE          000010000:
ADDR1           932 Wright               :
CITY            Chicago        :
STATE           IL:
ZIPCD           60615:



Bottom
F3=Exit     F12=Cancel
```

Test Data

In the panel in Figure I-27, you specify the test data which the panel tester will use to display your screen as if it were put out by a program. This lets you fix problems even before you hit the program phase. In this example, we put in some vendor information as in Figure I-27, as well as the status of indicator 44 (1 for on and 0 for off).

Figure I-28 Output of SDA Display Panel Test

```
                    Vendor Inquiry


    Enter Vendor Number:      28

    Name and Address                         Balance Owed

    C ENGRAVING CO                              100.00
    932 Wright
    Chicago          IL 60615




              F3    End of Job
```

As you can see in Figure I-28, the panel reflects the test data which we used. If we had set indicator 44 to a "1" then the field would have been shown in reverse-image. Notice that there is no sign in *VNDNBR* and *ZIPCD* and that the "hundred dollars" in *BALOWE* is nicely edited as we prescribed.

Display File in a Program

The next step is to merge the file with a program. For your edification, Figure I-29 shows an RPG program, which sends out a display of   vendor information from the database using this panel The logic of the program is as follows:

RPG Display File Program Logic

The program starts with a Do-While-Equal (DOWEQ) statement. This tells the compiler to keep running the same set of statements, from 0005 to 0010 until something happens. That "something" occurs if indicator 03 (a switch that gets tested) has turned to the ON state from the OFF state.

Figure I-29 RPG program (NEW) for Display File (NEW)

```
 Columns . . . :    1  71            Browse                HELLO/QRPGSRC
 SEU==>                                                              NEW
 FMT FX.....FFilenameIPEAF........L..I........Device+......KExit++Entry+A....U
    ************** Beginning of data *************************************
0001.00    FNEW      CF  E                    WORKSTN
0002.00    F* LOGICAL FILE VENDMST BUILT OVER VENDORP WITH KEY
0003.00    FVENDMST IF  E            K        DISK
0004.00    I                       'VENDOR NOT FOUND  'C          ERRMSG
0005.00    C         *IN03    DOWEQ*OFF                    CF03 = 03
0006.00    C                  EXFMTVENDFMT
0007.00    C         VNDNBR   CHAINVENDMST              90     90 = NOT FOU
0008.00    C         *IN90    IFEQ *ON
0009.00    C                  MOVELERRMSG      NAME
0010.00    C                  ENDIF
0011.00    C                  ENDDO
0012.00    C                  MOVE *ON          *INLR
    ***************** End of data ***************************************

 F3=Exit    F5=Refresh    F9=Retrieve   F10=Cursor   F11=Toggle   F12=Cancel
 F16=Repeat find          F24=More keys
 ©) COPYRIGHT IBM CORP. 1981, 2000.
```

You may recall that in our SDA display panel, we assigned Command Key 3 to the indicator 03. Thus, when indicator 03 (*IN03) is turned on by the display file, it is a signal to the program that the program user wants to end the program. The DOWEQ then moves to statement 0012 and sets on LR (last record), which is how RPG programs end.

Within the repeating Do-Loop, at statement 0006, the program sends out the VENDFMT panel from our SDA-built display file. The EXFMT operation in RPG sends a panel and then waits in the program for a user to enter data and hit ENTER. When the user types the vendor number and hits ENTER, the typed information becomes available in the program, inside the field *VNDNBR*.

In the next statement, 0007, the program uses the VNDNBR data to CHAIN to (access) the vendor file. If the vendor number entered is on file, the database information for that vendor is available to the program immediately after the CHAIN operation. If the record is not found, the operation turns on switch # 90 (indicator 90) to let the program know that a record was not found.

At statement 0008, the program tests the status of indicator 90 to see if it is on - meaning that a record was not found. At statement 0009, if the record was not found, the program loads an error message into the *Vendor Name* field of the display panel. Statement 10 ends this not-found error routine that began at statement 0009.

The next statement at 0011 is the ENDO. This works with the DOWEQ in statement 0005 to define the part of the program which repeats until the user hits Command Key 3. The ENDDO passes control back to statement 0005 and if the user has not hit Command Key 3, control is passed to the "loop" at statement 6.

At statement 6, the second and subsequent times through the DOWEQ loop, the output part of the operation sends out the data from the database, or the error message in NAME, while the input part of the operation brings in the next VENDOR number as well as an indication that the ENTER key or Command key 03 has been pressed. The program continues in the loop until the user takes the appropriate ending action - by pressing Command key 03.

Simple RPG Inquiry Program with Display File

In this inquiry example, the input is vendor number and the output is name and address information, as defined on the panel, which you built in this QuikCourse. After you, or a programmer in your organization, have compiled your RPG program, you call the program, (CALL NEW) enter a vendor number, and press enter. The name, address and balanced-owed information are then displayed.

When this happens, you have been successful.

Summary and Conclusions

In this SDA QuikCourse, we covered just about every SDA main menu option in a brief tutorial fashion. You can now use the results of your efforts in this chapter to move on to bigger and more sophisticated programming examples, using subfiles and other different advanced tools such as pop-up windows. You've now got the basic tools you need to move forward. Best wishes at your next stop in creating interactive IBM i applications.

☺ **Good News:** SDA Subfiles are covered in QuikCourse S which is included in this book

QuikCourse J. AS/400 & IBM i Data File Utility (DFU)

What is DFU?

I thought you'd never ask: "What is the Data File Utility?" Shall I say, "Oh, That's DFU?" No, you'd get mad and I'd feel like I had not given you a scrap of information.

In fact, DFU is a utility for defining, creating, and maintaining data base applications. It is primarily oriented to data entry, inquiry or file maintenance. DFU allows you to update files without creating a program . . .   and it works with every file type of file in the AS/400 Library File System. The files can be sequential, indexed, or direct.

DFU Is Database Aware

DFU is aware that the AS/400 is an integrated database machine. Yet, not only can it get its definition information from database objects, it can also use definitions from RPG II File and Input (F&I) specifications or Interactive Data Definition Utility (IDDU) definitions. The latter two methods are so that DFU works nicely with the System/36 way of doing things on the AS/400 and IBM i.

Great for Programmers

This utility is very convenient for programmers and more technically oriented end-users who want to quickly develop data entry, inquiry or file maintenance functions within applications. DFU, however, does have some limitations as far as data validation and verification that might be provided in more sophisticated high-level language (HLL) programs. However, the utility is also very good for general entry and update of data and for those times when 'fixing' data requires only simple maintenance.

Though an AS/400 shop may not necessarily turn DFU over to its user community in all of its regalia and ad-hoc-icy, many pre-create what they call DFUs, to add additional / missing functionality to application menus. Other shops build DFU menus for personnel who must enter data on a regular basis. If IBM ever chose to rid itself of DFU for any reason, there would be a scream from the gallery loud enough to get IBM to change its mind.

Auditing at its Best

DFU also creates a very nice paper log of all your file changes, so you can keep track of any and all changes to your data bases. This comes in handy when the auditors drop by for a look-see.

DFU Case Study

To get DFU going on your system, type STRDFU from a command prompt. As with most WebSphere Development Studio traditional development utilities, you are immediately taken to a main menu for the product, in this case - DFU. The menu is shown if Figure J-1

Create a DFU Program

From the Main DFU Menu, you just select an option (2 in this case) and press the ENTER key. You will be happy to know that there is lots of HELP available with DFU. If you forget how to use it, the Help panels will basically teach you what to do. In fact, there are even cursor-sensitive help text always available by pressing the Help key

Figure J-1 IBM i and AS/400 Data File Utility

```
                        AS/400 Data File Utility (DFU)


  Select one of the following:


        1. Run a DFU program

        2. Create a DFU program

        3. Change a DFU program

        4. Delete a DFU program

        5. Update data using temporary program




  Selection or command

  ===> 2_____



  _____

  F3=Exit        F4=Prompt        F9=Retrieve        F12=Cancel

                                    C) COPYRIGHT IBM CORP. 2000, 2000.
```

The DFU Main Menu

So, what does the DFU menu enable you to do?   (1) You can run a
DFU program that has already been created by taking option "1" on
the menu. (2) You can create a new DFU program by taking   option
"2" on the menu.   (2)You can change an already existing DFU
program by taking option "3" on the menu. (4)You can delete (if you
have the authority) an existing DFU program by taking option "4" on
the menu.

What Are We Going to Do?

In this QuikCourse, you will learn how to create and run a DFU. The
process of changing a DFU program or deleting a DFU program
flows smoothly from this menu. Once you create your own DFU and
you understand how to use it against data files, dressing it up with the

Change option, or deleting a DFU, to clean up your library, become second nature.

Additionally, you can update a file without defining anything to the system.   The DFU will create a temporary program based upon utility defaults and   data base definitions.   If you select this powerful option, no customization can be done to the DFU program. This "no options" DFU is available from PDM's *Work with Objects* panel, by placing an 18 next to a file object.

To be honest, this (18 from PDM) is my favorite function of DFU since it helps in program testing. It is a very quick and easy way to change data without burdening yourself with creating a program. After you have completed the updating of your data, the temporary program is deleted.

If you want to create a new DFU, from the main menu, you would select option 2 as in the Figure J-1, and then press the ENTER key.

The Steps to Creation

Let's create a simple DFU program by taking option 2 on the main panel.

Figure J-2 Create a DFU Program

```
                             Create a DFU Program

    Type choices, press Enter.

        Program  . . . . . . . . . .    DFUQUIK____    Name, F4 for list
           Library  . . . . . . . . .      HELLO_____    Name, *CURLIB

        Data file  . . . . . . . .      VENDORP____    Name, F4 for list
           Library  . . . . . . . . .      HELLO_____    Name, *LIBL, *CURLIB




     F3=Exit      F4=Prompt      F12=Cancel
```

The to-do list for the panel shown in Figure J-2 is as follows:

1. Select a name for your DFU
2. Select the file that you want to use
3. Press F4 to see a list of existing files or DFU   programs

Name the DFU

In order to create a new DFU program, you must enter a program name and library where that DFU program is to be placed. If you want to see a list of the existing DFU programs in a library, place the cursor in the DFU program name position on the screen, and press F4. You will see a list of DFU programs in that library. This is helpful when you are trying to create a new DFU program and you need a unique name.

Pick the Database File

You will need to enter a database file that you want to use for the DFU program.   If you do not remember the name of the file, place the cursor in the Data File name position on the screen and press F4. This will show you a list of files in the library you entered in the Data File Library line.   You may then select one of these files to be used by your DFU program.

After you have entered the DFU program name & library and the Data File name & library, press the ENTER key.

```
Figure J-3 General Information for Create DFU
              Define General Information/Nonindexed File

Type choices, press Enter.

    Job title . . . . . . . . . . . .    DFUQUIK
    Display format  . . . . . . . . .    2           1=Single,   2=Multiple
                                                     3=Maximum,  4=Row oriented

    Audit report  . . . . . . . . . .    N           Y=Yes,  N=No
    S/36 style  . . . . . . . . . . .    N           Y=Yes,  N=No
    Suppress errors . . . . . . . . .    N           Y=Yes,  N=No
    Edit numerics . . . . . . . . . .    N           Y=Yes,  N=No
    Allow updates on roll . . . . . .    Y           Y=Yes,  N=No
    Record numbers:
      Generate  . . . . . . . . . . .    N           Y=Yes,  N=No
      Store in a field  . . . . . . .    N           Y=Yes,  N=No
      Heading . . . . . . . . . . . .    *RECNBR


    Processing  . . . . . . . . . . .    2           1=Direct
                                                     2=Sequential

F3=Exit      F12=Cancel       F14=Display definition
```

Providing General Information

There are two different shapes to the type of panel shown in Figure J-3. If you were working with an indexed file, or a logical file with a key, the heading would say indexed file. Moreover, the record number generator as seen in Figure J-3, would not be present on the panel. DFU can work with indexed, direct and sequential files. The indexed label is one of the ways it differentiates these types.

On this General Information panel, you specify information about how you want your DFU program to work. There are lots of options as you can see. You can also select to produce an audit report showing the work done against a file during this session. You should always enter a job title that is relevant to the DFU program we are describing.

One or Two Columns? Multiple or Maximum?

You have a number of options as to how you want the display to look. A display format of single, for example, will design the display such that the prompting for fields will all be along the left side of the display in a single column.   All entry fields will also be aligned in a single column.

A display format of multiple will design the display such that data on the screen can be formatted into 1, 2, 3, or 4 columns depending on the number and size of the fields. A display format of maximum will design the display such that as many fields as possible will appear on the data display. The fields may or may not line up in columns.

Row Oriented - Power Record Keying.

The fourth (4= Row oriented) display format option allows the user to further define how the data entry screen appears. This option must be taken if multiple record processing is desired.   Data fields will appear in a left-to-right row orientation rather than in a top-to-bottom columnar fashion. This option is very powerful, especially when a row of data fits across the screen. DFU will produce a screen with as many as sixteen records, which you can view and update at one time.

Give Me an Audit Report!

If you specify 'Y' to Audit report, a report will be produced after each run of the DFU program. This report will show all changes, additions and deletions to the data file that is used by the DFU program.

Make My DFU Display System/36 Style!

If you specify 'Y' to S/36 style, then the DFU will format the display with S/36 structure and command key implementation. If you wish to suppress decimal data errors, then answer 'Y' to the 'suppress errors' prompt. Typing a 'Y' to "edit numerics," allows you to use numeric editing for the fields. Also, specifying a 'Y' for "Allow updates on roll" permits the roll keys to update data records, without a prior Enter key.

Generate Record Numbers!

If you are using a sequential or direct access data file, then you can generate record numbers. These can be stored in a field in the file. Sometimes they are and sometimes they are not. If the record number represents the relative record number of a record, it is not stored as a field within a record.

The processing prompt allows you to distinguish between direct or sequential processing of a non-indexed file. After completing the general information screen, press the ENTER key to continue with Panel I-4.

Figure J-4 Select Record Formats

```
                    Work with Record Formats
File . . . :   VENDORP                    Library  . . . . :   HELLO

Type options, press Enter.  Press F21 to select all.
   2=Specify   4=Delete


Opt  Format     Defined  Description
 _2  VNDMSTR       N     VENDMAST DB FORMAT



                                                          Bottom
F3=Exit                    F5=Refresh        F12=Cancel
F14=Display definition      F21=Select all
```

Selecting Database Record Formats

In the panel in Figure J-4, select which record format to use. In this case, the file contains only one record format. A physical database file contains only one format. A logical file may contain more than one record format, all of which DFU can process. The database file record format is a set of fields establishing the layout of a record for DFU to process. After selecting the record format, press ENTER.

Select and Sequence Fields

Figure J-5 Select and Sequence Fields - DFU

```
                        Select and Sequence Fields

  File  . . . . . . . . . . . . :    VENDORP      Library  . . . . :    HELLO
  Record Format . . . . . . . :    VNDMSTR

  Select fields and their sequence or press F21 to select all; press Enter.


  Sequence   Field      Attr     Length   Type       Description
  _____   VNDNBR              5,0      PACK       VENDOR NUMBER
  _____   NAME                25       CHAR       NAME
  _____   ADDR1               25       CHAR       ADDRESS LINE 1
  _____   CITY                15       CHAR       CITY
  _____   STATE               2        CHAR       STATE
  _____   ZIPCD               5,0      PACK       ZIP CODE
  _____   VNDCLS              2,0      PACK       VENDOR CLASS
  _____   VNDSTS              1        CHAR       A=ACTIVE,D=DELETE,S=SUSPEN
  _____   BALOWE              9,2      PACK       BALANCE OWED
  _____   SRVRTG              1        CHAR       G=GOOD,A=AVERAGE,B=BAD, P=

                                                                        Bottom
  F3=Exit          F5=Refresh        F12=Cancel         F14=Display definition
  F20=Renumber     F21=Select all
```

In Figure J-5, select which fields you want to include for your DFU program by typing a number under "Sequence." The number you type indicates the order of the fields on the display. You can also press F21 to select all fields. If "select all" is a viable option for you, it makes the selection task that much easier. After selecting the fields you want for your DFU program, press ENTER.

Along the way to the panel in Figure J-6, you will be asked to confirm your selections. If you have selected option 21, DFU will bring back a panel with each field, numbered in sequence from which you would press ENTER. If you are happy with the selections, press ENTER to accept them and you will then get the Extended Definitions panel in Figure J-6.

Figure J-6 Extended Definitions - Work With Fields

```
Define Fields

                              Work with Fields


  File   . . . . . . . . . :   VENDORP        Library . . . . :   Sample

  Record Format . . . . . . :  VNDMSTR


  Type options, press Enter.   Press F21 to select all.

      2=Specify extended definition

      4=Delete extended definition




                              Extended

  Opt    Field          Definition    Heading

      _    VNDNBR            N            VENDOR_____

      _    NAME              N            NAME_____

      _    ADDR1             N            ADDRESS LINE 1_____

      _    CITY              N            CITY_____

      _    STATE             N            STATE_____

      _    ZIPCD             N            ZIP_____

      _    VNDCLS            N            VENDOR_____

      _    VNDSTS            N            ACTIVE_____


More3=Exit                         F5=Refresh              F12=Cancel

    F14=Display definition     F21=Select all
```

Working with Fields

On the panel in Figure J-6, you can define different headings than the
DB defaults for the fields selected, or indicate that any field requires
an extended definition. Extended definitions give the opportunity to
provide additional information for editing and displaying fields.

Select option 2 for each field, for extended definitions and heading
information.   If you want extended definitions for all fields, press
F21.   After you have selected the fields, press ENTER. Since all the
work you must do, has been completed, you are taken to the DFU
Exit panel as in Figure J-7 in which you will have several decisions to

make including (1) whether to save your DFU program, and (2) whether to run the program before leaving the DFU environment.

Exit DFU

Figure J-7 Exit DFU Prompt

```
                          Exit DFU Program Definition

Type choices, press Enter.

    Save program  . . . . . . . . .  Y              Y=Yes, N=No
    Run program . . . . . . . . . .  Y              Y=Yes, N=No
      For choice Y=Yes:
        Type of run . . . . . . . .  1              1=Change, 2=Display
    Modify program  . . . . . . . .  N              Y=Yes, N=No
    Save DDS source . . . . . . . .  N              Y=Yes, N=No

    For Save program Y=Yes:
      Program . . . . . . . . . . .  DFUQUIK        Name
        Library . . . . . . . . . .    HELLO        Name, *CURLIB, . . .
      Authority . . . . . . . . . .  *LIBCRTAUT     Name, *LIBCRTAUT, . . .
      Text  . . . . . . . . . . . .  DFUQUIK

    For Save DDS source Y=Yes:
      Source file . . . . . . . . .                 Name
        Library . . . . . . . . . .    *CURLIB      Name, *CURLIB, . . .
      Source member . . . . . . . .  DFUQUIK        Name

F3=Exit       F14=Display definition      F17=Fast path
```

In the Exit DFU prompt, enter 'Y' at the *Save program* entry to save the DFU program in the library you specified when you started defining the DFU. Optionally, you may also save the DDS for the display file which DFU creates for you. You may then alter this DDS to allow for customization of the screen. The default is NOT to save the DDS.

Save DDS?

If you choose to save the DDS to modify the DFU display file later, enter the name of the DDS source file in which you would like the DDS created.

Enter 'Y' for the Run Program entry if you want to run the DFU immediately after creating the program.   The type of DFU run should be "Change," so that the data in the fields can be changed and not just viewed. Recheck your work to be sure that you entered the proper DFU program name and library. Default public authority to the newly   created DFU program will be *CHANGE. You should enter descriptive text in the program to help identify it for the future. When you have completed, press ENTER.

Running Your DFU Program

If you choose to immediately run your DFU program, you will get a prompt with all of the particulars you entered at DFU start time–program name, file name, libraries. Press ENTER and you will see a DFU ENTRY panel similar to that of Figure J-8. If you fully exited the DFU process, you can execute your newly created DFU by entering the DFU change data command as follows:

CHGDTA DFUPGM$\left(\text{HELLO/DFUQUIK}\right)$

FILE$\left(\text{HELLO/VENDORP}\right)$

Whichever way you get to DFU– either via the exit panel or via the CHGDTA command– you will see the DFU entry panel, only if your file contains no data records. If, on the other hand, you come in after having entered some data in a previous session, you will not see the DFU ENTRY panel. Instead you will be presented with the DFU CHANGE panel as shown in Figure J-9.

Entry DFU Panel

Note that the mode shown in the upper right corner in Figure J-8 is "ENTRY." Enter the values in the fields as shown.   Note, that you are in Entry mode. After you have keyed the information, press Enter. Key as many records as you wish, while in ENTRY mode. To Exit, press F3. If you have multiple formats from a logical file and you want to enter into a different format, press F5.

Change DFU Panel

To switch to CHANGE mode, press F11. You will see a panel similar to that in Figure J-9.

Figure J-8 DFU ENTRY Panel

```
DFUQUIK                                Mode . . . . :    ENTRY
Format . . . . :    VNDMSTR            File . . . . :    VENDORP


VENDOR NUMBER:    _____
NAME:                    _____
ADDRESS LINE 1:          _____
CITY:                    _____
STATE:             __
ZIP'CODE:            ____
VENDOR CLASS:      __
ACTIVE CODE:       _
BALANCE OWED:       _____
SERVICE RATING:    _


F3=Exit             F5=Refresh           F6=Select format
F9=Insert           F10=Entry            F11=Change
```

Figure J-9, DFU Change Panel.

```
DFUQUIK                                   Mode . . . . :    CHANGE

Format . . . . :    VNDMSTR               File . . . . :    VENDORP


*RECNBR:




F3=Exit             F5=Refresh            F6=Select format

F9=Insert           F10=Entry             F11=Change
                                    © COPYRIGHT IBM CORP. 1980, 2000.
```

Note, from the upper right corner of the panel in Figure J-9, that you are in DFU CHANGE mode. To change a record, type in the number of the record, and it is displayed for update. For keyed (indexed) files, the record key may be entered instead of the record number. To change to Entry mode, from Change mode, press F10. You can also Press F9 to add a record. This option also takes you to ENTRY mode. In all cases, when you have typed or changed the data in the displayed record, hit ENTER to add or to update the data.

End Data Entry

When you decide that you have had enough entering and maintaining data, press F3 to exit, and you will be taken to the *End Data Entry* screen as seen in Figure J-10. This panel shows the number of records added, changed or deleted. It also asks you if you really want to end data entry. If you answer "Y," DFU will gracefully end.

That's a wrap!

Figure J-10 End Data Entry

```
                              End Data Entry
      Number of records processed

      Added   . . . . . :          1
      Changed   . . . . :          0
      Deleted   . . . . :          0

 Type choice, press Enter.

    End data entry  . . . . . . .    Y            Y=Yes,  N=No

 F3=Exit        F12=Cancel
```

Summary and Conclusions

Well, there you have it. We created our own DFU from scratch and used it to update the APOPENP data file. Congratulations.

In this QuikCourse you learned the power of the data file utility (DFU) program generator, and you used it to create a program which enabled you to enter data, update files, and make file inquiries. You did not need a programming language to use DFU. You created the program by merely responding to a series of displays. DFU then created a program for you based on your input.

DFU also provides you with a quick way of updating a file using a temporary program. You do not have to define a DFU program first. Because it is so easy to use, and so database-aware DFU enables you to create database maintenance programs significantly faster than you could by using a programming languages (for example, RPG).

One DFU program can perform several jobs. For example, a single DFU program can allow you to enter new records into a file, update fields within existing records, or perform file inquiry tasks. It does this by creating data entry programs from definitions based on the descriptions of existing database files. These descriptions are used during the definition of your DFU program. After you have defined a program, as you learned, you can recall and run that program as often as required.

DFUs can be run from the main DFU menu, or they can be placed in user menus, to augment application packages and/or home-grown code. The program fills in the gaps that are always present in business applications. It is a very powerful tool and as you learned, it is reasonably easy to master.

Best wishes as you enter, display, and update your files to your heart's content!

QuikCourse S.   AS/400 and IBM i Subfile Programming Case Study

Subfiles: an Advanced Topic?

Now, you have arrived at a QuikCourse which some may argue presents an advanced subject. Subfiles are certainly an advanced topic. There is no denying that. However, there is little need for concern. You will not be exposed in this section to all of the wonderment of subfiles. It would be too overwhelming. But, you will learn how to build an inquiry subfile and you will be exposed to how to drive database update operations from subfiles.

The treatment of the topic in this QuikCourse is a combination of a succinct and pithy lecture with a presentation style which is mostly tutorial in nature. We hope you enjoy this brief Case Study and that you emerge with some good tools to help you become a master of subfiles.

What Is a Subfile?

In a nutshell, a subfile is a memory file. The part that you can see on the screen is like a window into a part of memory. Though a subfile is implemented via a display file, it is not a display file. Again, it really is a memory file. You declare a subfile record with "display file DDS," and with DDS, you link it to a control record format, which you must also declare in the display file. The control record format performs special functions such as initializing and clearing all records in the memory file. Additionally, it provides a special keyword

(SFLDSP) which, when enabled, causes the records in the subfile to be displayed one section or window at a time on your display.

Subfile Size and Page Size

Subfiles may contain a few or a few thousand records. The case study subfile, which you build in this section is to be set at 500 records and it is to have a window space (a subfile page) of ten records. In this case study then, the "sliding" window into the memory file (subfile) can hold just 10 records.

Subfile Productivity Benefits

When subfiles work with programs, they provide a number of productivity benefits. For example, programmers need only define one record line, and SDA builds all of the rest. If a subfile has four fields, for example, and ten records are what needs to be shown on the display, the programmer saves keying 36 screen panel field definitions into the makeup of the display file. That is big time productivity.

No Drudge Coding

Besides the elimination of this drudge coding, the subfile mechanism also saves on sophisticated design and coding time. As an example, the internal subfile code knows how to deal with multiple records on one display panel. In fact, for the most part, you not only do not have to code for multiple records on the display, but you don't even have to do much coding all to get the benefit of what the subfile does for you.

More Than You Would Expect

When you send a subfile to a screen, the subfile does the screen manipulation work itself. It enables the roll keys so that, without coding any special keys or rolling functions, once a panel is on a display, the user can roll backward and forward to his heart's content. Your program does not even know it is happening. You don't need any program code at all. You can roll up. You can roll down. You can even change records while you are rolling them by. When the user finally hits the ENTER key, or another key besides ROLL, your program gets control again. But, the subfile itself remembers any records in memory which the user may have changed.

Language Support for Subfiles

High Level Languages (HLL) have some special operations to work with the nuances of subfiles. For example, RPG has the READC operation (Read Changed) and COBOL has the "READ-SUBFILE- NEXT-MODIFIED" operation. These are used to read changed subfile records. When a user hits ENTER after editing a subfile, control comes back to the program. The READC opcode then directs the system to read, from the subfile, only the records that were changed by the user during the roll period.

> √ Note: Since RPG's READC is shorter than COBOL's READ-SUBFILE-NEXT-MODIFIED, we will use READC in this QuikCourse to refer to the facilities in both languages.

Suppose there are 500 records in the subfile – as in this case study, and the user has changed just five of them. The READC is satisfied just five times, until it receives an end-of-file indication telling the program that there are no more changed records to be read. The program reads only those five records, using five read operations, and it tells the READC operation when there are no more changed records to read. It is a very powerful operator. Similar function is also provided for the COBOL programmer.

How Does a Subfile Get Loaded?

We have already briefly discussed initializing, clearing, and displaying the records in a subfile, but we have not talked yet about how to get records into a subfile. Our example case study is a type 1 subfile: Inquiry for multiple records. In order to use a subfile for inquiry, of course, you first have to get the records into the subfile; otherwise, you won't have meaningful records to display when the subfile is viewed / shown.

There are four simple steps to loading and processing a subfile:

1. Activating
2. Loading
3. Displaying
4. Processing

Activation is simply the process of performing a write operation to the subfile. There is a DDS keyword SFLINZ which is typically used to initialize a subfile to prepare it for action. In sample and actual code, you will typically see this function occurring before other subfile activity.

Loading is the process of writing records to a subfile. First, data must be accessed from databases to get the data records which are being requested. In this case study, the records come from the Vendor Master file. Imagine an input variable that represents the relative record number of the *to-be-written record* in the subfile. This tells the *database-read program* which record number to write to the subfile. As you would expect, when loading the subfile, this variable is set to one and then incremented with each subfile write operation until the record number is equal to the size of the subfile.

So, records are read from the database file, and are written to the memory file until the memory file is full or until all records have been read from the database file. This program does not have to know the number of records to write to the subfile. A subfile load loop will typically continue to read records from a database and write them to the subfile, until one of two things occurs:

1. The database file (VENDORP in this case study) reaches an end-of-file condition and will give no more records.

2. The subfile is full, and a message is returned to the program indicating no more records can be written to memory. If the page size is 500, as is our case study, this would mean that 500 records have been written before the subfile full indicator would be raised.

Though the write operation to the subfile format name is typically used to fill a subfile, there is one trick. A relative record field is associated with the file description. This field must be primed with the record number in the subfile which is to be written, before the record is written. Imagine a loop incrementing a relative record number, reading from the Vendor file, writing each relative record, one at a time to the subfile, and eventually filling the subfile. Once the subfile is filled (in memory), you probably want to display it. **Displaying** is the process of sending out the control record for the display file with a request (SFLDSP keyword) to display the subfile. At the time of this operation, a disconnect from the program occurs as discussed above. The Roll keys can then be used to view records in the subfile. The displayed records can also be changed in the memory file as they are viewed.

Processing occurs when the ENTER, or command key is pressed, and control is passed back to the program. All records in the memory subfile can then be accessed by a relative record number loop using a CHAIN operation to the file, or by using the very powerful READC (read changed) operation.

With READC, as noted above, the subfile returns only those records which have been changed by the user. As the subfile is providing the changed records, one-at-a-time, the program can process them. If the AP case study were enhanced for update, and say the balance field (BALOWE) was changed, the next likely thing to happen in the program would be for that specific master record to be read and updated to reflect the change.

Purposes for Subfiles

There are three major purposes for subfiles:

1. Inquiry for multiple records
2. Inquiry with update for multiple records
3. Data Entry for multiple records

Subfiles are the perfect medicine if you can envision a panel with ten or so lines of repetitive data records. In our simple case study example, the objective is to display   vendor information including balance owed, for all the vendors whose numbers are higher than a value which is input to the process. Take a look at Figure S-1 and you can immediately see which portion of the display represents the subfile window. Once the panel in Figure S-1 is sent to the display, the operator can roll through as many records as are contained in the subfile (500, in this case study, specified by keyword SFLSIZE).

Figure S-1 VENDSRCH Subfile Program Output

```
                   VENDOR MASTER INQUIRY    18:18:35  6/18/02

       ENTER STARTING VENDOR NO:     25          F3=  END OF JOB

       VENDOR NO.    VENDOR  NAME           STATE    BALANCE OWED

          00025      A MACHINE CORP.          IL       7,500.00
          00026      B MACHINERY              OK       1,495.55
          00028      C ENGRAVING CO           IL         100.00
          00030      D CONTROLS               IL         900.25
          00032      I POWER EQUIPMENT        PA         250.00
          00034      ROBIN  COMPANY           PA         153.00
          00036      F STEEL CO               PA         290.00
          00038      J B COMPANY              PA         100.00
          00040      SCRANTON INC             PA         250.00
          00042      PASS PAX INC             PA         300.00
```

Inquiry for Multiple Records

The subfile in Figure S1 certainly shows multiple records. This is a simple design for a subfile inquiry program. The static and input information is on the top, and the dynamic subfile information is on the bottom. This panel has two record formats:

1. Subfile Control   The Subfile Control Record is used to provide the normal prompts for a display (column headings, etc. as well as for the control of specific functions for the memory file. In this case study, it is visible in the panels shown in Figure S-1. It is located on the top of the screen before vendor # 25.

2. Subfile Record   The second record format is the definition of the subfile page itself. You define the shape of one line and the number of lines, and the subfile handles the rest.

In this "inquiry for multiple records," example, the data in the vendor file is in sequence by vendor number. The user inputs a vendor number. The program places a file cursor before that particular vendor in the database and begins to read the file. Each time it reads a record from the database, it writes a record to the subfile. When the READ hits end-of-file in the database or when the subfile is full, the program sends out the control record with the SFLDSP keyword enabled. This tells the display file to send out both the top of the screen, as well as the bottom (subfile).

The subfile records are displayed in the subfile page (10 records). The display file then "disengages" from the program, and its control from the program. The program waits for the subfile to give it back control. During the "disengagement," the display file itself is in control, independent of the program. The user can roll forward or backward through the subfile records until the inquiry is completed. This is an effective way to handle an inquiry with multiple records. When the user presses the ENTER key or a command key, the display file passes control back to the program.

Inquiry with Update for Multiple Records

Though we do not show the code for this type of access, it is reasonably easy to achieve. Let us resume the "Inquiry for multiple records" scenario, in order to transform it to an update program. Suppose the user decides to change one of the balances, then another, and still yet another – each on different pages of the subfile. As the user rolls through the subfile, which, at the time is   "disconnected" from the program and under the control of the display file, changes are being recorded in subfile memory. When finished, the user hits ENTER, and the subfile contents are ready to be queried by the program.

How do these changes, which were made only to a memory file, get reflected back into the database file on disk, from which the initial values were originally loaded? The user just assumes it will be done. Here's how it works:

When the program gets control back, it goes into a READC loop, reading against the subfile. In this example, since the vendor number is in the subfile, it is returned for each successful READC operation. The program can then use the vendor number as the search argument for the CHAIN (random access by key) to the Vendor file. When the random database read by key is successful to the Vendor file, and the proper record has been accessed, the program can then issue an UPDATE operation to the Vendor file to reflect the new balance, as changed by the user, and as stored in the subfile record.

What If Vendor # Is Not in Subfile?

By the way, if the specific vendor number in any of the READCs, were not stored in the subfile, and if access by key were essential to the update, you could still accomplish the update mission. However, as you filled the subfile, you would have to build a separate, but related, table by relative record number. When the changed record were accessed, you could then access the table by the relative record number to obtain the vendor number or whatever key you stored. This key value could then serve as your means of accessing and updating the Vendor database. Of course, it is much easier if you can cram the key into the subfile record.

Data Entry for Multiple Records

In this scenario, there is no need to load the subfile. However, it must be initialized before being displayed. The SFLINZ keyword is your best bet for getting this done. It initializes all records in the subfile on an output operation to the subfile control record format. The fields in each subfile record are initialized to blanks for character type fields, to nulls for floating-point type fields, to zeros for other numeric type fields, or to the constant value specified on input-only fields if the DFT keyword is specified.

> ☺ Hint: When the operator hits the ENTER key after typing application information, you must make sure that your program processes the data before the SFLINZ is issued again or the data will be deleted. Any record previously written or typed into the subfile as data entry is overwritten and no longer has its earlier value.

When the subfile is displayed (on an output operation to the subfile control record), all records in the subfile are displayed with the same values (the initialized defaults). To the user, this should look like a blank subfile screen. In our case study example, if the data were to be entered, rather than displayed, forty fields, four for each line of the subfile would appear in default state awaiting data entry. When the user finishes typing one page of data, he or she could roll to the next page of blank lines and enter more data.

Subfile Correction

The programming required for correcting data entered via a subfile can be tricky. There are various changes that certain program opcodes and options may make to the status of record. For example, the READC operation and the UPDAT, with the SFLNXTCHG option affect the subfile records' status in exactly the opposite way. (The SFLNXTCHG record is specifically designed to force users to make corrections). READC turns off the "changed" flag in each record after a read so that a subsequent READC does not get those records previously read. An UPDAT with SFLNXTCHG, turns on the "change" flag so that the program gets a second look at error records.

What is SFLNXTCHG?

OK, SFLNXTCHG looks like a mean keyword to me. Let's say we don't have it as a tool to use. Big deal! Right? Let's see. Suppose that you want to edit the data, which was keyed to the Entry subfile. Your program processes the whole subfile and marks the errors in each record, but you do not specify the SFLNXTCHG on the error records when you mark them because the keyword does not exist.

User Control of Data Quality

If you do not specify the SFLNXTCHG parameter, since it does not exist, then the work station user can simply press the ENTER key, and ignore the program's request to fix the errors. When the user is presented with a subfile full of errors, instead of correcting the program-detected errors, the user can decide to do nothing. Your program will not read the error records with a READC the next time through. Since your program reads with the READC, it gets no records because the *get-next-changed operation* (READC) finds no changed records the second time the ENTER key is pressed. The user errors persist. The user, not the program was in control of the quality of the data That's a real gotcha! Whoa! SFLNXTCHG does exist! Pshaw!

Program Control of Data Quality

So, for corrections, one approach is to use the SFLNXTCHG keyword since it actually does exist. Well, what does it do? Basically, it marks a record which is updated with the keyword operative as "changed." Thus, when the error record is displayed, the user must correct the error before hitting ENTER or the READC will get the bad records again and keep sending them for correction. Without SFLNXTCHG, the user can just decide to make it an early weekend on errors.

It's simple. After all the records in error have been updated, the program sends an output/input operation to the subfile control record format to display the subfile again. With the subfile displayed again, the work station user types the data again and presses the ENTER key. If the data is correct, the program does not display the subfile again.

So, SFLNXTCHG is good because it forces the user to deal with and correct errors. It forces the user to fix any outstanding subfile errors before continuing. It does this by causing the "changed" attribute to be on in any subfile record in error. The next READC gets the record. An ENTER cannot bypass the check because the next READC will get it.

> √ Note: OK, so that's enough for the three major uses of subfiles. Though we described how to accommodate more complex scenarios than Inquiry with multiple records, the code for those more complex scenarios is not in this QuikCourse. Our belief is that, once you can light up your display panel with a multiple record inquiry subfile, you will feel that the rest is a cake walk other than the normal RPG coding. You don't need this QuikCourse to get you all the way, even though you may need the start which this module certainly gives.

Coding Examples:

A picture is worth a thousand words. Let's start by showing the record layouts for the two files used in the case study. The first, in Figure S-2 is the VENDORP physical file, which has no key. The second file, in Figure S-3 is the VENDMAST logical file, which orders the file with its vendor number key.

Figure S-2 VENDORP Physical File

```
 Columns . . . :    1  71              Browse              HELLO/QDDSSRC
SEU==>                                                         VENDORP
FMT A*  .....A*. 1 ...+... 2 ...+... 3 ...+... 4 ...+... 5 ...+... 6 ...+... 7
        *************** Beginning of data ************************************
001.00      A*  VENDOR MASTER PHYSICAL FILE
002.00      A                                    REF(HELLO/VENDORPA)
003.00      A           R VNDMSTR                TEXT('VENDMAST DB FORMAT')
004.00      A             VNDNBR    R
005.00      A             NAME      R
006.00      A             ADDR1     R
007.00      A             CITY      R
008.00      A             STATE     R
009.00      A             ZIPCD     R
010.00      A             VNDCLS    R
011.00      A             VNDSTS    R
012.00      A             BALOWE    R
013.00      A             SRVRTG    R
        ***************** End of data ************************************

F3=Exit   F5=Refresh   F9=Retrieve  F10=Cursor  F11=Toggle   F12=Cancel
F16=Repeat find        F24=More keys
                                   ©) COPYRIGHT IBM CORP. 1981, 2000.
```

Figure S-3 VENDMAST Logical File (In Subfile Program)

```
 Columns . . . :    1  71              Browse              HELLO/QDDSSRC
SEU==>                                                        VENDMAST
FMT LF  .....A..........T.Name++++++.Len++TDpB......Functions++++++++++++++++++
        *************** Beginning of data ************************************
0001.00     A           R VNDMSTR                PFILE(HELLO/VENDORP)
0002.00     A                                    TEXT('VENDMAST DB FORMAT')
0003.00     A             K VNDNBR
        ***************** End of data ************************************

F3=Exit   F5=Refresh   F9=Retrieve  F10=Cursor  F11=Toggle   F12=Cancel
F16=Repeat find        F24=More keys
                                   ©) COPYRIGHT IBM CORP. 1981, 2000.
```

The Final Design Panel

Now, let's look at the finished SDA design for the display file as shown in Figure S-4. Notice that it also includes the subfile definition. That's the ten lines, which look like records underneath all of the prompts. As you work through the tutorial, coming up shortly, you will see that one of the beauties of a subfile, among others, is that you need only define its first record. The display file handles the rest of the records. We specified the four fields directly under the titles and SDA did the rest. You just say there are 500 records and that only ten are visible on the screen at one time, and the display file worries about how to manage them. Yes, you only have to define one subfile record — even if your display holds 20 or more.

Figure S-4 SDA Subfile Design Panel for Vendor Case Study

```
                          VENDOR MASTER INQUIRY      TT:TT:TT DD/DD/DD

         ENTER STARTING VENDOR NO:     33333-          F3=  END OF JOB

         VENDOR NO.    VENDOR NAME                 STATE    BALANCE OWED

            66666      OOOOOOOOOOOOOOOOOOOOOOOOOO   OO   6,666,666.66-
            66666      OOOOOOOOOOOOOOOOOOOOOOOOOO   OO   6,666,666.66-
            66666      OOOOOOOOOOOOOOOOOOOOOOOOOO   OO   6,666,666.66-
            66666      OOOOOOOOOOOOOOOOOOOOOOOOOO   OO   6,666,666.66-
            66666      OOOOOOOOOOOOOOOOOOOOOOOOOO   OO   6,666,666.66-
            66666      OOOOOOOOOOOOOOOOOOOOOOOOOO   OO   6,666,666.66-
            66666      OOOOOOOOOOOOOOOOOOOOOOOOOO   OO   6,666,666.66-
            66666      OOOOOOOOOOOOOOOOOOOOOOOOOO   OO   6,666,666.66-
            66666      OOOOOOOOOOOOUUUOOOOOOOOOOO   OO   6,666,666.66-
            66666      OOOOOOOOOOOOOOOOOOOOOOOOOO   OO   6,666,666.66-




Work screen for VENDCTL. VENSUB displayed as additional record.

*****************************************************************
```

Show Me the Money!

Now, for the curious at heart, the incessant programmer among us, show me the money! Show me the code. Here is the DDS first for the display file with subfile, followed immediately by the RPG program code, which will drive this subfile. There can be a lot of learning accomplished between the two Figures S-5 and S-6.

Figure S-5 Display File DDS for Vendor Subfile

```
       SUBFILE DDS -- VENDSRCH
       *************** Beginning of data *****************************************
0001.00        A*%%TS  SD  20020618  180918  BKELLY      REL-V5R1M0  5722-WDS
0002.00        A*SUBFILE DDS -- VENDSRCH
0003.00        A*
0004.00        A*%%EC
0005.00        A                                 DSPSIZ(24 80 *DS3)
0006.00        A                                 REF(*LIBL/VENDORP)
0007.00        A                                 PRINT
0008.00        A            R VENSUB             SFL
0009.00        A*
0010.00        A              VNDNBR    R     O  9 12TEXT('VENDOR NUMBER')
0011.00        A              NAME      R     O  9 23TEXT('NAME')
0012.00        A              STATE     R     O  9 50TEXT('STATE')
0013.00        A              BALOWE    R     O  9 54TEXT('BALANCE OWED    ')
0014.00        A                                 EDTCDE(J)
0015.00        A*
0016.00        A            R VENDCTL            SFLCTL(VENSUB)
0017.00        A*%%TS  SD  20020618  180918  BKELLY      REL-V5R1M0  5722-WDS
0018.00        A                                 SFLSIZ(0500)
0019.00        A                                 SFLPAG(0010)
0020.00        A                                 CF03(99 'END OF JOB')
0021.00        A  81                             SFLDSP
0022.00        A  81                             SFLDSPCTL
0023.00        A  88                             SFLINZ
0024.00        A N81                             SFLCLR
0025.00        A  98                             SFLMSG('INVALID VENDOR NO.'
0026.00        A                              3 29'VENDOR MASTER INQUIRY'
0027.00        A                              3 54TIME
0028.00        A                              3 63DATE
0029.00        A                                 EDTCDE(Y)
0030.00        A                              5 10'ENTER STARTING VENDOR NO:'
0031.00        A              VENDNO   5S 0I  5 38DSPATR(HI)
0032.00        A                              5 53'F3=  END OF JOB'
0033.00        A                              7 10'VENDOR NO.   VENDOR NAME '
0034.00        A                              7 48'STATE    BALANCE OWED'
```

Subfile Definition

The source code for the Vendor subfile screen (DDS) is shown in Figure S-5. Notice that the subfile is defined at statement eight with the SFL keyword. Its name, as you can see in the subfile record format ®), at statement 0008, is VENSUB. Lines 0010 through 0013 define the four fields in the memory file that IBM calls the subfile. One of the fields, BALOWE, is to be edited with commas and decimals when it is written. You can see the *edit code* "J" at line 14. One other thing of note, is that the starting line # (0009) for the subfile, when displayed, is given in each of the four fields that make up the subfile. You can see this in statements 0010 to 0013.

Carriage or Horse?

By rule, IBM insists that the *subfile record* (SFL) must come first in the DDS – before the *subfile control record* (SFLCTL). If you can read

DDS, you may think there are an awful lot of keywords on the record format named VENDCTL. There are, and we'll talk about them shortly.

There are only two record formats in this whole display file. That is the least number of record formats that can exist in a display file that contains a subfile. There must be a subfile record (SFL), and there must be a subfile control record (SFLCTL)

Subfile Control Record

The subfile control record is called VENDCTL, and is specified at line 0016. You can see the link in the SFLCTL keyword which points the control record to the subfile record, VENSUB. That's how VENDCTL knows that it is controlling VENSUB; you tell it with the VNDCTL keyword and it remembers.

Since any read or write operations to the VENSUB subfile record format are treated as memory file reads and writes, and not display file reads and writes, there must be a tool to let us control the visible and invisible parts of the subfile. There is such a tool and that's why they call it the control record.

Through the control record, for example, you can specify the size and the page size of the subfile. You can also initialize the subfile, clear the subfile, or display the subfile. You can also send out an error message when things are not completely correct. The control commands for this are given in statements 0018 thru 0025. Notice some of these are conditional and some are unconditional. The RPG program in Figure S-6, does all that is necessary to work with the display file in Figure S-5. Its job is to turn the indicators on and off so that the proper functions occur, or do not occur as intended.

Statements 25, to the end of the program, are the constant text for the top half of the screen. Notice that this text can be specified in the subfile control record format. At statement 31 the input field is defined. This is where the vendor number is entered. It serves as the starting point for the whole program when it is executing.

Figure S-6 RPG Subfile Program-VENDSRCH

```
          F*                                        VENDSRCH
0001.00   FVENDSRCHCF   E                 WORKSTN
0002.00   F                               RRN    KSFILE VENSUB
0003.00   FVENDMASTIF   E        K        DISK
0004.00   C                      MOVE *ON      *IN88
0005.00   C                      WRITEVENDCTL
0006.00   C                      MOVE *OFF     *IN88
0007.00   C         *IN99        DOWEQ*OFF
0008.00   C                      MOVE *ON      *IN81
0009.00   C                      EXFMTVENDCTL
0010.00   C                      MOVE *OFF     *IN81
0011.00   C                      WRITEVENDCTL
0012.00   C                      MOVE *OFF     *IN60
0013.00   C                      Z-ADD0        RRN     50
0014.00   C         VENDNO       SETLLVENDMAST
0015.00   C         *IN60        DOWEQ'0'
0016.00   C                      READ VENDMAST         60
0017.00   C         *IN60        CABEQ'1'      FULL
0018.00   C                      ADD  1        RRN
0019.00   C                      WRITEVENSUB           82
0020.00   C         *IN82        CABEQ'1'      FULL
0021.00   C                      ENDDO
0022.00   C         FULL         TAG
0023.00   C                      ENDDO
0024.00   C                      MOVE '1'      *INLR
```

RPG Program

The RPG program in Figure S-6 is quite small for such a powerful program. The WORKSTATION file is defined at statement 1. This links to the name of the compiled DDS from Figure S-5, which is the display file named VENDSRCH. The workstation file is set up as a combined file ("C" in column 15), because it uses both input and output operations to the display station. On line two, the additional subfile information is defined to the program. The RPG compiler finds out that the format named VENSUB represents the subfile, and that it will be accessed via the relative record number field called RRN.

More File Descriptions

The next statement is the database file description, which is a logical file called VENDMAST over a physical file named VENDORP. It is defined as an input disk file, which will be processed by key. Both files have an "E" in column 19, which says that the input specifications will come from data descriptions in the database rather than from hard-coded program specifications.

The Basic Subfile Program Loops

In statements 4 thru 6, the subfile is being initialized. Indicator 88 is set on to communicate to the subfile that statement 23 in DDS is to run. This combination of the RPG write to the subfile control record at RPG statement 00o5, with indicator 88 on (statement 0004) , and the SFLINZ keyword in DDS at statement 23 cause the subfile to be initialized for action. The DDS is shown in Figure S-6. You will get an I/O error if you do not activate the subfile, either by writing records to it, or by using the SFLINZ operation as we did in the example.

Since indicator 81 is not on during the RPG write at RPG statement 0005, the clear operation (SFLCLR) at DDS line 24 is also performed but it is superfluous at this time since there are no real records in the subfile. SFLINZ activates the subfile and writes meaningless default records to it. SFLCLR at DDS statement 24 empties the subfile immediately after it is activated and initialized.

RPG statement 0006 turns off indicator 88 so that the subfile will not be initialized again. Since this code is before the DO-While-Equal loop, it gets executed just once in this program.

At RPG statement 7, a Do-While-Equal control loop is established with the RPG operation DOWEQ. This keeps the program alive and looping through statement 23, until the F3 key (Command key 3) is pressed. With each iteration of the DOWEQ loop, from statements 0008 through 0010, the program first sets on indicator 81 to pass to the display file. It then uses an EXFMT to send out both the subfile control record format, VENDCTL, and the subfile record format, VENSUB. This displays the prompts and the subfile records. This RPG code is executed unconditionally, whether the subfile is empty or full. The first cycle, of course, the subfile is empty.

Though the RPG code executes unconditionally, the program does set on indicator 81 at RPG statement 0008 to trigger the display of both the subfile and the subfile control record (prompts). The program passes the indicator status to the display file. The DDS in Figure S-6 show that indicator 81 controls lines 0021, 0022, and 0024. Lines 21 and 22 use the *ON condition of indicator 81 to display the subfile and the subfile prompts. Line 24 in DDS uses the *OFF condition of indicator 81 to clear the subfile.

At RPG statement 10, indicator 81 is set off so that the next operation to the subfile does not display the panel. This permits output operations to be directed to the subfile control record without the panel displaying for the user. At RPG statement 0011, for example, the program writes to the subfile control record with indicator 81 in the *OFF status. This links with DDS statement 24 to trigger the SFLCLR operation to clear the subfile.

As the program is looping, each time at statement 0009, it accepts a new vendor number from the prompted panel. When the user enters the number, the clear operation is triggered so that the subfile memory records from the last vendor display are cleared before the program begins to write new records to the subfile.

Statements 12 and 13 provide some light housekeeping to turn off indicator 60, and reinitialize the subfile counter for the new vendor. At statement 14, the program sets the file cursor for the VENDMAST file with the set lower limit (SETLL) operation, so that subsequent reads will bring in records following the entered vendor number value. Then, at statement 15, another Do-While-Equal (DOWEQ) control loop is begun, which continues looping through statement 21. In this loop, the Vendor database is read, the relative record number of the subfile record to be written is incremented, and the record read is written to the memory subfile at that relative record position. The loop ends when the READ operation at statement 16 reaches the end of the vendor file and the program turns on indicator 60, which controls the loop.

Subfile Full, Display

This all goes on merrily until one of two things happens. Either the READ of the VENDMAST comes back with an end-of-file (indicator 60), or the subfile is full (indicator 82). In either case, the outer loop continues to unmercifully send out the results of the last subfile load and continues to ask for the next starting vendor number. When the workstation user chooses to hit F3, the program leaves its loop, drops to statement 24, and ends.

SDA Subfile Case Study.

That is probably enough setup work for this case study. Now for the show! This topic is about subfiles and SDA. However, we did not spend much time talking about SDA; we did it on purpose. We did not want to put the cart before the horse. We introduced a number of keywords which are really part of DDS. To use SDA for these, you must specify the DDS keywords specifically while in the SDA session.

We also explained the type of RPG programming that must be done in order to accommodate subfiles. This was all done so that you would have an appreciation for what subfiles are, how to use them, and how they look when they are defined in DDS. Now, we can do the really easy stuff and take you through a semi tutorial on SDA for subfiles. Let's not wait another minute.

Get SDA Started

To get started with SDA, you type the command STRSDA (Start SDA) from a command line and hit ENTER. You are taken to the *AS/400 Screen Design Aid (SDA)* main menu. From this menu, take option 1 to *Design Screens*, and press ENTER. Fill in the *Design Screens* menu as follows:

Source file	-	QDDSSRC
Library	-	HELLO
Member	-	VENDSRCH

When you have finished filling in this preliminary panel, hit ENTER again, and you will come to the *Work with Display Records* panel as shown in Figure S-7.

Figure S-7 SDA Work With Display Records

```
                    Work with Display Records

File . . . . . . :    QDDSRC            Member . . . . . . :    VENDSRCH
   Library . . . . :    HELLO            Source type  . . . :    DSPF

Type options, press Enter.
  1=Add                2=Edit comments        3=Copy          4=Delete
  7=Rename             8=Select keywords     12=Design image

Opt  Order    Record         Type      Related Subfile   Date      DDS Error
 1            VENSUB

   (No records in file)



                                                                  Bottom
F3=Exit                 F12=Cancel        F14=File-level keywords
F15=File-level comments F17=Subset        F24=More keys
```

Creating Subfile Record with SDA

Type a "1" in the first option field in the Work With Display Records
panel, as shown in Figure S-7. Type *VENSUB* as the name of the
subfile you are going to define. Then press ENTER. You will then
come to the Add New Record panel shown in Figure S-8.

Figure S-8 SDA Add New Record Format

```
                    Add New Record

File . . . . . . :    QDDSRC            Member . . . . . . :    VENDSRCH
   Library . . . . :    HELLO            Source type  . . . :    DSPF

Type choices, press Enter.

  New record  . . . . . . . . . . . . . . .    VENSUB      Name

  Type  . . . . . . . . . . . . . . . . . .    SFL         RECORD, USRDFN
                                                           SFL,    SFLMSG
                                                           WINDOW, WDWSFL
                                                           PULDWN, PDNSFL
                                                           MNUBAR

F3=Exit      F5=Refresh      F12=Cancel
```

Since you are defining the subfile, type the keyword "SFL" in the
type column. The panel should already be primed with VENSUB as
the name of the subfile record you are about to define. Press ENTER

Linking Subfile with Control Record

When you press ENTER from Figure S-8, the panel does not change much. You get an added line after the subfile information, which looks almost exactly like the following:

Subfile control record. . . <u>VENDCTL</u> Name

It does not have the name filled in. Next to *Name*, type VENDCTL, and press ENTER. The next panel you see will be titled: "Select Subfile Keywords." This panel asks for two types of keywords for the subfile - General keywords and Indicator keywords. There are no keywords necessary for the subfile record (VENSUB) in this display file; just press ENTER.

On the next panel, as shown in Figure S-9, SDA makes the link between your subfile record and the name of the subfile control record which you provided above. Since there is lots of work to do with this subfile and we chose no keywords for the subfile record, we get to do all of our work from the control panel.

Figure S-9 RPG Subfile Program-Vendsrch

```
                       Select Subfile Control Keywords

   Subfile control record . . . . . . . . . :    VENDCTL

   Type choices, press Enter.

                                       Y=Yes
       General keywords  . . . . . . . .    Y
       Subfile display layout  . . . . .    Y
       Subfile messages  . . . . . . . .    Y

       Select record keywords  . . . . .    __

       TEXT keyword . . . . . . . . . .  :_____


   _____

   F3=Exit    F4=Display Selected Keywords    F12=Cancel
```

Entering Subfile Keywords with SDA

Notice in Figure S-9 that the panel record name has changed from the subfile record name VENSUB, to the subfile control record named VENDCTL. The first time you build your subfile, you will be taken to this panel automatically, to complete the link between the subfile records and the subfile control record. Answer "Y" to the first three options as shown in Figure S-9, and you will be taken first to the Define General Keywords panel as shown in Figure S-10

Figure S-10 RPG Subfile Program-Vendsrch

```
                        Define General Keywords

Subfile control record . . . . . . . . . :     VENDCTL

Type choices, press Enter.                 Keyword
   Related subfile record . . . . . . .    SFLCTL     VENSUB       Name
   Subfile cursor relative record . . .    SFLCSRRRN  _____     Name
   Subfile mode . . . . . . . . . . . .    SFLMODE    _____     Name


                                                   Y=Yes          Indicators/+
   Display subfile records  . . . . . .    SFLDSP       Y           81  ___ ___
   Display control record . . . . . . .    SFLDSPCTL    Y           81  ___ ___
   Initialize subfile fields  . . . . .    SFLINZ       Y           88  ___ ___
   Delete subfile area  . . . . . . . .    SFLDLT                   ___ ___ ___
   Clear subfile records  . . . . . . .    SFLCLR                   N81 ___ ___
   Indicate more records  . . . . . . .    SFLEND
      SFLEND parameter  . . . . . . . .       *MORE     ___
      SFLEND parameter   . . . . . . . .      *SCRBAR   ___        *MORE ...
   Record not active  . . . . . . . . .    SFLRNA       ___
                                                                    More..
```

The keywords will be associated with the subfile control record, which is where the memory file is defined. In Figure S-10, the SFLCTL prompt provides the link from the control file named VENDCTL, to the subfile named VENSUB.

Fill in this panel exactly as above and press ENTER. Select a number of functions, and in all cases, condition them with indicators. As you can see, indicator 81 is used to control when the subfile (memory file) is displayed, and when the control record is to be displayed. Indicator 88 is used to initialize the memory subfile with default records. When the program writes the control record and indicator 81 is not on, the file will not display the prompts or the subfile. If indicator 81 is not on, and the display will not be shown, the code in this panel clears the subfile of any records from the last interaction. This happens when the control record is written and indicator 81 is not on.

Press ENTER when you have filled in all parameters as above. You will move on to define the display and memory layout for the subfile. The ENTER key will take you to Figure S-11.

Figure S-11 Display and Memory Layout for the Subfile

```
                    Define Display Layout

Subfile control record . . . . . . . . . :    VENDCTL

Type values, press Enter.

                                      Keyword   Number
     Records in subfile . . . . . . . . . .  SFLSIZ     500
       Program-to-system field  . . . . . .             _____

     Records per display  . . . . . . . . .  SFLPAG     _10_

     Spaces between records . . . . . . . .  SFLLIN     ____


F3=Exit    F12=Cancel
```

Subfile Size and Page Size

As you can see in Figure S-24, you set the subfile to hold 500 records
in memory, and to window the records through a 10-line portal.
When the subfile is displayed, the display file will put 10 lines out - at
a time - to the screen. Press ENTER, to continue when you have
completed filling in the panel in Figure S-11.

Figure S-12 Define Subfile Messages

```
                        Define Subfile Messages
Subfile control record . . . . . . . . . :    VENDCTL

Type values, press Enter.

   Indicators/+     SFLMSG - Message Text                    More  Ind
     98 __ __       INVALID VENDOR NO._____  _    _
     __ __ __       _____  _    _
     __ __ __       _____  _    _
     __ __ __       _____  _    _
     __ __ __       _____  _    _

                                                               Bottom
   _____

   ____

   Indicators/+     SFLMSGID  File          Library     Ind   Name
     __ __ __       _____  _____      _____     __   _____
     __ __ __       _____  _____      _____     __   _____
     __ __ __       _____  _____      _____     __   _____
     __ __ __       _____  _____      _____     __   _____
 Bottom
 F3=Exit    F12=Cancel
```

Subfile Messages

Subfile messages are a way of identifying items in the subfile and displaying error messages. You see the error and then it goes away. The coding in Figure S-12 says that if indicator 98 is turned on in the program, and this panel (VENDCTL) is sent to the display, the error message will appear.

When you finish entering the subfile error message indicator, and message text, hit the ENTER key, and you will be taken back to a panel, which you have already seen – Figure S-9 – *Select Subfile Control Keywords*. Press the ENTER key once more and you will be taken to the *Work with Display Records* panel as shown in Figure S-13.

Figure S-13 SDA Work with Display Records

```
                        Work with Display Records
   File  . . . . . . :    QDDSSRC              Member . . . . . . :    VENDSEARCH
     Library . . . . :      HELLO              Source type  . . . :    DSPF

   Type options, press Enter.
     1=Add               2=Edit comments        3=Copy          4=Delete
     7=Rename            8=Select keywords     12=Design image

   Opt   Order    Record        Type     Related Subfile   Date        DDS Error

   __     10      VENSUB        SFL                         06/18/02
   12     20      VENDCTL       SFLCTL   VENSUB             06/18/02




                                                                     Bottom
   F3=Exit                   F12=Cancel        F14=File-level keywords
   F15=File-level comments   F17=Subset        F24=More keys
   Record VENSUB added to member VENDSEROO.
 +
```

Define the Panel Images

We have now given all of the linking and important information, which is unique to the subfile case study. However, we have not defined any fields. We have nothing but links and parameters. If we closed out now, we would have done nothing. Just as with non subfile display files, you must define the layouts of the screen panels (a.k.a. record formats).

Let's define the top part of the panel first and make it part of the subfile control record. It is just constant text to be displayed along with one input field. Its purpose is to be displayed, and when the control record is written, this constant text will be written also. In other words, it is not the memory file / subfile. To define the control panel, type a 12 for *Design image*, next to the VENDCTL record in the VENDSRCH display file, and press ENTER. You will see the panel as shown in Figure S-14. Well, not exactly! What you see first is a blank panel. The image in Figure S-14 reflects what it will look like, after you press ENTER, and type the design image as shown.

Figure S-14 Design Image for Subfile Control Record

```
                              'VENDOR MASTER INQUIRY'      TT:TT:TT


          'ENTER STARTING VENDOR NO:' +33333              'F3=   END OF JOB'


          'VENDOR NO.     VENDOR NAME'                 'STATE      BALANCE
OWED'
```

Input & Constant Image

In Figure S-14, you see just the top half of the screen, since that is all the information you need to type at this point. You'll notice that we place "wads" of text within quotes. We do this so that they will be treated as a block. For the input field (+33333), you can use the database trick we taught you in the non-subfile example. With this "trick," you can place the vendor number field from the VENDMAST database on the display image. For this example, however, we show how the design would be accomplished if the database were unavailable. Press ENTER, and the panel will change. But you have to look close in Figure S-15 to see the change.

Figure S-15 Subfile Control Record Design

```
                              VENDOR MASTER INQUIRY       TT:TT:TT
DD/DD/DD
          ENTER STARTING VENDOR NO:     33333-           F3=   END OF JOB


          VENDOR NO.     VENDOR NAME                 STATE
BALANCE OWED
```

Completing the Control Record Image

Notice the subtle changes on the panel. There are no more quotes around "wads" of text. Additionally, the input field appears as 33333- to indicate that it is a signed numeric output field. Now that we have designed the control record, let's design the subfile record. To go from the Subfile Control Record Design panel, to the Subfile Design panel, you must go to the Work with Display Records panel, as shown back in Figure S-13. Press F12 to go back. From there, place a "12" next to the VENSUB record, and you are on your way to defining the subfile record.

Typing the Subfile Record Image

The next panel will look almost exactly the same as the panel in Figure S-16. There is just one big difference. The bottom information will not be there. Just as you had to type the top part of the panel, you have to type the four field definitions onto the panel, just as shown in Figure S-16. When you are finished typing the subfile line, press ENTER.

Figure S-16 Adding the Subfile Display

```
                       VENDOR MASTER INQUIRY      TT:TT:TT DD/DD/DD

         ENTER STARTING VENDOR NO:    33333-          F3=  END OF JOB

         VENDOR NO.   VENDOR NAME                STATE   BALANCE OWED

           +66666     +OOOOOOOOOOOOOOOOOOOOOOOOO +OO   +666666666
```

When you press ENTER, poof! The subfile immediately expands to 10 records, as shown in Figure S-17. You may recall that this is the size of the SFLPAG parameter given back in Figure S-11.

Figure S-17 Subfile Control Record Design

```
                    VENDOR MASTER INQUIRY     TT:TT:TT DD/DD/DD

      ENTER STARTING VENDOR NO:    33333-         F3=  END OF JOB

      VENDOR NO.   VENDOR NAME              STATE   BALANCE OWED
         66666    OOOOOOOOOOOOOOOOOOOOOOOOO   OO   *666666666
         66666    OOOOOOOOOOOOOOOOOOOOOOOOO   OO    666666666
         66666    OOOOOOOOOOOOOOOOOOOOOOOOO   OO    666666666
         66666    OOOOOOOOOOOOOOOOOOOOOOOOO   OO    666666666
         66666    OOOOOOOOOOOOOOOOOOOOOOOOO   OO    666666666
         66666    OOOOOOOOOOOOOOOOOOOOOOOOO   OO    666666666
         66666    OOOOOOOOOOOOOOOOOOOOOOOOO   OO    666666666
         66666    OOOOOOOOOOOOOOOOOOOOOOOOO   OO    666666666
         66666    OOOOOOOOOOOOOOOOOOOOOOOOO   OO    666666666
         66666    OOOOOOOOOOOOOOOOOOOOOOOOO   OO    666666666
```

Editing Subfile Record with SDA

In Figure S-17, we have added the field command '*' next to the first Balance Owed field in the panel. It is hard to see. This command enables you to change the attributes of the field. A numeric dollar amount looks nice edited with commas and decimal points. If out value for BALOWE were edited, the editing characteristics would appear in Figure S-17. It is not, however. We did not tell SDA to edit it. Let's do that now by leaving the asterisk and pressing the ENTER key. You will then see the *Select Field Keywords* panel in Figure S-18.

Figure S-18 Subfile Record Design - Field Editing 1

```
                        Select Field Keywords

 Field . . . . . :   FLD004          Usage . . :   O
 Length  . . . . :   9,0             Row . . . :   9    Column . . . :  57

 Type choices, press Enter.
                                     Y=Yes   For Field Type
    Display attributes  . . . . . . .   _     All except Hidden
    Colors  . . . . . . . . . . . . .   _     All except Hidden



    General keywords  . . . . . . . .   _     All types
    Editing keywords  . . . . . . . .   Y     Numeric Output or Both
    Database reference  . . . . . . .   _     Hidden, Input, Output, Both



    TEXT keyword  . . . . . . . . . .


 F3=Exit   F4-Display Selected Keywords   F12=Cancel
```

Type a "Y" for Editing Keywords" in the panel if Figure S-18, and
press ENTER. You will then come to the *Select Editing Keywords*
panel in Figure S-19.

Figure S-19 Subfile Record Design Field Editing 2

```
                        Select Editing Keywords

 Field . . . . . :   FLD005          Usage . . :   O
 Length  . . . . :   9,0             Row . . . :   9    Column . . . :  57

 Type choices, press Enter.
                                     Keyword
 More
    Edit code  . . . . . . . . . . . . .   EDTCDE   J   A-D,  J-Q,  W,  Y,  Z,  1-9
       Replace leading zeros with . . . .            *, $

    Edit word  . . . . . . . . . . . . .   EDTWRD   _____


    Edit mask  . . . . . . . . . . . . .   EDTMSK   _____




 F3=Exit    F12=Cancel
```

As you can see, select the "J" edit code from the Select Editing
Keywords panel in Figure S-19. This will provide the proper editing
for the BALOWE field in the subfile display. At this point, we have
not renamed the field yet, so it still shows as field name FLD005.

End-of-Job Indicator

Press Enter twice from the panel in Figure S-19 to return to the SDA
Work Image panel. It should look like we are all done but the
cooking. It's not. We have one more thing to do - define the end of
job indicator - F3. For now, press F12 from the image panel and you
will go back to the *Work With Display Records* panel as shown in
Figure S-20.

Figure S-20 Subfile Control Record Design

```
                    Work with Display Records

File  . . . . . . :   QDDSSRC            Member . . . . . . :   VENDSCHA
   Library . . . . :   HELLO             Source type  . . . :   DSPF

Type options, press Enter.
   1=Add              2=Edit comments       3=Copy          4=Delete
   7=Rename           8=Select keywords    12=Design image

Opt  Order   Record       Type      Related Subfile   Date        DDS Error

___    10    VENSUB       SFL                          06/18/02
___    20    VENDCTL      SFLCTL    VENSUB             06/18/02


                                                                   Bottom
F3=Exit                     F12=Cancel      F14=File-level keywords
F15=File-level comments     F17=Subset      F24=More keys
Image updated for record VENSUB.
```

You'll have a message on the bottom of the screen saying: "Image
updated for record VENSUB." This means that your work is in the
work file waiting to be saved. Press F14 to add file level keywords,
and you will see come to the panel in Figure S-21.

Figure S-21 Select File Keywords for File Indicators

```
                              Select File Keywords
Member . . . :     VENDSRCH


Type choices, press Enter.


                                          Y=Yes
    General keywords  . . . . . . . .  _
    Indicator keywords . . . . . . .   Y
    Print keywords  . . . . . . . . .  _
    Help keywords . . . . . . . . . .  _
    Display sizes . . . . . . . . . .  _
    Alternate keywords  . . . . . . .  _
    DBCS conversion . . . . . . . . .  _
    Window Borders  . . . . . . . . .  _
    Menu-bar keywords . . . . . . . .  _

F3=Exit    F4=Display Selected Keywords    F12=Cancel
```

Place a "Y" in the column marked "Indicator keywords" in the panel in Figure S-21 and press ENTER. You will get the *Define Indicator Keywords* panel in Figure S-22.

Figure S-22 Define Indicators Keywords

```
                         Define Indicator Keywords
    Record . . . :     VENDCTL

    Type keywords and parameters, press Enter.
      Conditioned keywords:        CFnn CAnn CLEAR PAGEDOWN/ROLLUP PAGEUP/ROLLDOWN
                                   HOME HELP HLPRTN
      Unconditioned keywords:      INDTXT VLDCMDKEY SETOF CHANGE

    Keyword    Indicators/+ Resp Text
    CF03       __ __ __      99  END OF JOB_____
    _____     __ __ __      __  _____
    _____     __ __ __      __  _____
    _____     __ __ __      __  _____
    _____     __ __ __      __  _____
    _____     __ __ __      __  _____
    _____     __ __ __      __  _____
    _____     __ __ __      __  _____
                                                                    Bottom
    F3=Exit    F12=Cancel
```

Fill in the information for CF03 to turn on indicator 99 and provide the text *"END OF JOB."* Press ENTER three times to return to the *Work with Display Records* panel, last shown in Figure S-20.

Exiting SDA, Creating Display File

Now, you should be able to get this thing cooked. Let's get it done. When you are finished tuning all the panels, return to the Work with Display Records panel again, as shown in Figure S-20.

From the panel in Figure S-20, let's create our display file by hitting F3 and working through SDA exit beginning with the panel as shown in Figure S-23.

Figure S-23 SDA Exit Panel - Create Display File

```
                    Save DDS - Create Display File

Type choices, press Enter.

    Save DDS source  . . . . . . . . . . .    Y           Y=Yes
       Source file  . . . . . . . . . . . .   QDDSSRC     F4 for list
          Library  . . . . . . . . . . . . .  HELLO       Name, *LIBL ...
       Member . . . . . . . . . . . . . . .   VENDSRCH    F4 for list
       Text . . . . . . . . . . . . . . . .   ***


    Create display file  . . . . . . . . .    Y           Y=Yes
       Prompt for parameters  . . . . . . .               Y=Yes
       Display file . . . . . . . . . . . .   VENDSRCH    F4 for list
          Library  . . . . . . . . . . . . .  HELLO       Name, *CURLIB
       Replace existing file  . . . . . . .   Y           Y=Yes

    Submit create job in batch . . . . . .    Y           Y=Yes

    Specify additional
       save or create options . . . . . .                Y=Yes

F3=Exit    F4=Prompt    F12=Cancel
```

Fill the panel in as above, and hit the ENTER key twice to save the DDS and to create the Display File. You will then be brought back to the Design Screens panel, as shown in Figure S-24

Figure S-24 Design Screens Panel

```
                         Design Screens

    Type choices, press Enter.

        Source file . . . . . . . .    QDDSSRC     Name, F4 for list

           Library . . . . . . . . .    HELLO      Name, *LIBL, *CURLIB

        Member  . . . . . . . . . .    VENDSRCH    Name, F4 for list



    F3=Exit      F4=Prompt      F12=Cancel
```

From the Design Screens panel in Figure S-24, you have the opportunity to make the great escape. Press F3 to get to the main SDA panel as shown in Figure S-25.

Figure S-25 SDA Main Panel

```
                        AS/400 Screen Design Aid (SDA)

    Select one of the following:

         1. Design screens
         2. Design menus
         3. Test display files



    Selection or command
    ===>
   _____

    F1=Help    F3=Exit    F4=Prompt    F9=Retrieve    F12=Cancel
```

Checking DDS

If you take F3, in Figure S-25, you will be officially out of SDA temporarily. Take the chance and leave for a while.

Figure S-26 DDS For Subfile

```
0001.00    A*%%TS  SD  20020618  200627  BKELLY     REL-V5R1M0  5722-WDS
0002.00    A*%%EC
0003.00    A                                         DSPSIZ(24 80 *DS3)
0004.00    A           R VENSUB                       SFL
0005.00    A*%%TS  SD  20020618  200627  BKELLY     REL-V5R1M0  5722-WDS
0006.00    A             FLD002        5S 00   9 13
0007.00    A             FLD003       25A  O   9 24
0008.00    A             FLD004        2A  O   9 51
0009.00    A             FLD005        9Y 00   9 57EDTCDE(J)
0010.00    A           R VENDCTL                      SFLCTL(VENSUB)
0011.00    A*%%TS  SD  20020618  183003  BKELLY     REL-V5R1M0  5722-WDS
0012.00    A   81                                     SFLDSP
0013.00    A   81                                     SFLDSPCTL
0014.00    A   88                                     SFLINZ
0015.00    A  N81                                     SFLCLR
0016.00    A                                          SFLSIZ(0500)
0015.00    A  N81                                     SFLCLR
0016.00    A                                          SFLSIZ(0500)
0017.00    A                                          SFLPAG(0010)
0018.00    A   98                                     SFLMSG('INVALID VENDOR NUMB
0019.00    A                                       3 30'VENDOR MASTER INQUIRY'
0020.00    A                                       3 55'TT:TT:TT'
0021.00    A                                       3 64'DD/DD/DD'
0022.00    A                                       5 11'ENTER STARTING VENDOR NO:'
0023.00    A                                       5 54'F3=  END OF JOB'
0024.00    A                                       7 11'VENDOR NO.   VENDOR NAME'
0025.00    A                                       7 49'STATE    BALANCE OWED'
0026.00    A             FLD001        5  0I   5 39
```

If you followed the instructions in the tutorial, you will have five field names to change with SEU. We did not use the database option with the subfile as we did in the General SDA QuikCourse. However, we can change the field names with SEU while we look at the job SDA did for us.

Change Field Names with SEU

To get it done, go into PDM, and select VENDSRCH from PDM, using the SEU option 2. You are about to change the fields with SEU. It's easier than going through SDA again. Additionally, it shows the work that the SDA tool has done. See Figure S-26.

Figure S-26 shows all of the DDS source, which SDA just built for us. The generic field names built in the source code are displayed below. Across from each of these "fake" names, is the name you are to change the source to. Just roll through SEU until you see the source code and make the changes as noted below:

Statement Number Name	SDA Field Field Name	Real
6.	FLD002	VNDNBR
7.	FLD003	NAME
8.	FLD004	STATE
9.	FLD005	BALOWE
26.	FLD001	VENDNO

Final Steps to Execution

Now, that you have made the changes, you can exit SEU. Then, you can use option 14 of PDM to compile your new file. Since the file has changed, to avoid a level check, you should also recompile the RPG program.

Running the Subfile Program

When it is all compiled, find a command entry panel. Assure that HELLO is in your library list. Type CALL VENDSRCH and press ENTER. You will immediately get a panel similar to that in Figure S-27.

Figure S-27 Running the VENDSRCH Program - Input

```
                          VENDOR MASTER INQUIRY      23:46:33
 6/19/02

        ENTER STARTING VENDOR NO:        10           F3=  END OF JOB

        VENDOR NO.    VENDOR  NAME                STATE    BALANCE OWED
          00000                                                    .00
          00000                                                    .00
          00000                                                    .00
          00000                                                    .00
          00000                                                    .00
          00000                                                    .00
          00000                                                    .00
          00000                                                    .00
          00000                                                    .00
          00000                                                    .00
```

As you can see in Figure S-27, there is a little editing which we can
do on the first panel to prevent the zeros from showing. We'll do that
another day. When you type the number 10, as the vendor number,
you will set the panel to the first key since the lowest key in the file is
25. When you hit ENTER, you will get the filled subfile page as
shown in Figure S-28. At this point, the program has disconnected
from the display file. The display file is now in control.

Figure S-28 VENDSRCH Program - First Panel Output

```
                    VENDOR MASTER INQUIRY    23:47:56  6/19/02

   ENTER STARTING VENDOR NO:                      F3=  END OF JOB

   VENDOR NO.    VENDOR   NAME                STATE   BALANCE OWED

        00025    A MACHINE CORP.               IL       7,500.00
        00026    B MACHINERY                   OK       1,495.55
        00028    C ENGRAVING CO                IL         100.00
        00030    D CONTROLS                    IL         900.25
        00032    I POWER EQUIPMENT             PA         250.00
        00034    ROBIN   COMPANY               PA         153.00
        00036    F STEEL CO                    PA         290.00
        00038    J B COMPANY                   PA         100.00
        00040    SCRANTON INC                  PA         250.00
        00042    PASS PAX INC                  PA         300.00
```

Roll the Subfile

See how nice the panel looks in Figure S-28 for this simple inquiry
display file case study. Since the program and file are disconnected,
and we did not code for ROLL or Paging keys in the display or
program, let's test the subfile notion by giving it a ROLL. When you
roll forward, since the sample file has just fourteen records, the panel
which we get on the first roll has the last four records from
VENDMAST displayed.

Figure S-29 VENDSRCH Program - Roll Panel Output

```
                    VENDOR MASTER INQUIRY    23:47:56
 6/19/02

    ENTER STARTING VENDOR NO:   _____       F3=  END OF JOB

    VENDOR NO.    VENDOR   NAME               STATE   BALANCE OWED

         00044    J B EQUIP INC               PA          50.00
         00046    K D BUTTS WALLACE INC       PA         500.00
         00048    DENTON AND BALL             PA       3,500.00
         00049    JOHN STUDIOS                PA         325.00
```

Changing the Displayed Subfile?

If we had coded the subfile record using input rather than output type
fields, then we would be able to type over any of the fields shown,

and the subfile could be changed in disconnected mode. There are no underlines on the panel other than the starting vendor input field. Therefore, on this panel, there will be no alteration of the memory file.

Ending it!

To end our program, it is quite simple. You may recall that we coded the F3 command key at the file level. This means that it does not matter whether we are in disconnected mode or we are accepting more input. We can end the program from either the subfile record or the subfile control record. Let's press F3 now and get out of town.

At this point, you would return to the command screen from which you started the VENDSRCH program.

Summary and Conclusions.

You can't help liking subfiles. They are powerful, exciting, and they save lots of time and effort for a common and necessary function. Whether the objective is inquiry, mass file updates, or even data entry, there is a subfile program out there just waiting to be written. Enjoy!

QuikCourse B.   AS/400 and IBM i Work Management

Part I: What is Work Management?

Thought you'd never ask!   The idea of how an AS/400 gets its work done is cleverly referred to as Work Management. To navigate around an AS/400, it helps to have a basic idea of how it goes about getting its work done. Operating System/400, a.k.a. OS/400 is the AS/400 and IBM i component that brings you the notion of work management.

Work management is the topic that answers the question: "How do it do it?" There is lots to it, but it is all understandable. After this QuikCourse, you should be smart enough, if you are not already, to be one lesson away from being dangerous. More importantly, you'll be able to share with your friends your work management quips, and your answers to their work management questions. Of course your quips and answers will all end in: "...and that's how it do it!"

> ☺Note: Originally, this course was presented as one big chapter. It was also slotted to be placed as the second QuikCourse in this book. However, because of its length, and because it is an advanced topic, the readers recommended, in the beta review, that it be placed at the end of the book. They also suggested that it be broken into smaller "chapters" to make it digestible in smaller chunks.

Same on All Models

If you closely examine all AS/400 system models, regardless of how many processors they may have, from the smallest model 250 to the largest Power4 model 890 Regatta – the behemoth mainframe IBM i, you will see that they basically get all their work done in the same way. Of course the bigger machines get more done in the same period, but all systems run the same operating system code - OS/400.

There is a simple underlying assumption regarding the way work gets done on the AS/400 (a.k.a. Work Management). When the system can handle all of the work in total, one particular type of work, should not cripple the system's ability to perform other work by "hogging" system resources.

Work Management then, is a term used for how the AS/400 or IBM i manages the work (also called Jobs) which runs in the system. This includes the active allocation of memory, processor, and other system resources to specific activities called processes or threads, as necessary.

What Runs Where?

Everything must run some place. The work management rules on AS/400 and the configuration you establish, determine what work runs where, when it runs, and how well it runs, when it runs, compared to all other competing work on the system. If there is no competing work on the system, there is little need for work management. It is the big impresario of a big balancing act. How well it does its job often determines how pleased you are with the performance of your system.

Work management depends upon a number of object types, which we will discuss, and in fact create in this QuikCourse. The king of work management objects is designed specifically to split up the system's resources in a meaningful way. Its function is in its name, *Subsystem*. Objects such as user profiles, which we discuss first, as well as job queues, output queues, classes, and job descriptions, all have a role in work management. By the time you finish this QuikCourse, you will be introduced to them all. In fact, some may even become your friends.

Navigating the AS/400

Since you may wish to use this QuikCourse in somewhat of a tutorial fashion, it helps to know the easiest ways to **walk** around inside of the system. Hold off on the **run** for just awhile! As a developer, once you sign on to an AS/400, depending on how your system administrator has set up your profile, you will probably see a standard AS/400 panel such as the AS/400 Main Menu or the Program Development Manager (PDM) menu. In either case, unless your administrator specifically locks you out from being able to type in system commands (an option in the user profile object), when you sign on, you should see a two-line area at the bottom of the screen with a heading that says:

Selection or command

We'll operate in this QuikCourse as if you have been granted the appropriate authority from your system administrator. It's time to give it a run. Sign on, to your AS/400 now. Hopefully, you will see a command line as in the main AS./400 menu as shown in Figure B-1

Getting a Command Line

If you do not see a command line as in Figure B-1, and you cannot get authority to execute this course on your shop's AS/400, you can still gain by taking this course using the book. However, you will have to envision what happens by following the screen sequences and the instructions in this QuikCourse.

> ☺ **Hint: For this QuikCourse, you should ask your administrator to give you special security officer power for the duration of the course. Life would be much easier for you, and you would actually be able to learn more if you can follow along by doing.   If you are the security officer, but you are still an AS/400 neophyte just be careful since you can mess up your AS/400 using the commands we show you in this course.**

Figure B-1, AS/400 Main Menu With Command Line(s)

```
MAIN                        OS/400 Main Menu
                                            System:   HELLO
Select one of the following:

     1. User tasks
     2. Office tasks
     3. General system tasks
     4. Files, libraries, and folders
     5. Programming
     6. Communications
     7. Define or change the system
     8. Problem handling
     9. Display a menu
    10. Information Assistant options
    11. Client Access/400 tasks
90. Sign off
    Selection or command
===>WRKUSRPRF
_____
F3=Exit    F4=Prompt    F9=Retrieve    F12=Cancel    F13=Info Assistant
F23=Set initial menu                                              ©)
COPYRIGHT IBM CORP. 1980, 2000
```

☺ **Tip: Ideally, you should be using a test machine. Then, you will
not have a system integrity risk factor. Since we have been
discussing ways that you may be excluded from hands-on
participation in this course, before we cover the objects which are
typically associated with Work Management, let's first look at one
of the most powerful objects involved in the process - the user
profile. If you have been excluded, the shut-off valve for your
activity was applied in your user profile. The user profile is your
gate as to whether and how you get your work done on the AS/400.
In many ways it is the prime mover.**

Part II: The Work Mgt. User Profile

Looking at the User Profile

One of the key work objects on your AS/400 is the user profile
(*USRPRF object). Without a user profile, you simply don't get in.
Without a password for your user profile, you don't get in. Without
authority to perform protected or restricted functions, you don't get
to do them. Without entries such as a functional job description, a
menu, a startup program, and proper coding for a number of other
powerful parameters, you don't get operational flexibility. With a
well-shaped user profile, however, you are afforded many benefits as
an AS/400 or IBM i user. It's an important object.

Again. If you don't have a profile with enough capability, and you have been shut off from full access, you can follow-along in the text. Let's first look at a user profile object in detail so that you know why it is so powerful. Once you are sure you have a command line, type in the following command as shown in Figure B-1:

WRKUSRPRF *ALL

Then Press ENTER. You will be taken to a panel, which looks very similar to the one in Figure B-2. If you are following along on your own machine, when you get a panel similar to Figure B-2, you can look up your own profile name, rather than "ARETHAF," among the many profiles you will see in the list. Use the Roll keys or Page Up and Page Down keys to traverse the list.

Figure B-2 Work With User Profiles

```
                        Work with User Profiles
                                    Type options, press Enter.
    1=Create    2=Change    3=Copy    4=Delete    5=Display
    12=Work with objects by owner

       User
Opt    Profile     Text

  2    AREFRAN     Aretha Frankspin
  _    AMMCGIN     Amy McGin - Accounting Dept
  _    APGL        AP/GL for Amy McGin
  _    AMYLETT     Amy Letts  - IT Dept - Operations
  _    ANGEDICK    Angie Dickinson- Order Entry Dept
  _    ANGELL      Angel Lollonip-- Night Shift
  _    ANITASO     Anita Soleman - Order Entry Dept
  _    ANHEUSER    Bud Man II
  _    FROG        FROG USER PROFILE
                                                        More...
Parameters for options 1, 2, 3, 4 and 5 or command
===>
F3=Exit    F5=Refresh    F12=Cancel    F16=Repeat pos. to    F17=Position
F21=Select assistance level            F24=More keys
```

Check Out Your Own Profile

Place a "2" next to any user's profile or your own profile, in the panel
shown in Figure B-2. Pick the profile you want to change, and press
ENTER. You will receive a panel similar to the panel in Figure B-3
for the user you have selected.

Figure B-3 Change User Profile Command Initial Parameters

```
                    Change User Profile (CHGUSRPRF)
Type choices, press Enter.

User profile . . . . . . . . . . > ARETHAF        Name
User password  . . . . . . . . .   *SAME          Character value,*SAME,*NONE
Set password to expired  . . . .   *NO            *SAME, *NO, *YES
Status . . . . . . . . . . . . .   *DISABLED      *SAME, *ENABLED, *DISABLED
User class . . . . . . . . . . .   *USER          *SAME, *USER, *SYSOPR...
Assistance level . . . . . . . .   *SYSVAL        *SAME, *SYSVAL, *BASIC...
Current library  . . . . . . . .   STARS          Name, *SAME, *CRTDFT
Initial program to call  . . . .   STARSMN        Name, *SAME, *NONE
  Library  . . . . . . . . . .     STARS          Name, *LIBL, *CURLIB
Initial menu . . . . . . . . . .   *SIGNOFF       Name, *SAME, *SIGNOFF
  Library  . . . . . . . . . .                    Name, *LIBL, *CURLIB
Limit capabilities . . . . . . .   *YES           *SAME, *NO, *PARTIAL, *YES
Text 'description' . . . . . . .   'Aretha Frankspin'
                                                             Bottom
F3=Exit    F4=Prompt    F5=Refresh    F10=Additional parameters  F12=Cancel
F13=How to use this display           F24=More keys
```

For new AS/400 developers, there are lots of insights, which can be
gained by examining the user profile object. Even for us old timers,
IBM keeps adding items to the object and thus, the shape of the
profile object we may have in our memories, may not be the shape of
the object today or tomorrow. Therefore, it is worthwhile to take a

look at the user profile object from time to time, since a capability that was not there yesterday, may very well be there tomorrow.

With more and more users on Version 5 of OS/400, and with all the additions since Version 1 (1988), there's certainly lots to see. Considering the user profile object was first built for the System/38's announcement in 1978, over the years the original object has had plenty of time to grow in power, function, and completeness.

Roll For More

There are far too many parameters in the user profile object for just one screen snapshot, such as that in Figure B-3. To get to the rest, press F10 (*Additional Parameters*) and you can roll through all of them. Give it a try. You will see the many settings contained within the user profile object. If you don't want to do that right now, that's OK. We did it for you already – on our machine. In fact, we took all of the subsequent roll panels together, and made one oversized amalgamated panel from them. Don't expect to find a display on your system with this many lines. If you did, it would look like the "panel" shown in Figure B-4.

Figures B-3 and B-4 together represent the totality of the user profile object. As we explain some of the more significant parameters in the profile, we will refer to both of the panels as shown in Figures B-3 and B-4.

Figure B-4 Amalgamation of Additional CHGUSRPRF Parameters

```
                        Additional Parameters

Special authority  . . . . . . .      *SPLCTL        *SAME, *USRCLS, *NONE...
            + for more values
Special environment  . . . . . .      *NONE          *SAME, *SYSVAL, *NONE, *S36
Display sign-on information  . .      *SYSVAL        *SAME, *NO, *YES, *SYSVAL
Password expiration interval . .      *SYSVAL        1-366, *SAME, *SYSVAL, *NOMAX
Limit device sessions  . . . . .      *SYSVAL        *SAME, *NO, *YES, *SYSVAL
Keyboard buffering . . . . . . .      *SYSVAL        *SAME, *SYSVAL, *NO...
Maximum allowed storage  . . . .      *NOMAX         Kilobytes, *SAME, *NOMAX
Highest schedule priority  . . .      3              0-9, *SAME
Job description  . . . . . . . .      QDFTJOBD       Name, *SAME
   Library  . . . . . . . . . . .      QGPL           Name, *LIBL, *CURLIB
Group profile  . . . . . . . . .      STARG          Name, *SAME, *NONE
Owner  . . . . . . . . . . . . .      *GRPPRF        *SAME, *USRPRF, *GRPPRF
Group authority  . . . . . . . .      *NONE          *SAME, *NONE, *ALL...
Group authority type . . . . . .      *PRIVATE       *PRIVATE, *PGP, *SAME
Supplemental groups  . . . . . .      *NONE          Name, *SAME, *NONE
            + for more values
Accounting code  . . . . . . . .      MUSIC
Document password  . . . . . . .      *SAME          Name, *SAME, *NONE
Message queue  . . . . . . . . .      ARETHAF        Name, *SAME, *USRPRF
   Library  . . . . . . . . . . .      QUSRSYS        Name, *LIBL, *CURLIB
Delivery . . . . . . . . . . . .      *NOTIFY        *SAME, *NOTIFY, *BREAK...
Severity code filter . . . . . .      0              0-99, *SAME
Print device . . . . . . . . . .      *WRKSTN        Name, *SAME, *WRKSTN, *SYSVAL
Output queue . . . . . . . . . .      *WRKSTN        Name, *SAME, *WRKSTN, *DEV
   Library  . . . . . . . . . . .                     Name, *LIBL, *CURLIB
Attention program  . . . . . . .      *SYSVAL        Name, *SAME, *SYSVAL...
   Library  . . . . . . . . . . .                     Name, *LIBL, *CURLIB
Sort sequence  . . . . . . . . .      *SYSVAL        Name, *SAME, *SYSVAL, *HEX...
   Library  . . . . . . . . . . .                     Name, *LIBL, *CURLIB
Language ID  . . . . . . . . . .      *SYSVAL        *SAME, *SYSVAL...
Country ID . . . . . . . . . . .      *SYSVAL        *SAME, *SYSVAL...
Coded character set ID . . . . .      *SYSVAL        *SAME, *SYSVAL, *HEX...
Character identifier control . .      *SYSVAL        *SAME, *SYSVAL, *DEVD...
Locale job attributes  . . . . .      *SYSVAL        *SAME, *SYSVAL, *NONE...
            + for more values
Locale . . . . . . . . . . . . .      *SAME

User options . . . . . . . . . .      *NONE          *SAME, *NONE, *CLKWD...
            + for more values
User ID number . . . . . . . . .      754            1-4294967294, *SAME
Group ID number  . . . . . . . .      *NONE          1-4294967294, *SAME, *GEN...
Home directory . . . . . . . . .      *SAME
                                                                   Bottom
F3=Exit   F4=Prompt   F5=Refresh   F12=Cancel   F13=How to use this display
F24=More keys
```

User Profile Object

From top to bottom in Figure B-3, you can see that ARETHAF's password is not expired, but it is disabled. Profiles get disabled by the security officer, or after an administrator-specified excessive number of invalid signon attempts. The number is set by the security officer and is stored in the system value named *QMAXSIGN*. On a new AS/400, this value is typically set to 3. It should be set low so that hackers do not have all day to crack into your system by guessing your profile and password by programmed retries.

> ☺Hint: To follow along on your AS/400, each time we provide a system value for you to learn. Go look at it on your system. If you are on a production box, please do not change it. You can affect operations negatively by "messing" with system values. Rather than using the *work with system values* command (WRKSYSVAL) which permits you to change values, each time we show a nice juicy system value, substitute the name of the value for QMAXSIGN as in the following: DSPSYSVAL QMAXSIGN. Type the command on a command line, press ENTER, and look at how your system is set.

User Class

This is another important parameter. You get to choose the general type of user authority that you would like the user profile to possess. With this parameter, you specify whether the type of user associated with this user profile is a security officer, security administrator, programmer, system operator, or a plain old user.

Based on the user class value, different classes of users will see different options on their IBM menus. For a user to receive all of the authority that IBM believes should be given to a user of a particular class, you need to make sure that you specify the special authority parameter (SPCAUT) in Figure B-4 as *USRCLS.

Assistance Level

The next parameter shown in Figure B-3, for the profile is Assistance Level. Based on a selection of *BASIC, *Intermediate, or *Advanced, this user either gets lots of information and help on   the system panels for a given function, a modest amount, or very little. Most shops default this to the system value called QASTLVL, and most system values are set to an intermediate help / assistance level.

Current-Library

The next parameter is Current-Library. Each user, through their profile can be assigned a specific, possibly unique library that will always be accessible in the user's library search list. When the system is looking for the location of referenced objects (programs, files, queues, etc.), it will search the current library prior to any other libraries in the user library list.

Initial Program

The next parameter is the "Initial program to call (INLPGM)." This parameter specifies a startup program for the user profile. This enables the same or a different program to be called for each user at the time the user signs on, to an interactive job. This program is often used to tailor the user's operating environment and begin the user's primary application.

Initial Menu

The next parameter is the "Initial Menu" parameter. The AS/400 uses a menu object to provide lists of options to users. From the menu, the user selects various options to perform certain functions, such as application programs (Payroll, A/R, etc.) The initial menu allows the system administrator to tailor each user's profile so that they will be presented with an initial menu that reflects the type of work in which they are engaged.

Limited Capabilities

The next parameter is the one, which may have originally prevented you from getting a command line as we discussed above. The "Limited Capabilities" parameter in the user profile specifies whether the user can run commands from a command line. If you could not run commands from the command line, this parameter was set to *YES.

Lots of Tuning Available in User Profile

As you can see in the amalgamation panel in Figure B-4, there are lots of other knobs and switches and bells and whistles that you can control from the user profile object. This is a critical element in managing the system– a. k. a.   Work Management.

Before you leave the amalgamation in Figure B-4, go down about 1/4 through the parameters. Take a look at Job Description parameter. The job description object itself will be explained later. For now, make a note to yourself that there is a job description in the user profile, and it is a major source of execution attributes for a user at signon. You will see, as we go on to explain how a job is routed, that the routing data parameter in the job description referenced in the user profile has a major role in job initiation.

To learn more about any of the parameters in the amalgamation, when you are working with your AS/400, position your cursor to a given parameter and hit F1 or the HELP key. You will get a ton of text explaining the item you have selected.

Part III: Work Management Objects - Subsystems

Checking Out the QINTER Subsystem

We all know from QuikCourse A that the AS/400 is an object-based system. When a particular item has a particular purpose, it is fashioned as a system object for cross system uses. There are six objects, including the user profile object, along with a number of object attributes that are used in the work management process. These object types are highlighted and briefly explained in the list below. This list is followed by another list of object attributes that are also very important to the notion of work management.

After each object or attribute is briefly explained, we supply the commands necessary for you to look at an IBM supplied object of that type. For this exercise, we have chosen the QINTER subsystem and its associated set of objects, since QINTER is supplied by IBM, and it is not a complicated subsystem. If your system uses IBM's QBASE for interactive work, rather than QINTER, feel free to substitute QBASE for QINTER in the representative commands.

Subsystem Description Object

A Subsystem Description is an AS/400 object (*SBSD type) used to allocate systems resources among various types of workloads. The basic work element in the system is a job. Jobs run in subsystems. No job runs outside a subsystem. An interactive job is initiated when a user signs on, and is terminated when the user signs off. A batch job is submitted to a job queue (holding area) until it is first in line. It is then selected for execution and runs until it ends. Batch jobs typically end when a file reaches a point in which there are no more records to read, or a trigger code is read which tells the program to begin termination.

Subsystem descriptions hold many attributes, which govern, or facilitate the execution of jobs in one way or another. These include the attribute types in Table B-1:

Table B-1 Subsystem Attributes

Attribute	Description
Operational attributes:	Maximum jobs, signon display file, etc.
Pool Definitions:	Shared and private pool definitions and activity levels
Autostart Job Entries:	Work entries to start jobs when susbsystem is started.
Work Station Name Entries:	Specific or generic terminals to run in the subsystem
Work Station Type Entries:	Terminal types to run in subsystem - 3197, *cons, etc.
Job Queue Entries:	Job Queue objects attached to this subsystem, to run jobs
Routing Entries:	Used in job initiation to give a job a memory pool, class, etc.
Communications Entries:	Entries which enable SNA jobs to start in subsystem
Remote Location Name Entries:	Location attributes for communications entries
Prestart Job Entries:	Used to speed up program start requests

The best command to display a subsystem to show all that it contains is the display subsystem description (DSPSBSD) command as follows:

DSPSBSD QINTER

When you type this command and hit ENTER, the Display Subsystem Description menu then appears as in Figure B-6A.

Because a subsystem is a collection of attributes and entries, and to show them all at once, would be overwhelming, OS/400 presents this menu of options (Figure B-6A) for you. In order for you to gain a better appreciation of what is in a subsystem, we recommend that you take each of these options on your own system. If there are elements, within the panels, that you do not understand, and you would like more information, press the HELP key on your terminal or F1 on your PC to get the Help text that explains the item.

Figure B-6A Ten Parts to a Subsystem

```
                        Display Subsystem Description
                                                    System:    S103LR7M
 Subsystem description:    QINTER          Library:   QSYS
 Status:    INACTIVE

 Select one of the following:

      1. Operational attributes
      2. Pool definitions
      3. Autostart job entries
      4. Work station name entries
      5. Work station type entries
      6. Job queue entries
      7. Routing entries
      8. Communications entries
      9. Remote location name entries
     10. Prestart job entries

                                                             More...
 Selection or command
 ===>



 F3=Exit    F4=Prompt    F9=Retrieve    F12=Cancel
```

To get a good feel for this very important work management object, we will examine each of these QINTER options in the following section. While we are covering these ten parts of a subsystem, we will also show how the object behind the entry (if there is one) was created, and how it was added to the subsystem. For now, take option 1 from the menu and press ENTER. You will see a panel similar to that in Figure B-6B.

Figure B-6B Operational Attributes

```
                        Display Operational Attributes
                                                    System:
 S103LR7M
  Subsystem description:    QINTER            Status:    INACTIVE

  Subsystem description  . . . . . . . . :    QINTER
    Library  . . . . . . . . . . . . . :    QSYS
  Maximum jobs in subsystem  . . . . . . :    *NOMAX
  Sign-on display file . . . . . . . . . :    QDSIGNON
    Library  . . . . . . . . . . . . . :    QSYS
  System library list entry  . . . . . . :    *NONE


  Press Enter to continue.

  F3=Exit    F12=Cancel
```

Operational Attributes

By looking at the attributes in the panel shown in Figure B-6B, the first thing you may notice is that the subsystem does not limit the amount of work that can be processed at once (*NOMAX). The other piece of information that is important here is that the QDSIGNON display file in QSYS is established as the sign on screen panel for the subsystem. The source code for this display panel is available in the QDDSSRC file in the QGPL library. By modifying the source, and re-creating this file, you can have a customized signon display panel for the QINTER subsystem.

After reviewing this panel, take option 2 from the main subsystem menu to look at the subsystem pool allocations. You will see a panel similar to that in Figure B-6C.

Figure B-6C Display Pool Definitions

```
                        Display Pool Definitions
                                                        System:
S103LR7M
  Subsystem description:   QINTER          Status:    INACTIVE

  Pool         Storage       Activity
   ID          Size (K)      Level
    1             *BASE
    2          *INTERACT
    3          *SHRPOOL2


Bottom
 Press Enter to continue.

 F3=Exit    F12=Cancel
```

Pool Definitions

As you can see in the panel shown in Figure B-6C, there are three pools defined in this subsystem description object. They are known as subsystem pools 1, 2, and 3 respectively. Each subsystem pool happens to be assigned to a shared pool. Subsystem pools 1, 2, and 3, are assigned to the shared pools, *BASE, *INTERACT, and SHRPOOL2, respectively.

After reviewing this panel, take option 3 from the subsystem menu to look at the Autostart Job Entries. You will see a panel similar to that in Figure B-6D.

Figure B-6D Autostart Job Entries

```
                     Display Autostart Job Entries
                                                      System:
S103LR7M
Subsystem description:    QINTER          Status:    INACTIVE

Job            Job Description      Library

   (No autostart job entries)



Bottom
Press Enter to continue.

F3=Exit    F12=Cancel
```

Autostart Job Entries

As you can see in the panel shown in Figure B-6D, there are no
Autostart Job Entries in the QINTER subsystem. So that you can see
what one of these entries looks like, we copied an entry from QCTL,
the controlling subsystem, as shown immediately below:

Job   Job Description

QSTRUPJD   QSTRUPJD   QSYS

If you are a programmer, you may be wondering where the CALL
statement is. There is none. However, an Autostart Job Entry does
provide a spot that lets you specify a job description. In this case, the
job description name is QSTRUPJD and it is in the QSYS library.
IBM created all of the programs that get called when this job
description fires up. You can retrieve the CL source for the main
startup program (QSTRUPJ in QSYS) using the RTVCLSRC
command if you want to customize your signon panel.

In order to use an Autostart Job Entry for a program that you want to
start, each time the system comes up, you must first get the program
working. Then, you create a job description and specify the CALL
program name in the Command section of the job description. When
that is complete, you invoke the *Add Autostart Job Entry* command to
place the entry in the QINTER subsystem. Use the following
command to accomplish this:

ADDAJE SBSD(QINTER) JOB(MYSTART) JOBD(HELLO/MYSTART)

In this command, the name of the job is MYSTART, and the program we wrote is called MYSTART. It is located in the HELLO library.

When you have your Autostart Job Entry completed, from the main subsystem menu, pick option 4 to look at the Workstation Name Entries. You will see a panel similar to that in Figure B-6E.

Figure B-6E   Display Work Station Name Entries

```
                    Display Work Station Name Entries
                                                      System:
S103LR7M
Subsystem description:   QINTER        Status:    INACTIVE

Type options, press Enter.
  5=Display work station name details

Opt  Name           Opt  Name          Opt  Name          Opt  Name
 __   BRIAN*




Bottom
F3=Exit    F9=Display all detailed descriptions    F12=Cancel
```

Workstation Name Entries

What is a workstation entry? Quite simply, it is a flag and a little piece of information that get added to the subsystem description. It enables the subsystem to perform interactive work. Additionally, it specifies the names or types of the devices that are presented signon screens from the subsystem.

The QINTER subsystem comes from IBM with no workstation entries. An interactive subsystem cannot be built that has no Work Station Name or Type entries. Since QINTER definitely started with no Work Station Name Entries, when it arrived from IBM, as an interactive subsystem, you can only conclude that it must have

Workstation Type entries. Otherwise it would be incapable of interactive work.

We created a generic workstation name entry called BRIAN* in the QINTER subsystem, as shown in Figure B-6E. This means that any terminal device or emulated terminal device (Client Access), with a name that begins with B-R-I-A-N, will automatically be assigned to the QINTER subsystem at subsystem startup – if there are no name or type conflicts.

The device description does not have to be created for the entry to take. If a device description is created with that name, or its name has the first five letters of this generic entry, it will run in the QINTER subsystem. When it is varied on, it will get a signon screen from the QINTER subsystem.

Adding Generic and Specific Entries

Though we demonstrated a generic entry, if you do not put an "*" at the end, it becomes a specific name entry.   The two commands below add generic and specific workstation name entries respectively to the QINTER subsystem:

ADDWSE SBSD(QINTER) WRKSTN(BRIAN*)
JOBD(*USRPRF) MAXACT(*NOMAX) AT(*SIGNON)

ADDWSE SBSD(QINTER) WRKSTN(BRIANK)
JOBD(*USRPRF) MAXACT(*NOMAX) AT(*SIGNON)

If a device is created that is named BRIANK, and both of these name entries (generic and specific) have been added to the QINTER subsystem, the second is redundant. It is not needed. Any device starting with B-R-I-A-N is assigned to QINTER by the generic entry, so the BRIANK entry is not needed. However, if JOEMAC were substituted for BRIANK, it would take, and it would be useful.

A Note about Work Entries

When you create a subsystem, there is little value to it. You must add lots of stuff to make it a complete environment. The ADDWSE command stands for Add Workstation Entry. The entry types that we have added so far, are all work entries. So, can we conclude that work management needs work entries? Well, not exactly! Subsystems need work entries so they can be connected to their sources of work.

An *Autostart Job Entry* provides a vehicle to have work started in the subsystem before anybody signs on. A Workstation Name Entry gives a subsystem, such as QINTER, a means of doing interactive work. A subsystem with no workstation name or type entries, cannot have any workstations, real or virtual, attached to do interactive work.

Does this mean that all I have to do is add a valid workstation name or type entry to the QBATCH subsystem description, and it becomes an interactive subsystem? Yes, it does! However, there may be some other attributes that make QBATCH less than an ideal environment for interactive work, such as its memory pool designations and its execution attributes, such as priority and time slice end.

Are there more sources of work entries that we will be examining? Yes! These are shown in subsystem options 5, 6, 8, and 10.

For now, if you go back and take option 5 from the main subsystem menu, and you press ENTER, you can view the Workstation *Type* entries for QINTER as shown in Figure B-6F

Figure B-6F   Display Work Station Type Entries

```
                        Display Work Station Type Entries
                                                      System:    S103LR7M
Subsystem description:    QINTER          Status:   INACTIVE

Type options, press Enter.
  5=Display work station type details

Opt   Type             Opt   Type        Opt   Type            Opt   Type
      *CONS
 __   *ALL
 __


Bottom
F3=Exit    F9=Display all detailed descriptions    F12=Cancel
```

Workstation Type Entries

As you can see in Figure B-6F, there are two workstation types:
*ALL, and *CONS. The *ALL ENTRY means that all workstation
types will do their work in the QINTER subsystem. They will also
get their signon screen from this subsystem (QINTER). The types of
devices include devices with 5250, ASCII, and 327x device types.

The device type *CONS says that the system console can attach to
this subsystem. This entry overrides the *ALL or a device type entry
that specifies the same device type as the device being used as the
console.

Is there a conflict between the BRIAN* name entry and the *ALL
entry? From a user's perspective, the answer today is no! Both entries
place the device in the QINTER subsystem. Though it makes no
difference, it is redundant work. However, if later on, you move the
name to another system, there will be a conflict.

It would make a big difference if the *ALL were in QINTER, and we
put the BRIANK entry in another subsystem. IBM says that
unpredictable results will occur. Neither name nor type entries have
priority. If there are conflicting live subsystems, either subsystem may
get the device. I have seen situations in which the device will not
change subsystems. I have seen other situations, in which each
signoff, prompts a signon from the other subsystem to the device.

Creating a Type Entry

The way you would create the *ALL Workstation Type entry in the QINTER subsystem is as follows:

ADDWSE SBSD(QINTER) WRKSTNTYPE(*ALL)
JOBD(*USRPRF) MAXACT(*NOMAX) AT(*SIGNON)

Now, it's time to move on to the next item in the subsystem display menu, Display Job Queue Entries:

Figure B-6G Display Job Queue Entries

```
                        Display Job Queue Entries
                                                    System:
S103LR7M
  Subsystem description:    QINTER        Status:    INACTIVE

  Seq  Job                       Max    ---------Max by Priority----------
  Nbr  Queue      Library      Active   1   2   3   4   5   6   7   8   9
  10   QINTER     QGPL         *NOMAX   *   *   *   *   *   *   *   *   *
  20   QS36MRT    QGPL         *NOMAX   *   *   *   *   *   *   *   *   *



Bottom
Press Enter to continue.

F3=Exit    F12=Cancel
```

Job Queue Entries

As you can see in figure B-6G, there are two job queue entries in the QINTER subsystem. Just as Autostart Job Entries provide a means of automatically performing work in a subsystem at startup, and Work Station *Name and Type* Entries provide a vehicle for interactive work to be accomplished in a subsystem, a Job Queue Entry provides a way for regular batch work to be accomplished.

Before you can have a Job Queue Entry,, you must have a job queue object, created. As you can see in the panel in Figure B-6G, the QINTER job queue is in the QGPL library If you want to check the queue to see if there is anything in it, you can type the following Display Job Queue command and hit ENTER:

DSPJOBQ QINTER

The system checks the library list and finds the QINTER job queue object. The DSPJOBQ command then peeks into the QINTER job queue container to see if anybody put a job in there, hoping it would execute someplace. Whether or not you have added a job queue entry, for a specific job queue object, to a subsystem, you can still submit jobs to it, and you can still display them from it. The job queue is an object independent of all subsystems. However, jobs in an unattached queue will not execute until you place a Job Queue Entry in a subsystem. A job queue becomes capable of feeding work to a subsystem when, and only when, a Job Queue Entry is added to a subsystem on its behalf.

Since there are no jobs that have been submitted recently to the QINTER subsystem, the DSPJOBQ command replies with a panel with one valuable piece of information:

$$\left(\text{No jobs in job queue} \right)$$

Creating a Job Queue Object

There are no jobs in the Queue. The command we would have used to create a job queue named QINTER in QGPL, would be as follows:

CRTJOBQ JOBQ(HELLO/QINTER) TEXT('QINTER Job Queue')

Submit Jobs to JobQ

Once the Job Queue is built, you can submit jobs to it using the SBMJOB command as follows:

SBMJOB CMD(DSPLIBL OUTPUT(*PRINT))
JOBQ(QGPL/QINTER)

Add Job Queue Entry to Subsystem

In order for a job queue to actually feed jobs to a subsystem, you must add it to the job queue entries of the subsystem, using the following Add Job Queue Entry command:

ADDJOBQE SBSD(QGPL/QINTER) JOBQ(QGPL/QINTER)

The QINTER Job Queue is attached to the subsystem, but, unless QINTER has routing entries, jobs will not be able to be initiated and routed for execution. Let's go back again and take option 7 from the Main Subsystem Menu to see if the QINTER subsystem has any routing entries. You will be taken to a panel that looks a lot like the one in Figure B-6H

Figure B-6H Display Routing Entries

```
                         Display Routing Entries
                                                       System:
S103LR7M
Subsystem description:    QINTER           Status:    INACTIVE

Type options, press Enter.
  5=Display details

Start
Opt    Seq Nbr    Program      Library      Compare Value        Pos
  _        10     QCMD         QSYS         'QCMDI'              1
  _        15     QCMD         QSYS         'QIGC'               1
  _        20     QCMD         QSYS         'QS36MRT'            1
  _        40     QARDRIVE     QSYS         '525XTEST'           1
  _       700     QCL          QSYS         'QCMD38'             1
  _      9999     QCMD         QSYS         *ANY

Bottom
F3=Exit    F9=Display all detailed descriptions    F12=Cancel
```

Subsystcm Routing Entries

I see routing entries. For each job that gets routed to a subsystem, a routing entry is selected from the routing table in the subsystem description. The selection is based mostly on information that comes from the   job description objects and SBMJOB commands. The routing entry that gets selected, matches the routing data that is provided. The entry then gives important execution parameters to the job. For example, from the routing entry, the job picks up its memory pool, and its *CLASS object, which gives it its execution priority.

If a job were routed to the first routing entry (#10) as in Figure B-6H, it would pick up the attributes associated with the detailed routing entry. You may ask: "What are these?" Well, Let's go see!

To look at the detailed routing entry, place a "5" next to the first entry as shown in Figure B-6H, and press ENTER. You will see the detailed routing entry as shown in the panel in Figure B-6I

Figure B-6I Display Routing Entry Detail

```
                          Display Routing Entry Detail
                                                      System:    S103LR7M
    Subsystem description:    QINTER         Status:    INACTIVE

    Routing entry sequence number . . . . . . . :    10
    Program . . . . . . . . . . . . . . . . . . :    QCMD
      Library . . . . . . . . . . . . . . . . . :      QSYS
    Class . . . . . . . . . . . . . . . . . . . :    QINTER
      Library . . . . . . . . . . . . . . . . . :      QGPL
    Maximum active routing steps  . . . . . . . :    *NOMAX
    Pool identifier . . . . . . . . . . . . . . :    2
    Compare value . . . . . . . . . . . . . . . :    'QCMDI'

    Compare start position  . . . . . . . . . . :    1


    Press Enter to continue.

    F3=Exit    F12=Cancel    F14=Display previous entry
```

Detailed Routing Entry

As you can see in Figure B-6I, this job will be routed to subsystem pool 2, it will be able to execute an unlimited number of steps, and it will use the QINTER class object to get more execution attributes, such as execution priority.

By the time a job is finished being routed through an entry such as this, it is in memory, and it is competing with other jobs for machine resources.

QINTER is QOK!

Now, we have verified that QINTER is a potentially functioning subsystem, since we have assured that it has had all the necessary ingredients added to the subsystem description object. The next three subsystem entries are not as important, but we will cover them briefly. When you complete item seven of the display subsystem menu, you really have seen all that matters. If you were building the QINTER subsystem, it would be as complete as you would want, since it does not need the last three entries.

Communications Entries - Option 8

There are no communications entries in QINTER. If you would like to see communications entries, you can display the QCMN or QBASE subsystems and take option 8. IBM pre-loads these subsystems with SNA entries so that IBM code, such as Client Access and Remote Support can function as intended. Now that the world has gone TCP/IP, the need for communications entries, will more than likely go away.

What you would see are the communications entries defined in the subsystem description by device name or by device type. For each one, you would be able to see the name of each device, the mode name, the job description used, the default user profile, and the maximum number of jobs allowed.

Remote Location Name Entries- Option 9

Again this is used for SNA communications. The Remote Location Name Entries display shows the communication entries defined in the subsystem description by remote location name vs. device. The information given is the name of each remote location (instead of the device name), the mode name, the job description used, the default user profile, and the maximum number of jobs allowed.

Prestart Job Entries - Option 10

Prestart jobs are typically communications jobs that are waiting to be used. By starting the jobs ahead of time, the wait time to make a connection is lessened, since the initial program does not have to be loaded . The display would shows the Prestart Job entries defined in the subsystem description. Each Prestart Job entry contains the program name, user profile, and other information that is needed by the subsystem to create and manage one pool of identical Prestart jobs.

The jobs are typically started when the subsystem is started, but there is a Start Prestart Jobs command (STRPJ) that can be used at any time. After it is pre-started, and waiting, the job is selected for execution, when an incoming request has a program name that matches the Prestart Job program name.

Now that we have examined all of the entries that make up a subsystem description, there are still a few more items to examine to complete our discussion of work management objects. Clearly, the subsystem, and all of its accouterments, is the most important work management object. Yet, work cannot get done by a subsystem alone. You need some other objects.

Part IV: Work Management Objects - Other Than Subsystems

Getting Class

Let's re-start our work management object discovery process with the *CLS object. During the subsystem section, the *CLS object appeared several times. Each time we treated it lightly, though it is a very important element in routing and job execution. Let's take a little deeper look this time.

Class: *CLS   Object

A Class is a work management object used to provide initial execution attributes to a job being initiated. During the job routing process, as a job is sent through the subsystems at initiation time, it picks up attributes from the CLASS object that is referenced in the subsystem detailed routing entry. The class attributes include priority, time slice, and memory purging characteristics. The importance of these in understanding work management is explained as you proceed through this QuikCourse.

To display the QINTER class, type the following and press ENTER:

DSPCLS QINTER

The elements included in the *CLS object are shown in the panel in Figure B-6J.

Figure B-6J Display Class

```
                    Display Class Information
                                              System:    S103LR7M
Class . . . . . . . . . . . . . . . . . . . . . :   QINTER
  Library . . . . . . . . . . . . . . . . . . . :     QGPL
Run priority  . . . . . . . . . . . . . . . . . :   20
Time slice in milliseconds  . . . . . . . . . . :   1000
Eligible for purge  . . . . . . . . . . . . . . :   *YES
Default wait time in seconds  . . . . . . . . . :   30
Maximum CPU time in milliseconds  . . . . . . . :   *NOMAX
Maximum temporary storage in megabytes  . . . . :   *NOMAX
Maximum threads . . . . . . . . . . . . . . . . :   *NOMAX
Text  . . . . . . . . . . . . . . . . . . . . . :   Interactive Subsystem Class
Press Enter to continue.
F3=Exit   F12=Cancel
```

Job Queue: *JOBQ Object

A Job Queue is an object that provides a holding area or waiting line for batch type jobs that you intended to execute in a subsystem. Interactive users' jobs and other batch jobs submit work *to job queues* for batch execution. The jobs wait in these queues or "waiting lines" until they move up to be first in line. Then they are selected for execution. The command which places a job in the job queue is called *submit job* or SBMJOB.

Other commands for job queues are as follows:

ADDJOBQE   Adds a job queue to a subsystem description. The queue assigned will then feed jobs to that particular subsystem.

CRTJOBQ   Creates a Job Queue

WRKJOBQ   Displays all job queues on the system in one-line format

WRKJOBQ (name)   Displays the jobs in the named job queue waiting to be executed

To display the QINTER job queue, type the following and press ENTER:

DSPJOBQ QINTER

Since there are no jobs right now in the QINTER job queue, the best you would get would be a message telling you that.

Output Queue: *OUTQ Object

An output queue is an object that provides a holding area for printouts produced by jobs while they are executing. The printouts remain in the queue until they are printed on a printer, or they are removed from the queue. Just like a job queue is a waiting line for jobs to run, an output queue is a waiting line for printouts from jobs that already ran. The print files in an output queue are waiting for a print writer to print them on a physical printer. The Print Writer or "Writer" as it is most often called, is the software driver that links the output queue to the printer.

IBM does not supply an output queue named QINTER in its standard definitions. There are a number of other standard output queues supplied, however. One is called QPRINT. Let's take a look at this output queue. Just as with the job queue display, when you issue the display command, it shows you the items in the queue that are waiting. In job queues, the items waiting are jobs. In output queues the items waiting are printouts.

To display the QPRINT output queue, type the following and press ENTER:

DSPOUTQ QPRINT

The meat of an output queue display for QPRINT is shown below:

```
File      User     User Data   Sts   Pages   Copies   Form Type   Pty
QSYSPRT   STEVES   DBPLSTPR    RDY     7        1      *STD         5
MSG0001P  QPGMR    MSG0001R    HLD     1        1      *STD         5
MSG0001P  QPGMR    MSG0001R    HLD     1        1      *STD         5
MSG0001P  DAVIDD   MSG0001R    HLD     1        1      *STD         5
```

Job Description: *JOBD Object

*Job Description: *JOBD*   A job description is a specific set of job-related attributes that can be used by one or more jobs.   The attributes determine how each job is run on the system.   The values in the job description are usually set as the default values of the corresponding parameters in the Batch Job (BCHJOB) and Submit Job(SBMJOB) commands when their parameters are not specified. They can also be overridden by these commands.

There are a number of important job parameters that are typically supplied by the job description. These include the Job Queue and Output Queue, as well as routing data, request data or command, library list, logging level, job switches, and many others.

I like to think of a job description as a container. It is like a cookie jar for job attributes. Using the job description name (the cookie jar itself) instead of supplying all of the attributes, one-by-one, makes it lots easier, and it saves a lot of work in getting jobs going.

The *COMMAND* parameter in the job description enables a command to be placed within a job description. If a *Submit Job (SBMJOB)* command does not specify a command, the AS/400 command in the COMMAND parameter of the job description is executed. Of course, it follows the normal route of going through a job queue prior to being dispatched for execution. A job description with a command specified is also the way you designate a command to execute within a subsystem auto-start job entry.

To display the QINTER job description, type the following and press ENTER:

DSPJOBD QINTER

The job description parameters in QINTER are as follows

```
User profile . . . . . . . . . . . . . . :   *RQD
CL syntax check  . . . . . . . . . . . :   *NOCHK
Hold on job queue  . . . . . . . . . :   *NO
End severity . . . . . . . . . . . . . :   30
Job date . . . . . . . . . . . . . . . :   *SYSVAL
Job switches . . . . . . . . . . . . . :   00000000
Inquiry message reply  . . . . . . . . :   *RQD
Job priority (on job queue)  . . . . . :   5
Job queue  . . . . . . . . . . . . . . :   QBATCH
   Library . . . . . . . . . . . . . . :      QGPL
Output priority (on output queue)  . . :   5
Printer device . . . . . . . . . . . . :   *USRPRF
Output queue . . . . . . . . . . . . . :   *USRPRF
   Library  . . . . . . . . . . . . . . :
Message logging:
   Level  . . . . . . . . . . . . . . . :   4
   Severity . . . . . . . . . . . . . . :   0
   Text . . . . . . . . . . . . . . . . :   *NOLIST
Log CL program commands  . . . . . . . :   *NO
Accounting code  . . . . . . . . . . . :   *USRPRF
Print text . . . . . . . . . . . . . . :   *SYSVAL

Routing data . . . . . . . . . . . . . :   QCMDI

Request data . . . . . . . . . . . . . :   *NONE

Device recovery action . . . . . . . . :   *SYSVAL
   Time slice end pool  . . . . . . . . :    *SYSVAL
Job message queue maximum size . . . . :   *SYSVAL
Job message queue full action  . . . . :   *SYSVAL
Allow multiple threads . . . . . . . . :   *NO
Text . . . . . . . . . . . . . . . . . :   Interactive etc.
```

User Profile: *USRPRF Object

*User Profile: *USRPRF:* The User Profile object identifies a user to the system. We have already exhaustively covered this object. Through attributes in the profile, you can customize the way the system appears to a user. Important attributes contained within a user profile include the user's password, default job description, group profile, authorities, startup programs and menus, library list, current library, output queue, message queue, home directory, etc. Many of these attributes, such as the routing data supplied by the referenced job description, are important for work management. See Figures B-3 and B-4 above.

Work Management Commands

You will learn in QuikCourse D about the CL command structure. Right now, it would help for a very brief introduction. We have been discussing work management objects. Later, we will specifically create some objects in order to demonstrate how this all works. For now, it is good to understand that all objects can be created, displayed, worked with, and deleted. If you take the three characters *CRT* for create, *DSP* for display, *WRK* for work with, and *DLT* for delete, and if you merge them with the object type, you have the commands for creating displaying, working with and deleting objects. Here is a sampling:

CRTJOBQ	Create Job Queue
DSPSBSD	Display Subsystem Description
WRKOUTQ	Work With Output Queue
DLTCLS	Delete a class

Other Definitions

Though the following items are not objects, it would help for us to have these items better defined as we discuss how work management objects can be used to help optimize your system.

Job

The basic work unit on the system is called a *job*. Thus, each piece of work on the system is performed in a job and each job has a unique name within the system. Jobs start and end. All jobs, with the exception of system jobs, run within subsystems. A job can enter the subsystem from any of the subsystem's work entries as described when we dissected the QINTER subsystem. Additionally, these entries are built from scratch and discussed in detail in the case study at the end of this QuikCourse. They are also listed as part of Table B-1.

The subsystem work entries, in review, consist of Job Queue Entries, Workstation Entries, Communications Entries, Autostart Job Entries, and Prestart Job Entries. No job enters an AS/400 subsystem without going through one of these work doors. The entries therefore provide a means for work, in the form of jobs, to be initiated within subsystems.

To display the current job, in which you are engaged, type the following and press ENTER:

DSPJOB *

When you think of all of the attributes a job pick up from the user profile to the job description, to the routing entry, to the class, it is no wonder that it takes two screen panels just for the DSPJOB menu. The following choices appear on the display job menu:

1. Display job status attributes
2. Display job definition attributes
3. Display job run attributes, if active
4. Display spooled files
10. Display job log, if active or on job queue
11. Display call stack, if active
12. Display locks, if active
13. Display library list, if active
14. Display open files, if active
15. Display file overrides, if active
16. Display commitment control status, if active
17. Display communications status, if active
18. Display activation groups, if active
19. Display mutexes, if active
20. Display threads, if active
21. Display media library attributes, if active
30. All of the above

Because a job is a collection of governing attributes, representing an execution environment, there is a lot to a job. You can see by the list above that a job has many parts. The system keeps track of them all within the job environment itself. Thankfully, like most things on the AS/400 and IBM i, you do not have to understand all of the pieces in order to be able to work with the whole. Very few professionals understand all of the job parts in the above list.

When you display a job, such as your job, OS/400 presents this menu of options for you. For educational purposes, to give you a better appreciation of what is in a job, we recommend that you take each of these options, and see what is behind each. If there are elements, within the panels, that you do not understand, as there will be, remember how to get Help. Press the Help key on your terminal or F1 on your PC to get the Help text that explains the item.

Library List

The library list is just one job attribute. It is picked up during job initiation (routing). As a job runs, the library list can be modified by the job itself. A common command used for changing a library list is the Change Library List command (CHGLIBL). However, there are a number of other commands that can be used to change the list.

The Add Library list entry command (ADDLIBLE), for example, adds one library to the list. The Remove Library List Entry command (RMVLIBLE) does just the opposite. It removes one library from the list.

For interactive users, the favorite library list command is the Edit Library List (EDTLIBL). Unlike the CHGLIBL, which, when run interactively, displays all of the libraries in the list, and permits you to change the list, the EDTLIBL produces a multi-column display of all the libraries in the list along with sequence numbers and empty slots to add entries. In addition to accommodating changes, additions, and removals to the list, this panel also provides a simple means, via sequence number, of re-sequencing the listed libraries.

A better term for a library list is *library search list* and it is somewhat analogous to a PC path. The list for a job can contain as many as 250 library names. To overtly specify that the list is to be used, rather than a single library, you can specify the special value *LIBL*, for *library list* as you would a single library name in a command. Of course, the default, when neither the *LIBL value, nor the name of a library is given in a command, is the job's library list.

The library search list is used when a job is looking for a particular object that is not qualified by its specific path (library). The system searches each of the libraries in the list for the object until it either finds it, or it completes searching all the libraries in the library list, without finding the object.

To display the library list for your job, type the following and press ENTER:

DSPLIBL

Up to 250 libraries can be in a library list. The following is a sample list from a live AS/400.

Library List:

Library	Type
MGDSYS	SYS
QSYS	SYS
QSYS2	SYS
QHLPSYS	SYS
QUSRSYS	SYS
MGDOBJ	USR
MGDDTA	USR
MGDSRF	USR
MGDS	USR
QSYS38	USR
QGPL	USR
QTEMP	USR
MGDSMODS	USR
QIWS	USR
WOFACE	USR
HELLO	USR
MGDGPL	USR
MGDCHK	USR
MGD2OBJ	USR
DBU60	USR

Part V: Job Routing

The Key to Understanding

The key to understanding how jobs get started, and how they run, is to understand routing. There are two big time attributes used in routing. One is called *routing data*. The other is called a *routing entry*. They have a key / lock relationship to each other.

Routing Data - The Key

Let's first examine the key and then we will study the locks. Routing data is provided as an attribute of a job description. For interactive jobs, IBM's job descriptions often provide a value of "QCMDI" as the routing data. This has no significance by itself. However, the five letters "QCMDI" are certainly shaped differently from the five letters "HGDVB." As five letter terms, they are not even close.

Try to envision *routing data* as the shape of a key that opens something. You would expect that a key shaped like "QCMDI" would open a different lock than a key shaped like "HGDVB." It certainly would.

Now, that you have the notion of a routing key, known as *routing data,* where does it come from? Where do you get this key? At job initiation, it is always supplied by the job description's routing data,

It just happens that the routing data attributes for the QINTER job description, which we discussed above, as shipped by IBM, looks exactly as the following:

Routing data . . . . . . :   QCMDI

With poetic license, we removed some of the dots above so the full prompt and parameter combination from the job description could fit on one line. If the job description provides a key of "*QCMDI,*" as above, then where are the locks that this key may open?

Routing Entry Compare Value- the Lock

In a word, the locks exist in functioning subsystems. In a functioning subsystem, there is a " lock" on each routing entry. However, when you first create a subsystem, there are no locks at all. Such subsystems, as they are built, are non-functional until all of the necessary entries are added. In fact, a new subsystem description contains nothing but a memory pool allocation. For routing entries to exist, they must be added to the subsystem using the Add Routing Entry command (ADDRTGE).

A new subsystem has no means of getting any work done. No, I am not kidding. If you were to create a new subsystem, right now, it would contain no entries with locks for job routing. In addition to having no routing entries, a new subsystem would have no work entries. Without at least one work entry, such as a Workstation Entry, a Job Queue Entry, or an Auto Start Job Entry, no work could ever be done in the subsystem.

Subsystem work entries are the means the system uses to get work started in specific subsystems. Without subsystem work entries, therefore, no jobs can get started in a subsystem.   Without the routing entries, no jobs can get routed to memory, and no jobs can pick up the necessary execution attributes in order to be able to run within the subsystem environment.

You may recall that at the beginning of this section, as we examined the routing data (QCMDI), in the QINTER job description, we posed the question:

Where are the locks that this key may open?

For the answer to this question, you must go back to the QINTER subsystem description that we examined briefly above, and you must look at the routing entries. The routing entries are the locks. One routing entry is selected for each job that is started in a subsystem.

When you execute a *WRKSBSD* (work with subsystem description) command, option 7 lets you look at the basic portion of all the *routing entries* (routing locks) that can fit on a screen. If you were to look at the *routing entries* for the QINTER subsystem, they would appear similar to those in Figure B-7.

Figure B-7, Routing Entries for QINTER

```
                         Display Routing Entries
                                                    System:    HELLO
     Subsystem description:   QINTER          Status:    INACTIVE
     Type options, press Enter.

       5=Display details


     Opt    Seq Nbr    Program       Library       Compare Value          Start
     Pos
      _        10      QCMD          QSYS          'QCMDI'                   1
      _        15      QCMD          QSYS          'QIGC'                    1
      _        20      QCMD          QSYS          'QS36MRT'                 1
      _        40      QARDRIVE      QSYS          '525XTEST'                1
      _       700      QCL           QSYS          'QCMD38'                  1
      _      9999      QCMD          QSYS          *ANY

     F3=Exit    F9=Display all detailed descriptions    F12=Cancel
```

The routing locks that you are looking for, are under the column
Compare Value in Figure B-7. You may have already noticed that
there does not seem to be a lock for "HGDVB." Thus, a key shaped
as "HGDVB" has as much value in QINTER as an old key on your
key ring, which opens nothing.

Whoops! I spoke too soon. Notice the last compare value of sequence
9999. It has a value *ANY*. This means that any key shape will open
this routing entry (lock), even good old "HGDVB."

You've probably also noticed that there is a specific lock for
"QCMDI." at sequence 0010.   If you "place" the "QCMDI" key,
from the QINTER job description, into this lock, you will open the
specific entry door, which the "QCMDI" lock protects.

Getting the Right Key

During a process called routing, when an interactive or a batch job is
initiated, one of the first things that happens is that it picks up its job
description. Since an interactive job exists from signon to signoff, at
signon, system work management typically goes to the user profile
object associated with the user, who is signing on, to get the job
description for the new job. Once the job description is found, the job
picks up all of the attributes within the job description object, and
adds them to the attribute set for the job being routed. The routing
data attribute (QCMDI), found in the job description (QINTER) is
then used as the key to unlock the rest of the attributes during the
routing process.

If Not User Profile - Subsystem Name

In some subsystem configurations, the job description for an interactive job does not come from the user profile. How then, you may ask, is this determined? If the subsystem attributes for the workstation are not set to use the user profile object, then the interactive job uses a job description that is specified in the subsystem.

Where in the subsystem is this specified, you may again ask? The answer is that this information is stored within the workstation type entries and the work-station name entries in the subsystem. In order to see a workstation type entry for QINTER, you would first display the QINTER subsystem with the following command:

DSPSBSD QINTER

From the *Display Subsystem Description* panel, take option 5 for *Work Station Type Entries* and press ENTER. From the Display Work Station Type Entries panel, pick a work station entry, such as *ALL by placing a "5" next to it as shown immediately below:

```
Opt   Type
      *CONS
 5    *ALL
```

For an interactive job, the line in the QINTER subsystem's workstation type entry, that governs where the job description for the job is to be found is as follows:

Job description . . . . :   *USRPRF

Thus, the subsystem QINTER is set to direct interactive jobs from all terminals to the user profile object to pick up their job descriptions. If this were not the case, the job description name "QINTER" would be used as the name of the job description. The Workstation type entry you would see instead of the above would be as follows:

Job description . . . . :   QINTER

In this case, the job description whose name is the same as the subsystem name would be used. This was the only option when the idea of work entries in subsystems was introduced for the System/38. Over the years, the operating system became more flexible by permitting the interactive work entry to defer the job description to the user profile, rather than forcing all users within a subsystem to use the same job description.

The Default Job Description - Interactive

If you recall the user profile amalgamation in Figure B-4, you may remember that the job description for the profile shown is QDFTJOBD. This is the system default job description. It happens that, just as with the QINTER job description, IBM chose 'QCMDI' as its routing data (routing key for the QDFTJOBD job description. So, for an interactive job, running in QINTER, for this profile, the routing key again is "QCMDI."

Job Description - Batch

For batch jobs, there are no special subsystem entries required to point to a job description A batch job typically gets its routing data directly from its job description. However, it can also get routing data from the commands, which initiate a batch job. The most frequently used command for initiating a batch job is the *submit job* (SBMJOB) command.

When you issue a SBMJOB command to start a batch job, you specify the job description name as a parameter of the command. Thus, the SBMJOB can point to any job description just by referencing its name –   QINTER, QDFTJOBD, or any other job description. With SBMJOB, by default, the system supplies routing data "QCMDB." This overrides the routing data in the job description. To defer to the job description, you can change the routing data parameter in your SBMJOB command by specifying routing data in the SBMJOB command as follows:

Routing data . . . . . *JOBD* or

RTGDTA(*JOBD)

From the job description or the SBMJOB, the job picks up its routing data (routing key). If you specify routing data in the SBMJOB, such as QCMDI, rather than defer to the job description (*JOBD), the routing data in the SBMJOB command overrides any routing data that you may supply in the job description.

Let's Open the Lock

For this example, let's say that "QCMDI," is the routing data, picked up by the interactive or batch job, through job description QDFTJOBD. This "key" is designed to open the routing entry in subsystem QINTER that has the "QCMDI" compare value (routing lock).   What happens when the lock opens?

If you place a "5" next to the entry that we want to examine in Figure B-7 (Sequence # 10), you can get a peak at the goodies available to the job being routed. These goodies are presented in Figure B-8, showing the detail within the open "QCMDI" routing entry.

Figure B-8 Detailed Routing Entry for QCMDI

```
                 Display Routing Entry Detail
                                      System:   HELLO
Subsystem description:   QINTER        Status:   INACTIVE
Routing entry sequence number . . . . . . . :   10
Program . . . . . . . . . . . . . . . . . . :   QCMD
   Library . . . . . . . . . . . . . . . . . :     QSYS
Class . . . . . . . . . . . . . . . . . . . :   QINTER
   Library . . . . . . . . . . . . . . . . . :     QGPL
Maximum active routing steps  . . . . . . . :   *NOMAX
Pool identifier . . . . . . . . . . . . . . :   2
Compare value . . . . . . . . . . . . . . . :   'QCMDI'
Compare start position  . . . . . . . . . . :   1
Press Enter to continue.
F3=Exit   F12=Cancel   F14=Display previous entry
```

If you take a look at the open routing entry in Figure B-8, you will notice that there are just three new pieces of information shown. They are as follows:

1. **Class – QINTER**
2. **Max act. routing steps – *NOMAX**
3. **Pool Identifier – 2**

Working from the top, let's look at all of the attributes (goodies), one at a time. Through the process of routing, with the "QCMDI: routing data as the key, and the routing entry compare value "QCMDI" as the lock, the job being routed grabs all of the attributes, at which you are looking in Figure B-8.

These are the attributes that your job obtains by opening the "QCMDI" door in the QINTER subsystem during job initiation. The first item behind (also in front of the door) is the program, "QCMD." This is the AS/400's command processor. It is the program used to process the job that is being routed. Please note that this is not "QCMDI," our routing data, it is "QCMD," the system command processing program. In many ways it is like the CMD (COMMAND) program in a PC system. It is the program that analyzes the commands, invokes syntax checkers, and gets things going. QCMD very nicely interprets and processes the command language statements in the job and gets the work done for the job.

Of course, you do not have to open the door to find QCMD. It is shown on the Routing Entry display as seen in Figure B-7.

You've Got Class

The next item is the CLASS object reference. The CLASS used is QINTER. This attribute tells the routing process to fetch a class object called QINTER. The job being routed then picks up the QINTER class's execution attributes from the object in the QGPL library.

During the routing process, as you are observing, a job picks up all of its initial values including its class attributes. These are referred to as *initial* values because, after the job is running, these attributes can be changed to other values.

You have also seen in this example that the QINTER *Class* object, as shown in Figure B-9, is obtained by opening the proper routing entry. You know that during the initial job routing process, QCMDI is the routing data that selects the QCMDI compare value in the QINTER subsystem routing table. This key opens the sequence # 0010 *routing entry* using the QCMDI routing data. This selected entry then routes the new job to the QINTER class, to pick up some more execution attributes.

Max Routing Steps

Continuing the move down the detailed routing entry for QCMDI in Figure B-8, you come across the "Maximum active routing steps" parameter. Notice that it is set to *NOMAX. This means that a newly routed job won't be artificially ended, even if it goes through tons of different routing steps.

Memory Pool Identifier

The next item in the routing entry, called "Pool Identifier," is very important. This points to the specific subsystem memory pool, in which this job's pages will be loaded and managed, when it is active and executing. Thus, from this little key, you can route a job into its proper memory pool, and through the class object, you can assign it a priority, a time slice, and other execution characteristics, thereby giving it a full set of attributes for execution. After the trip through the routing entry, the job is routed and executing in memory.

Figure B-9 Interactive Class Definition

```
                        Display Class Information
                                                System:     HELLO
Class . . . . . . . . . . . . . . . . . . . . . :   QINTER
    Library . . . . . . . . . . . . . . . . . :     QGPL
Run priority . . . . . . . . . . . . . . . . :   20
Time slice in milliseconds . . . . . . . . . :   2000
Eligible for purge . . . . . . . . . . . . . :   *YES
Default wait time in seconds . . . . . . . . :   30


Text . . . . . . . . . . . . . . . . . . . . . :   Interactive Subsystem
Class

Press Enter to continue.
F3=Exit    F12=Cancel
```

Priority

You may notice in Figure B-9, that the class priority is 20, and the
time slice end is 2000 milliseconds. Priority is relative, with the
highest priority being the lowest number - "1," and the lowest priority
being the highest two-digit number - "99." When a task with the
lowest numbered (highest) priority wants the processor, it is
preemptively dispatched to that task - even if the processor were
doing lower priority work at the time. Priority provides the divvying
rules for sharing the central processor resource, when jobs are
competing for CPU time.

Time Slice / Activity Levels

Like all virtual memory management systems, performance
degradation experienced from paging delays is directly related to the
amount of real memory installed in your AS/400 or IBM i. If the
amount of real memory installed is less than the required amount of
memory for the task at hand, a phenomenon called "thrashing" can
occur. This is exhibited when the machine spends most of its time
moving memory pages to and from disk versus doing real work.

Avoid Thrashing

The *time slice end* attribute and the *activity level* attribute have to do
with memory. Both of these attributes, if used properly, help avoid
thrashing.   For example, in a subsystem description, you set an
activity level for each memory pool. As its name implies, an activity
level limits the level of activity in a pool. By overtly limiting the
amount of activity, the rationale is that more jobs than feasible, say
fifty, will not be able to be occupy memory pages at the same time.

If you can fit five jobs, and fifty want to get in, you can either let them fight it out, or you can limit the number that can use storage, to the number that can fit. If you let them fight it out, thrashing will rule the day, and you will have pages being brought into memory and brought back out without even being used. Your CPU will be close to, or at 100% utilization, but your programs will not be able to get any CPU to get work done.

On the other hand, if you limit the memory use in a pool to the number of jobs that can fit on the average, then you will have a number of jobs that become ineligible (45) since they are ineligible and simply can't get into memory.

Ineligible Queue

On the AS/400, the place where jobs wait for an activity level slot is called the *ineligible queue*. It is where the jobs go that are not allowed in memory, so that you can avoid thrashing. The Kingston Trio would ask: "Do they ever return?" The answer is "yes." They stay in line and wait for the jobs that are eligible and in memory, to reach either a *time slice end* or a long wait (such as when a job sends out a panel with input fields).

When a job reaches one of these states, it loses its activity level, and the job at the top of the ineligible queue, if it is ready for action, is given the departing job's activity level. The newly dispatched job keeps its activity level until it eventually reaches *time slice end* or it enters a long wait state. Then it gives up its activity level.

It is highly likely that a job at number 45 in the queue would wait just a few seconds to become eligible again for memory. Thus, the idea of divvying up memory, rather than letting jobs fight it out for pages, conserves system resources. If all the jobs were competing with no governors, response time would be much worse than a few seconds, most of the time, in a memory constrained system. Moreover, very little real work would get done.

Using the governors, a job gets just a certain amount of time to execute. You set this time to a value that typically permits at least one interactive transaction to be completed. If you estimate well, by the time an interactive job is about to hit the ineligible queue, it has already sent out a screen panel and it is waiting for input. When the user hits ENTER, the job comes off the long wait queue and tries to get back an activity level. Since many of the other 50 users' jobs are also in a long waits, there is a good chance that the job gets dispatched immediately or after just a few seconds. That is lots better than indefinite response time, caused by 90% or more of the system's resources being chewed up, to manage thrashing.

Limit the Slots

Thus, by limiting jobs to slots big enough to permit them to execute without excessive paging, they can get productive work done. The system also has a mechanism called time slice end that penalizes jobs that have taken more than their share since getting an activity level. When the time slice end clock runs out, jobs go tot he ineligible queue to fight again with those waiting.

Purge?

The *Purge* parameter in the CLASS object adds another dimension to system resource conservation. With this parameter, you can decide what happens to a job's memory pages, when it gets kicked out of an activity level. The *YES or *NO options, on the *Purge* parameter, determine the answer to the question: "Should the system use demand paging (Purge *NO) to selectively remove the pages for a job when it loses an activity level or should it take them all out in one big swoop (Purge *YES)?

In constantly busy memory situations, Purge(*YES) is preferred, since it uses less resources to swap programs than to demand page them. In situations where there is more memory, Purge(*NO) is the ticket, since a job's pages would, more than likely, be in memory when it comes back from a long wait or a time slice end. With PURGE(*NO), the system would not have to load job pages back into memory since, if the system is not thrashing, there is a likelihood that the pages would still be there.

As you can see in Figure B-9, jobs routed using the QINTER class, are eligible to have their pages purged (Eligible for PURGE *YES), when they lose control of the CPU.

Other CLASS Attributes

The next attribute in the CLASS object in B-9 is *Default wait time*. This specifies the amount of time, a process using this CLASS, will wait, until it can obtain a resource that it needs.

The last set of attributes, picked up from the CLASS object, are the maximums to set, for the job being routed (initiated). These are:

```
Maximum CPU time in milliseconds
Maximum temporary storage in megabytes
Maximum threads
```

By default, these are set at no maximum (*NOMAX). Unless you are specifically interested in tuning with one of these governors, the recommendation is to stick with the defaults.

So far, you can see that any job routed using the QINTER job description with the QINTER subsystem, by now would have already picked up a lot of attributes. In fact, at this point, it would more than likely already be executing in subsystem memory pool 2.

If this all sounds like Greek, in a few months, you may want to read and re-read this section, and maybe even read a little bit of the IBM Work Management Guide. Once you "get" the notion of routing, and basic memory tuning, much of the mystery will be removed from your notion of the AS/400 and IBM i. You will still be happy that OS/400 is so helpful in getting things done for you. But things will be different. You will have a big understanding of just what the system is doing and how it is doing it. That my even be a little more scary at first.

Managing Performance

Rather than lump all work in a ball, all together, and say: "Hey if one thing doesn't perform well, nothing will perform well!" ... the AS/400 designers gave us a way to manage performance. They gave us a way in which we can divvy up workloads. Therefore, with a finite amount of processing power, various types of workloads could be optimized to run as well as possible, together in the same machine.

Part VI: Storage Pools

Defined in the Subsystem

You may recall from Figure B-6C, there are three memory pools defined in the QINTER subsystem. Pools 1 and 2 are defined by IBM, in its standard subsystem. We added pool 3 to make the subsystem more interesting.

The three subsystem pools were assigned to shared pools, *BASE, *INTERACT, and SHRPOOL2, respectively. Thus, you can use one subsystem to split up various workloads and direct them into different memory pools – up to 10 pools in one subsystem. The memory divvy can be extensive considering that an AS/400 can have 64 shared memory pools allocated at one time.

Divvy Up the Memory

The first memory pool, which the subsystem uses, is called the *BASE pool. The second is a special shareable pool called *INTERACT, and the third is a user shared pool (SHRPOOL2). To make it even more interesting, let's assign a private pool of 10000K, which, when the subsystem starts, will take 10000K of private, dedicated memory for its use, and only its use. It will be subsystem pool4.

*Base Memory Pool

The *BASE memory pool is shareable across all subsystems, so IBM gave it a name which helps us all know that it is a base requirement of every AS/400. Work directed into this pool competes for memory with other jobs from WDS, as well as work from other subsystems. Additionally, IBM uses it for transient system routines. Unlike the operating system nucleus in the Machine pool, the latter are in and out of memory as needed, and do not have to continually reside in memory. The *BASE* pool is often called system Pool 2 since it always exists, and it is always listed in the *Work With System Status* command (WRKSYSSTS) output, after Pool 1.

*MACHINE Pool

By the way, System Pool 1 is also very important, but it does not get allocated to any user subsystems. It is known as the Machine pool and it is where the nucleus of the operating system function resides and executes, when it is doing its work.

Private Pools

When you divvy up the memory, how do you know where your job is going to run?   The answer to this question again has to do with the routing data and the routing entries. A routing entry can point a job to just one memory pool. For the newly modified (4 pools) QINTER to be able to route work to all of these pools, there must be at least four routing entries, each pointing to a different memory pool. Likewise, to select the entries, you need jobs to be routed with four different sets of routing data to open the four different entry doors.

Monitoring Active Subsystems and Memory Pools

There is a very powerful command on the system, which keeps track of activity and memory usage. It is called, WRKSYSSTS. It provides a window into your system's performance, and it is often used as a first basis for system performance tuning. In addition to showing work, memory, and paging characteristics, it also permits you to change memory allocations and activity levels on the fly and to observe the impact on paging.

To invoke the command, type WRKSYSSTS and press ENTER. You will come to a panel similar to that in Figure B-10. We rolled once on our system and pasted the two additional lines to the panel.

Figure B-10 Work With System Status

```
                        Work with System Status                    HELLO
                                                    10/14/02   08:09:11
% CPU used . . . . . . . :        26.2    Auxiliary storage:
% DB capability  . . . . :          .0       System ASP . . . . . . :    473.8 G
Elapsed time . . . . . . :    00:00:25       % system ASP used  . . :    58.6413
Jobs in system . . . . . :        2745       Total  . . . . . . . . :    473.8 G
% perm addresses . . . . :        .047       Current unprotect used :    10417 M
% temp addresses . . . . :        .280       Maximum unprotect  . . :    17442 M

Type changes (if allowed), press Enter.

System    Pool    Reserved    Max    -----DB-----   ---Non-DB---
 Pool   Size (M)  Size (M)   Active  Fault  Pages   Fault  Pages
  1      344.99    199.15    +++++    .0     .0      5.3    7.3
  2     2480.38      6.33    422      .0     .0      3.7    9.7
  3      785.94       .03    74      5.1    14.5    13.2  116.9
  4       40.31       .00    19       .0     .0       .0     .0
  5       81.98       .00    23       .0     .0       .0     .0
                                                              More...


  6       96.37       .00    8        .0     .0       .0     .0
  7       10.00       .00    4        .7    1.1       .3     .9
                                                              Bottom

Command
===>
F3=Exit    F4=Prompt           F5=Refresh    F9=Retrieve    F10=Restart
F11=Display transition data    F12=Cancel    F24=More keys
```

You may recall a few pages ago, we discussed *Activity Level*. The column in the WRKSYSSTS display titled *Max Active*, in Figure B-10 shows the activity level of each memory pool. The *Pool Size* column represents the amount of memory allocated to a pool.

The *System Pool* number shown in Figure B-10, is not as simple to understand, as you would first presume. For pools after System Pool # 2, for example, the System Pool ID has to do with the sequence in which the subsystems are started. When the subsystems are started, memory is then allocated to their defined pools. We have learned that pools 1 and 2 are always the Machine pool and the *BASE pool respectively. The higher number System Pool IDs (3 to 7) represent pools that are allocated when the subsystems, in which they are defined, are started.

For example, pool ID 3 happens to be the *INTERACT shared pool but you cannot tell from this panel. It is pool 3 because the system numbered it when the QINTER subsystem, in which it is defined, was started. System pools 4 and 5, likewise were allocated when their associated subsystems were started. Since subsystems can have up to 10 pools defined, if a subsystem with three private pools were started before any others, the system would assign System Pool Ids, 3 to 5 to these memory pools.

At system startup, the Machine pool gets what it wants and all other memory is given to the second system pool known as *Base. As subsystems get started, they take memory from the *BASE pool (System Pool # 2). It gets reduced in size by the amount of memory needed by each new subsystem pool as the subsystem starts.

Auto Tuning

Though you can certainly struggle through the IBM Work Management Guide, and you can calculate the proper settings for your machine, manually tuning an AS/400 has gotten to be very involved. Though it is not impossible, it is not as necessary as it once was. There is a system value called QPFRADJ. My recommendation for tuning is to use the QPFRADJ system value and set it to a value of 2.

Shared Pools

There are sixty-four total shareable pools on the system. Besides the machine pool and the base pool, these are as follows:

*INTERACT   The shared memory pool specifically designated by IBM for interactive jobs.

*SPOOL   The shared memory pool specifically designated for spool readers and writers.

*SHRPOOL1   Thru *SHRPOOL60. These are generally available shared memory storage pools that you can use as your needs dictate.

*INTERACT

The *INTERACT pool exists on all AS/400s. However, a shop can choose to ignore this pool and use dedicated (private) pools or other shared pools for interactive work. However, most shops see the advantage for defining interactive work using this pool. The *INTERACT pool is typically defined in subsystems that perform interactive workloads.

Thus, if there were several interactive subsystems on your AS/400, all could have their interactive programs run in the shared *INTERACT memory pool.

*SPOOL

The specified pool definition is defined to be the shared pool used for spooled writers.   The size and activity level of the shared pool are specified using the CHGSHRPOOL command.

*SHRPOOL1 et al.

This pool definition is defined to be a general-purpose shared pool. There are sixty general-purpose shared pools, identified by special values *SHRPOOL1 to *SHRPOOL60.   The size and activity level of a shared pool are also specified using the Change Shared Pool (CHGSHRPOOL) command.

Setting the Size of Shared Pools

When you build a subsystem, you must specify at least one memory pool. If you pick *Base, *Interact, *Spool, or any shared pool, you cannot set the size of the pool when creating the subsystem description. Shared pools are freelance pools, not assigned to subsystems. Yes, you can set the share pool size and its activity level with the WRKSYSSTS command, but that is not the command designed for the purpose.

In order to set the size of the *INTERACT memory pool, and all other shared pools; you can use the CHGSHRPOOL command as noted above. However, there is a special command called *WRKSHRPOOL,* which makes the task easier. To help you visualize the various shared pools on the system, and how easy it is to set their sizes and activity levels, the first output panel of a WRKSHRPOOL command is shown in Figure B-11.

Notice in Figure B-11, that the size of the *INTERACT pool at the time of the snapshot is 785.94K with an activity level of 74. It is no coincidence that pool 3, in Figures B-10 is exactly the same size, with the same activity level.

Figure B-11: Work With Shared Pools

```
                        Work with Shared Pools
                                                        System:  HELLO
Main storage size (M)  . :        3840.00

Type changes (if allowed), press Enter.

             Defined    Max    Allocated   Pool  -Paging Option--
Pool         Size (M)  Active  Size (M)     ID   Defined  Current
*MACHINE      344.99   +++++     344.99      1   *FIXED   *FIXED
*BASE        2480.39     422    2480.39      2   *CALC    *CALC
*INTERACT     785.94      74     785.94      3   *CALC    *CALC
*SPOOL         81.98      23      81.98      5   *CALC    *CALC
*SHRPOOL1      96.37       8      96.37      6   *CALC    *CALC
*SHRPOOL2      40.31      19      40.31      4   *CALC    *CALC
*SHRPOOL3        .00       0                     *FIXED
*SHRPOOL4        .00       0                     *FIXED
*SHRPOOL5        .00       0                     *FIXED
*SHRPOOL6        .00       0                     *FIXED

More...
Command
===>

F3=Exit   F4=Prompt   F5=Refresh   F9=Retrieve   F11=Display tuning data
F12=Cancel
```

As a point of note, the underlined fields are changeable in this panel.
In fact, they are input-capable fields by default on AS/400. That
means you can change the size of the pools right on the status
display. If, for example, you knew that you were about to have a few
big interactive programs hit this pool, you could bump up the
*INTERACT memory numbers shown in Figure B-11 to
accommodate your need. You would type the changes right from the
WRKSHRPOOL panel as shown above.

The fourth column under Pool ID refers to system Pool ID. Thus,
this panel gives us another way of seeing the relationships between
the system pool ID #s and the shared pools.

Another field to examine on this panel is Paging Option, which for
*INTERACT is defined as *CALC. There is a detailed explanation
of this after Figure B-10D above. In a nutshell, this means that the
system dynamically adjusts the paging characteristics and the amount
of memory associated with the *INTERACT storage pool for
optimum performance. Believe me, there is nothing you want more
than the system balancing performance rather than you having to do
it. Under this scenario, you set the thermostat and the system tries to
achieve it.

A Look at *Spool

In Figure B-11, you can learn a few other interesting tidbits besides the size of *INTERACT. You can see the *MACHINE pool size, the *BASE pool size, and the print or *SPOOL size. The *SPOOL pool is a convenient way of assigning a tunable, specially designated shared memory pool for the system spooling function.

A Look at *SHRPOOLS

You can also see that there are more shared pools than are shown on the screen (*More* in lower right corner). In fact, as noted above, in V5RX, there are up to 60 user defined shared pools. With memory available in gigabytes, IBM is helping OS/400 give you some exciting ways to divvy up memory to have the system manage the pools, using the shared pool mechanism. The user defined shared pools (*SHRPOOLX* type pools) are also available for use with subsystems. Though sketchily defined by IBM, they are inert until a user gives them some memory and an activity parameter by making the pool a part of one or more subsystems that actually get started.

> ☺Tip Unless a subsystem is started (STRSBS) using its subsystem description, no memory pools defined in a subsystem are ever allocated.

A Look at the *BASE Pool

You may also notice that *BASE is not changeable using WRKSHRPOOL or WRKSYSSTS. You can see there is no underline in Figure B-11. This means that the field is not input-capable. Though you cannot set the value of *BASE memory, there is a system value accessible via the *WRKSYSVAL* (work with system values) command. It is called *QBASPOOL*. Through this value, you set the minimum size for the *BASE memory pool. You cannot set its exact size since *BASE is the pool, from which all other pools take their memory.

The actual size of *BASE is determined after all subsystems are started. Starting subsystems causes them to allocate needed memory in the sequence in which the subsystems, and the pools within the subsystems are started. After all the other system pools have been allocated during subsystem startup time, *BASE gets whatever is left. However, under no circumstances will the *BASE pool ever have less memory than the amount specified in the QBASPOOL system value.

If during startup, in order for a subsystem to get its full private memory allocation, *BASE would be taken below its minimum, the system does not permit this. *BASE gets its full minimum allocation and the subsystem that is starting then gets the memory that remains.

A Look at the *MACHINE Pool

The machine pool, *MACHINE is set by the QMCHPOOL system value. Unlike the QBASPOOL value, however, this defines how much memory is given to the nucleus of the machine when it is powered on. It is not a minimum setting. It is an actual number. Based on the size of the system and the number of concurrent processes expected, IBM makes a recommendation in the Work Management manual (SC41-5306) for the size of the pool.

If your system is set to not adjust memory based on workload, the value you specify is what you get. On the other hand, if the system is set to adjust memory based upon the various workloads in the subsystems, then the value of the QMCHPOOL is a startup value and, just as any other shared pool, it can be auto-adjusted upwards or downwards to accommodate workload during system operation.

This is a major advantage of a shared pool since private memory pools, such as WDS subsystem pool 3 (set at 10000K with an activity level of 2) cannot be tuned automatically by the system based upon workload. Without overt action by an operator / implementer, WDS pool 3 will have 10000K forever.

Part VII: Case Study– Building Work Management Objects from Scratch

One Object at a Time

By this time in this QuikCourse, you should certainly know more than you did when you started —. Lots more! There was probably a time mid-way that you may have felt that you knew even less than when you began. Those days are behind us. We are ready to move on!

Now, it is time to solidify our gains by creating a new subsystem and a matching set of work management objects, from scratch. The agenda for this part of the QuikCourse is just that. As we proceed, we first discuss the building task to be performed, and then we show the commands used to build the work management objects.

Logically Sequenced Exercises

You will find that this exercise is sequenced logically and in a way that you can understand each piece along the way. However, our bet is that you will find a few dependencies that you may not have counted on. If you get set back in any way as you are building these objects, because of prerequisite objects being necessary, feel free to break sequence and go to the step that shows you the command to build the prerequisite object, enter the command, and build the object.

Build Batch and Interactive Environments

Because batch and interactive subsystems prosper with different operational characteristics, this exercise creates both a batch and an interactive environment and associated objects. The commands used are the same, but some of the parameters are different. Take a look at the commands as you use them, so that you can be able to differentiate the things that are probably good for batch and the things that are probably good for interactive. This should help you in tailoring your own shop.

Use IBM's Manual

If after you complete this exercise, and you want to do more, you can go to the back of the IBM Work Management guide. All the parameters for the shipped IBM Work Management objects are there, in an easy to read format.

Using the shipped objects in the IBM manual as a guide, one exercise that would be helpful would be to display the objects on your system and compare them against what is in the manual (how they shipped). In this way, you can identify things that your shop has changed.

Another exercise would be to pick a subsystem environment that you may recognize, such as QBASE or QBATCH or QCTL, try to identify all of its associated objects, and create them with a new name in your library. For example, you may name the group TESTQ, instead of QINTER, QBATCH, etc.

Even is you choose not to do any additional exercises, just looking at the shipped objects in the back of the IBM Work Management Guide is an educational trip by itself.

Work Management Exercises

The Let's get on with our own exercise for the present. For each of the commands in the exercise, type it on the command line or type the command name and then use the prompter (F4) to help you fill in the command parameters. When you are finished, press ENTER to run the command.

The steps to setting up a Work Management Environment for both batch and interactive users are as follows:

1. Create a subsystem description for interactive:

CRTSBSD SBSD(HELLO/WDS)
POOLS((1 *BASE) (2 *INTERACT)
(3 10000 2))

2. Create a CLASS object for interactive:

CRTCLS CLS(HELLO/WDS) RUNPTY(20) TIMESLICE(2000)
PURGE(*YES) DFTWAIT(30)CPUTIME(*NOMAX)
MAXTMPSTG(*NOMAX) MAXTHD(*NOMAX)
TEXT('Interactive Class for WDS subsystem')

3.Create a subsystem description for batch:

CRTSBSD SBSD(HELLO/WDSBATCH)
POOLS((1 *BASE) (2 *SHRPOOL1)) TEXT('Batch Subsystem
Description For WDS Case Study')

4. Create a Class object for batch:

CRTCLS CLS(HELLO/WDSBATCH) RUNPTY(50)
TIMESLICE(5000) PURGE(*NO)DFTWAIT(30)
CPUTIME(*NOMAX) MAXTMPSTG(*NOMAX)
MAXTHD(*NOMAX) TEXT('Batch Class for WDSBATCH
subsystem')

5. Create a User profile for interactive:

CRTUSRPRF USRPRF(PGMR) PASSWORD()
STATUS(*ENABLED) USRCLS(*PGMR)
INLPGM(HELLO/MYPROG) JOBD(NEWJOBD)
GRPPRF(BIGGRP) SUPGRPPRF(DEPTGRP)
MSGQ(*USRPRF) PRTDEV(SECPRTR)
OUTQ(HELLO/SECPRTR) TEXT('Interactive')

When you create this profile, and later sign on using it, you can
submit batch jobs without creating a batch user profile. For example,
on the SBMJOB itself, when you submit the job tot he WDSBATCH
job queue, it will run in the WDSBATCH subsystem. For batch
routing data, you can provide the **NEWBJOBD** job description if it is
already built from having completed this exercise. You can also
directly specify "BATCH" as the routing data for the SBMJOB. As
long as all of the work management objects in this exercise are built,
you should have no problem submitting batch work with what
appears to be an interactive profile.

6. Create a Printer Device for a LAN attached printer:

This is a model for an IBM InfoPrint21. If you've got a different
model printer(s), check the printer manual and call IBM support if
you can't make it work. They often have the unpublished secrets.

CRTDEVPRT DEVD(SECPRTR) DEVCLS(*LAN)
TYPE(3812)MODEL(1) LANATTACH(*IP) PORT(2501)
ONLINE(*YES) FONT(011) FORMFEED(*AUTOCUT)
PRTERRMSG(*INFO) MSGQ(QSYSOPR) ACTTMR(170)
INACTTMR(*NOMAX) PARITY(*TYPE) STOPBITS(1)
TRANSFORM(*YES) MFRTYPMDL(*INFOPRINT21)
PPRSRC1(*LETTER) PPRSRC2(*LETTER)
ENVELOPE(*NUMBER10) RMTLOCNAME('192.168.5.200')
SYSDRVPGM(*IBMSNMPDRV) TEXT('Security Officers" Printer')

7. Create an Interactive Output Queue:

If you want to use a queue, which is not associated with a printer, use this command.

CRTOUTQ OUTQ(QUSRSYS/PGMR) DSPDTA(*NO)
JOBSEP(0) OPRCTL(*YES) TEXT('Programmer' Interactive Output
Queue')

8. Create batch Output Queue for batch work:

CRTOUTQ OUTQ(QUSRSYS/BATCHOUT) DSPDTA(*NO)
JOBSEP(0) OPRCTL(*YES) TEXT('Batch Output Queue')

9. Create an Interactive Job Description:

Use the same name as referenced in the User profile. You'll have to get this created before you sign on.

CRTJOBD JOBD(HELLO/NEWJOBD) JOBQ(HELLO/WDS)
RTGDTA(HGDVB) PRTDEV(*USRPRF) OUTQ(*USRPRF)
INLLIBL(*SYSVAL) ENDSEV(30) LOG(4 0 *NOLIST)
LOGCLPGM(*NO) TEXT('Interactive Jobd')

10. Create a Batch Job Description:

```
CRTJOBD JOBD(HELLO/NEWBJOBD)
JOBQ(HELLO/WDSBATCH) RTGDTA(BATCH)
OUTQ(HELLO/BATCHOUT)    INLLIBL(*SYSVAL)
ENDSEV(30) LOG(4 0 *NOLIST) LOGCLPGM(*NO)
TEXT('Batch Job Description')
```

11. Create an Interactive Job Queue:

Since a job queue is for Batch work, this queue permits the interactive subsystem to be used for batch work.

```
CRTJOBQ JOBQ(HELLO/WDS) TEXT('WDS JOB QUEUE')
```

12. Add a Job Queue Entry:

Add a Job Queiue Entry to the WDS Interactive Subsystem (WDS).

```
ADDJOBQE SBSD(HELLO/WDS) JOBQ(HELLO/WDS)
SEQNBR(350)
```

The newly created subsystem WDS would be capable of batch work, if you execute the above commands – item 11 and item 12. Of course, it may need a little more work to make it right. That's why we created a batch subsystem. For example, you would want a batch memory pool, so your batch jobs are not stealing your interactive pages. Moreover, if you submit work, you would want a routing entry and routing data that would select the batch pool and a batch class. You might be better off running in WDSBATCH!

13. Create Job Queue for Batch:

The Job Queue enables the WDSBATCH subsystem to perform batch work (WDSBATCH)

```
CRTJOBQ JOBQ(HELLO/WDSBATCH) TEXT('WDSBATCH
JOB QUEUE')
```

14. Add Job Queue Entry for Batch:

ADDJOBQE SBSD(HELLO/WDSBATCH)
JOBQ(HELLO/WDSBATCH) SEQNBR(350)

The newly created subsystem WDSBATCH is capable of batch work, if you execute the above commands – item 13 and item 14. When it gets it s routing entries below, the batch environment should be fine.

This subsystem can run interactive work if we choose to add some Work Station Entries. Of course, it may need a little more work to make it right. That's why we created the interactive subsystem. For example, you would want an interactive memory pool or *INTERACT to be used so your high priority interactive jobs are not preempting your batch jobs with lower priority. This could cause thrashing.

Moreover, if you really want interactive in a batch subsystem, you would want a routing entry and routing data that would select the interactive pool and an interactive class. The more you think about it, you might be better off running in WDS!

15 Add Workstation Entry to Interactive subsystem (WDS):

All displays starting with *WS* will be connected to this subsystem.

ADDWSE SBSD(HELLO/WDS) WRKSTN(WS*)
JOBD(*USRPRF)

16. Add a Routing Entry to WDS Subsystem:

(Interactive - HGDVB)

ADDRTGE SBSD(HELLO/WDS) SEQNBR(100)
CMPVAL(HGDVB) PGM(QCMD)
CLS(HELLO/WDS)POOLID(2)

17. Add a Routing Entry to WDSBATCH Subsystem (Batch - BATCH)

ADDRTGE SBSD(HELLO/WDSBATCH) SEQNBR(100)
CMPVAL(BATCH) PGM(QCMD)
CLS(HELLO/WDSBATCH)POOLID(2)

Getting Your Printouts to Check Work

Now that you have a user profile, a printer definition, and an output queue, how do you get to have your printouts arrive in your output queue? The answer is through the job description associated with the user profile (NEWJOBD or NEWBJOBD). The output queue is a parameter that is specified in the job description

Any printer can print from any output queue if you use the *start print writer* (STRPRTWTR) command such as shown below. Getting from the output queue to the printer is not hard to figure out. The command to start the system's main printer, which is often named PRT01, using the PGMR output queue is as follows:

STRPRTWTR DEV(PRT01) OUTQ(HELLO/PGMR)

So far, we have created a user profile, a printer, an output queue, a job queue, a job description, class, and a subsystem description. We have taken the subsystem descriptions and we have added a mix of batch sources of work (Job Queue Entry for WDSBATCH job queue) and an interactive source of work (WS* work station entry) for subsystem WDS. As a final step, we supplied routing entries for the subsystem. We did it all.

Create Your Own Subsystem!

It would serve you well to create a few more subsystems of your own as suggested in the exercises. You can also create the necessary work management objects, memory pools, workstation entries, job queue entries, and routing data to go along with them. Then you can start your subsystems, and try to get interactive jobs running (terminal name is important). Then submit jobs to your job queues and see them run in your subsystems. You will feel smart because when you can do that, you'll be way ahead on the work management game plan.

IBM Supplied Objects

IBM does not abandon its new AS/400 and IBM i users with a set of instructions to build all these objects before you can use your system. In fact, the collection of objects, which IBM supplies, is often regarded as must-haves instead of starter sets. Most AS/400 shops persist in using the IBM definitions for one reason or another. It certainly makes it easier when the replacement players come in to take your job.

There are three main environments supplied by IBM. One is System/36-like and uses a controlling subsystem called QBASE. One is System/38-like. The third is native OS/400. Native is so much like the System/38 environment that for our purposes in this QuikCourse, we combine them in the discussion. It uses a subsystem called QCTL as its controlling subsystem. Additionally, it uses subsystem QINTER for interactive, subsystem QBATCH for batch work, and subsystem QCMN for communications work.

With or without using the System/36 environment, some shops use the QBASE subsystem as their *controlling subsystem* since IBM shipped many AS/400 systems with this default. The controlling subsystem is defined in the system value *QCTLSBSD*.

Controlling Subsystem Starts Other Subsystems

At power-on, the AS/400 starts the subsystem whose name is contained in this system value, as the first subsystem after an IPL. If you look at your controlling system, you will find that there is an auto-start job entry for a program that then starts the other user work on your system, including the other subsystems.

If your environment is QBASE, then the QBASE subsystem itself is built to support interactive, batch, and communications jobs. It also has an Autostart job, which automatically starts the QSPL (Spooling) subsystem.

If your environment is QINTER, then your controlling subsystem is QCTL. Your batch work would be designed to run in a subsystem called QBATCH, and communications jobs would run in QCMN. In this mix, there are job queues and job descriptions, provided by IBM and named the same as the subsystem descriptions. Thus, QINTER would be the JOBQ for QINTER, etc. Additionally, each subsystem comes chocked full of routing entries, and, depending on the nature of the subsystem, the workstation entries and job queue entries are pre-built.

In the back of IBM's Work Management Guide, in Appendix C, all of the IBM supplied objects can be found, along with the commands to create them. Keep this in mind as you begin to explore doing your own work management setups.

Final Note

This was just a little primer on the subject of work management. But, if you have been able to follow after one or several reads, you have come a long way. The beauty of work management is that the basics have stayed the same since 1978. It was a good idea then, and continues to be a good idea.

Learn as much as you can, and as changes come about to the OS/400 operating system, you will find that most of the base concepts do not change. The starter values for the new mainframe size AS/400s are much different from the baby AS/400, however. That's why IBM wrote the Work Management Guide, to give you the starter values needed to get you going. If you can't find the starter values, then turn on the performance adjuster, and the values it gives right out of the gate are what you would have had to calculate.

Don't get locked out. Remember, you can create the key! Enjoy work management. You'll be amazed at what you can do with it. It can be a lot of fun.

Other Sources of Work Management Information

IBM's documentation on Work Management is fairly thorough and it would be a worthwhile read. It can be found on the Web by taking the following links

www.as400.ibm.com

After you get there, choose as follows:

1. Library
2. IBM i Information Center
3. IBM i Online Library (on the left frame)
4. English, GO
5. V5R1
6. Systems Management (Left frame)
7. Work Management (Left frame)
8. Introductory Work Management information becomes available in the right frame
9. Manuals and Redbooks
10. Work Management

When you finally get to the Work Management link, it brings down the Work Management Guide. When V5R2 was announced, this manual was still at the V4R5 level. In any case, the guide is very powerful and can still help you in understanding the details of the many topics in Work Management. Item seven in the above list is also helpful to get a simplified view from the Information Center itself, which can amplify your understanding of the topics presented in this QuikCourse.

As much as I'd like to tell you that this Pocket Guide is all you need to do all you need with Work Management that is not the purpose of this QuikCourse. In both the Mini Course provided in this IBM i Pocket Developer's Guide, or the Full Course in the IBM i Pocket Work Management Guide, the objective is to help you understand how work is accomplished in the system and to stage you for building your own subsystems and tuning systems.

In the Full Course, we carry the hands-on experience and tuning experience even further, walking you through the building of the objects necessary to create your Work Management environment, and giving solid tips for tuning performance.

Neither the Mini Course, nor the Full QuikCourse is as extensive in content as the IBM Work Management manual. Before you go digging in the IBM manual for some abstruse concepts, however, go through one of these pocket-sized QuikCourses. It will save a lot of time. These are intended to teach whereas the IBM manuals are intended to amplify your learning with concrete facts. As you learn Work Management, remember that the bite at a time theory definitely applies here.

We wish you the best!

Appendix A   IBM Documentation - How to Find it!

How to Find an IBM AS/400 or IBM i Manual Using IBM' S Web-Based Documentation

Many AS/400 and IBM i manuals are excellent. Though you will be able to amble somewhat through the wonderment of IBM i program development after taking these QuikCourse tutorials, for your details and specifics, unfortunately, you must access IBM's wealth of AS/400 manuals and other documentation.

There was once a time that every IBM manual had a form number which was very easy to locate. It was on the front cover of the book or manual. This was a nice way of uniquely identifying the manual you needed. Things have changed, mostly for the better. Now, you don't need any manuals at all per se, since all of IBM's AS/400 documentation is available on the web in HTML and/or PDM format. Thus, every manual for AS/400 and IBM i is just a Web access away. Throw your old manuals away. Save the trees. Clear up your desks.

How do you find the manual you need? For this book, you will position yourself to IBM's IBM i documentation web site. This will be your entree into the world of IBM documentation for version 5.X of the operating system. From here, for certain manuals, you will take very specific paths to get to the manuals of your choosing. For others, which are still referenced by manual number, and there is a ton of them, you will go to the supplemental manuals' page, a sample of the manuals there is shown in Figure AA-1.

Figure AA-1 IBM Supp. Manuals Page - Looking for a Manual

Title	Document Number
3270 Device Emulation Support	SC41-5408
ADTS for AS/400: Report Layout Utility	SC09-2635
ADTS for AS/400: Screen Design Aid	SC09-2604
ADTS for AS/400: Source Entry Utility	SC09-2605
ADTS/400: Application Dev. Manager API Reference	SC09-2180
ADTS/400: Application Dev. Mgr Intro and Planning	GC09-1807
ADTS/400: Application Dev. Manager Self-Study Guide	SC09-2138
ADTS/400: Application Dev. Manager User's Guide	SC09-2133
ADTS/400: Application Dictionary Svcs Self-Study Guide	SC09-2086
ADTS/400: Application Dictionary Services Users Guide	SC09-2087
ADTS/400: Advanced Printer Function	SC09-1766
ADTS/400: Data File Utility	SC09-1773
ADTS/400: File Compare and Merge Utility	SC09-1772
ADTS/400: Interactive Source Debugger	SC09-1897
ADTS/400: Programming Development Manager	SC09-1771
ADTS/400: Screen Design Aid for the S/36 Environment	SC09-1893
CL Programming	SC41-5721
COBOL/400 Reference	SC09-1813
COBOL/400 Users Guide	SC09-1812
ILE Application Development Example	SC41-5602
ILE C/C++ Compiler Reference	SC09-4816
ILE C/C++ for AS/400 MI Library Reference	SC09-2418
ILE C/C++ Language Reference	SC09-4815
ILE C/C++ Programmer's Guide	SC09-2712
ILE C for AS/400 Run-Time Library Reference	SC41-5607
ILE COBOL Programmer's Guide	SC09-2540
ILE COBOL Reference	SC09-2539
ILE COBOL Reference Summary	SX09-1317
ILE Concepts	SC41-5606
ILE RPG Programmer's Guide	SC09-2507
ILE RPG Reference	SC09-2508
ILE RPG Reference Summary	SX09-1315
Introducing ADTSet for IBM I	GC09-2088

REXX/400 Programmer's Guide	SC41-5728
REXX/400 Reference	SC41-5729
RPG/400 Reference	SC09-1817
RPG/400 User's Guide	SC09-1816
Sort Users Guide and Reference	SC09-1826
System Operation	SC41-4203
System/36-Compatible RPG II User's Guide and Ref.	SC09-1818
System/38-Compatible COBOL Reference Summary	SX09-1286
System/38-Compatible COBOL User's Guide and Ref.	SC09-1814
VisualAge RPG Language Reference	SC09-2451
VisualAge RPG Parts Reference	SC09-2450
Work Management	SC41-5306

Finding a Manual - IBM Process

Let's find a couple manuals. As an example, Let's say you are looking for database manuals. What is the first thing you do?   You want to go to IBM's documentation site. The easiest way to get there is to go to the main AS/400 / IBM i site at
WWW.AS400.IBM.COM

On the left frame, notice a link called Library. Take the link then, from the right panel, take the IBM i Information Center link. From there, you will get a panel, which lets you pick the version and release and the language. Pick   *V5R1* and *English,* then click on the GO button. You are now at IBM's English documentation site for V5R1.

To get to the database books, you have a few more links to go. After you press GO, for Database, 1. click on *Database and File Systems*, 2. Then click   *DB2 UDB For IBM i.*   3. Then click *Manuals and Redbooks.*

In this section, you will find two valuable manuals. The first, DDS Reference: Concepts, shows how to use DDS, and the second, *DDS Reference: Physical and Logical Files* shows how to create physical and logical database files. When we find these two manuals, we have found what we are looking for.

When I did my search, I noticed that neither of these manuals, taking this path, showed up with IBM form numbers. At least I could not find them. Now, let's try to find a few books which would come in handy in some of the QuikCourses you are studying. Suppose you were looking for books in any of the following topical areas:

Work Management
PDM - Program Development Manager
SEU - Source Entry Utility
DFU - Data File Utility
SDA - Screen Design Aid

As you are going through the main path as we did for database, you would notice that there is no stopping point for *Application Development*. So, how do you find the books above?

Instead of clicking on the *Database and File System* path, go down a bit further, until you see: *Looking for A Manual?* Take this link. You will then get a new browser window with all AS/400 and IBM i manuals listed by topical area. Page down this display. While paging, look at all the manuals you see and make a note of them for future reference. You will come to a section called *Supplemental Manuals.* For your edification, we cut out a sample of these supplemental manuals and made them available as Figure AA-1 above.

Please note that the list of five manuals, for which we were searching, are all available in this list. The SEU, DFU, etc. manuals are prefixed by ADTS which means the Application Development Tool Set. As you know, with V5R1, the ADTS is bundled with the 5722-WDS product called *WebSphere Development Studio for IBM i.*

As you move through the QuikCourses, especially those teaching a technical topic such as SEU or PDM, feel free to take a trip out to the Web and either download your own PDF version of these manuals or check it out in HTML form right from the Web. Like me, I would expect that you will be impressed with all that IBM has made available for your use, and how easy it is to access and find specific information.

LETS GO PUBLISH! Books by Brian Kelly: (Sold at www.bookhawkers.com; Amazon.com, and Kindle.).

LETS GO PUBLISH! is proud to announce that more AS/400 and Power i books are becoming available to help you inexpensively address your AS/400 and Power i education and training needs: Our general titles precede specific AS/400 and other technology books. Check out these great patriotic books which precede the tech books in the list.

<u>Seniors, Social Security & the Minimum Wage</u>
The impact of the minimum wage on Social Security Beneficiaries

<u>How to Write Your First Book and Publish It With CreateSpace</u>
This books teaches how to create a book with MSWord and then publish it with CreateSpace. No need to find a traditional publisher.

<u>Healthcare & Welfare Accountability The Trump Way</u>
Why should somebody win the Lottery & not pay back welfare?

<u>The Trump Plan Solves Student Debt Crisis</u>. .
This is the Trump solution for new student debt and the existing $1.3 Trillion student debt accumulation.

<u>Take the Train to Myrtle Beach The Trump Way</u>.
Tells all about the Donald Trump Plan to restart private passenger railway systems in America while it tells you how to get to Myrtle Beach by Train.

<u>RRRRRR The Trump Way</u>.
This book represents the overarching theme of the Trump campaign with verbs ready to reign in the excessive policies of the Obama Administration. These are the six verbs for the RRRRRR plan: Reduce, Repeal, Reindustrialize, Raise, Revitalize, Remember

<u>Jobs! Jobs! Jobs! The Trump Way!</u>
All about the jobs mess we ae in along with a set of Trump solutions

<u>The Trump Plan Solves the Student Debt Crisis</u>
Solution for new student debt and the existing $1.3 Trillion debt accumulation

<u>101 Secrets How to be a High Information Voter</u>
You do not have to be a low-information voter.

<u>Why Trump?</u>
You Already Know… But, this book will tell you anyway

<u>Saving America The Trump Way!</u>
A book that tells you how President Donald Trump will help America sn that Americans wind up on top

<u>The US Immigration Fix</u>
It's all in here. Finally an answer to the 60 million interlopers in America. You won't want to put this book down

<u>I had a Dream IBM Could be #1 Again</u>
The title is self-explanatory

<u>Whatever Happened to the IBM AS /400?</u>
The question is answered in this new book.

Great Moments in Penn State Football Check out the particulars of this great book at bookhawkers.com.

Great Moments in Notre Dame Football Check out the particulars of this great book at bookhawkers.com or www.notredamebooks.com

WineDiets.Com Presents The Wine Diet Learn how to lose weight while having fun. Four specific diets and some great anecdotes fill this book with fun and the opportunity to lose weight in the process.

Wilkes-Barre, PA; Return to Glory Wilkes-Barre City's return to glory begins with dreams and ideas. Along with plans and actions, this equals leadership.

The Lifetime Guest Plan. This is a plan which if deployed today would immediately solve the problem of 60 million illegal aliens in the United States.

Geoffrey Parsons' Epoch... The Land of Fair Play Better than the original. The greatest re-mastering of the greatest book ever written on American Civics. It was built for all Americans as the best govt. design in the history of the world.

The Bill of Rights 4 Dummmies! This is the best book to learn about your rights. Be the first, to have a "Rights Fest" on your block. You will win for sure!

Sol Bloom's Epoch ...Story of the Constitution This work by Sol Bloom was written to commemorate the Sesquicentennial celebration of the Constitution. It has been remastered by Lets Go Publish! – An excellent read!_

The Constitution 4 Dummmies! This is the best book to learn about the Constitution. Learn all about the fundamental laws of America.

America for Dummmies!
All Americans should read to learn about this great country.

Just Say No to Chris Christie for President two editions – I & II
Discusses the reasons why Chris Christie is a poor choice for US President

The Federalist Papers by Hamilton, Jay, Madison w/ intro by Brian Kelly
Complete unabridged, easier to read version of the original Federalist Papers

Companion to Federalist Papers by Hamilton, Jay, Madison w/ intro by Brian Kelly
This small, inexpensive book will help you navigate the Federalist Papers

Kill the Republican Party! (2013 edition and edition #2)
Demonstrates why the Republican Party must be abandoned by conservatives

Bring On the American Party!
Demonstrates how conservatives can be free from the party of wimps by starting its own national party called the American Party.

No Amnesty! No Way!
In addition to describing the issue in detail, this book also offers a real solution.

Saving America
This how-to book is about saving our country using strong mercantilist principles. These same principles that helped the country from its founding.

RRR:
A unique plan for economic recovery and job creation

Kill the EPA
The EPA seems to hate mankind and love nature. They are also making it tough for asthmatics to breathe and for those with malaria to live. It's time they go.

Obama's Seven Deadly Sins.
In the Obama Presidency, there are many concerns about the long-term prospects and

sustainability of the country. We examine each of the President's seven deadliest sins in detail, offering warnings and a number of solutions.   Be careful. Book may nudge you to move to Canada or Europe.

Taxation Without Representation Second Edition
At the time of the Boston Tea Party, there was no representation.   Now, there is no representation again but there are "representatives."

Healthcare Accountability
Who should pay for your healthcare?   Whose healthcare should you pay for?   Is it a lifetime free ride on others or should those once in need of help have to pay it back when their lives improve?

Jobs! Jobs! Jobs!
Where have all the American Jobs gone and how can we get them back?

Other IBM I Technical Books

The All Everything Operating System:
Story about IBM's finest operating system; its facilities; how it came to be.

The All-Everything Machine
Story about IBM's finest computer server.
Chip Wars
The story of ongoing wars between Intel and AMD and upcoming wars between Intel and IBM. Book may cause you to buy / sell somebody's stock.

Can the AS/400 Survive IBM?
Exciting book about the AS/400 in a System i5 World.

The IBM i Pocket SQL Guide.
Complete Pocket Guide to SQL as implemented on System i5.   A must have for SQL developers new to System i5. It is very compact yet very comprehensive and it is example driven. Written in a part tutorial and part reference style, Tons of SQL coding samples, from the simple to the sublime.

The IBM i Pocket Query Guide.
If you have been spending money for years educating your Query users, and you find you are still spending, or you've given up, this book is right for you. This one QuikCourse covers all Query options.

The IBM I Pocket RPG & RPG IV Guide.
Comprehensive RPG & RPGIV Textbook -- Over 900 pages.   This is the one RPG book to have if you are not having more than one.   All areas of the language covered smartly in a convenient sized book Annotated PowerPoint's available for self-study (extra fee for self-study package)

The IBM I RPG Tutorial and Lab Guide – Recently Revised.
Your guide to a hands-on Lab experience. Contains CD with Lab exercises and PowerPoint's. Great companion to the above textbook or can be used as a standalone for student Labs or tutorial purposes

The IBM i Pocket Developers' Guide.
Comprehensive Pocket Guide to all of the AS/400 and System i5 development tools - DFU, SDA, etc.   You'll also get a big bonus with chapters on Architecture, Work Management, and Subfile Coding.

The IBM i Pocket Database Guide.
Complete Pocket Guide to System i5 integrated relational database (DB2/400) – physical and logical files and DB operations - Union, Projection, Join, etc.   Written in a part tutorial and part reference style. Tons of DDS coding samples.

Getting Started with The WebSphere Development Studio Client for System i5 (WDSc). Focus is on client server and the Web. Includes CODE/400, VisualAge RPG, CGI, WebFacing, and WebSphere Studio. Case study continues from the Interactive Book.

The System i5 Pocket WebFacing Primer.
This book gets you started immediately with WebFacing.   A sample case study is used as the basis for a conversion to WebFacing. Interactive 5250 application is WebFaced in a case study form before your eyes.

Getting Started with WebSphere Express Server for IBM i Step-by-Step Guide for Setting up Express Servers
A comprehensive guide to setting up and using WebSphere Express. It is filled with examples, and structured in a tutorial fashion for easy learning.

The WebFacing Application Design & Development Guide:
Step by Step Guide to designing green screen IBM i apps for the Web. Both a systems design guide and a developers guide.   Book helps you understand how to design and develop Web applications using regular RPG or COBOL programs.

The System i5 Express Web Implementer's Guide.   Your one stop guide to ordering, installing, fixing, configuring, and using WebSphere Express, Apache, WebFacing, System i5 Access for Web, and HATS/LE.

Joomla! Technical Books

Best Damn Joomla Tutorial Ever
Learn Joomla! By example.

Best Damn Joomla Intranet Tutorial Ever
This book is the only book that shows you how to use Joomla on a corporate intranet.

Best Damn Joomla Template Tutorial Ever
This book teaches you step-by step how to work with templates in Joomla!

Best Damn Joomla Installation Guide Ever
Teaches you how to install Joomla! On all major platforms besides IBM i.

Best Damn Blueprint for Building Your Own Corporate Intranet.
This excellent timeless book helps you design a corporate intranet for any platform while using Joomla as its basis.
4
IBM i PHP & MySQL Installation & Operations Guide
How to install and operate Joomla! on the IBM i Platform

IBM i PHP & MySQL Programmers Guide
How to write SQL programs for IBM i

Joomla! books and many of the tech books above are only available at www.bookhawkers.com